SCHUMANN

SCHUMANN

The Faces and the Masks

Judith Chernaik

Alfred A. Knopf · New York · 2018

THIS IS A BORZOI BOOK
PUBLISHED BY ALFRED A. KNOPF

Copyright © 2018 by Judith Chernaik

Library of Congress Cataloging-in-Publication Data
Names: Chernaik, Judith, author.
Title: Schumann : the faces and the masks / by Judith Chernaik.
Description: First edition. | New York : Alfred A. Knopf, 2018. |
Includes bibliographical references and index.
Identifiers: LCCN 2017061535 (print) | LCCN 2017060796 (ebook) |
ISBN 9780451494474 (ebook) | ISBN 9780451494467 (print)
Subjects: LCSH: Schumann, Robert, 1810–1856. | Composers—
Germany—Biography.
Classification: LCC ML410.S4 (print) | LCC ML410.S4 C37 2018
(ebook) | DDC 780.92 [B]—dc23
LC record available at https://lccn.loc.gov/2017061535

Jacket image: Lithograph by Joseph Kriehuber, Vienna, 1839. Robert-
Schumann-Haus, Zwickau
Jacket design by Carol Devine Carson

Manufactured in the United States of America
First Edition

For my grandchildren,

Alice and Thomas

Jonah, Dan, and Mimi

CONTENTS

INTRODUCTION

Music is the most romantic of all the arts—one might almost say, the only genuinely romantic one—for its sole subject is the infinite.

—E. T. A. HOFFMANN

Schumann was a key figure in the new Romanticism of his age. He was a true Romantic in his embrace of poetry and feeling, his love of emotional extremes, his intermingling of life and art. He held passionate convictions about the art of music that was "food and drink" to his fellow musicians in their youth. He believed that music, like all the arts, must respond to the times, that it must be original and forward-looking while building on the greatest works of the past. His music was closely interwoven with the chief events of his life and the people he loved, especially his wife, Clara, herself a great artist. His major works have endured through all changes of taste up to the present time.

He was the most literary of composers. In his early years he was torn between literature and music and tried his hand at both. Fortunately for us, his early sketches for novels in the style of his favorite Romantic writers came to nothing. Instead we have the enduring magic of *Carnaval* and *Kinderszenen,* the great song cycles, a wealth of chamber music, four symphonies, the *Manfred* Overture, and many other orchestral and choral works. His ambition to become a virtuoso pianist had to be abandoned when he injured his right hand, having used his own ingenious invention to strengthen the weak middle fingers. His extraordinary artistic achievements must be set against recurrent illness, self-inflicted obstacles, and misjudgments, detailed in the following pages.

More than 150 years after his death in Endenich asylum, aged forty-six, Schumann's life and works still arouse partisan debate. Biographers disagree about whether to attribute his final illness to lifelong mental disorder or to the last stage of syphilis, contracted in his early youth. Performers argue about the merits of his late works: the Violin Concerto, which his close friend the violinist Joseph Joachim believed unworthy of publication; a song cycle setting the sentimental poems of a child poet for whom Schumann felt great enthusiasm; the haunting *Songs of Dawn* for piano, almost the last work he wrote before his breakdown. Some critics think these works reflect his mental decline; others see a master forging new artistic paths.

Questions still rage about Schumann's skill as a symphonist. Brahms and Clara Schumann were bitterly estranged following a quarrel about the respective merits of the first and final versions of Schumann's D Minor Symphony. Gustav Mahler, who championed Schumann's works, reorchestrated the symphonies with a heavy hand. In his performances and recordings of all four symphonies, the conductor George Szell defended them as supreme master-pieces against the opposition of virtually all his colleagues, but he too indulged in some reorchestration. Leonard Bernstein, a great admirer of Schumann, was one of the first conductors to return to Schumann's original scores.

Clara Schumann's role in Schumann's life remains a subject for debate, as her own works are rediscovered and newly assessed. Was she responsible for tempering the originality of Schumann's early works, urging him toward more conventional forms? Was her own genius stifled by Schumann's love of home and family? The complex relationship of these two great artists was central to the work of both, giving definitive shape to Clara Schumann's career and immortalized in Schumann's music.

Described by friends as an impractical dreamer, Schumann founded and edited a successful music journal with contributors in every major European city. No doubt his father's experience as a publisher, translator, and editor contributed to his own expertise. Like his father, he had to prove his financial competence before marrying the woman he loved. Throughout his life, he carefully noted all professional and household income and expenses, down to the last groschen for beer at his favorite tavern.

His diaries describe bouts of depression, fears, and phobias, and—details omitted in the early biographies—his sexual experience, his overindulgence in alcohol, his determination to reform, and his frequent lapses. It is possible that he suffered from what is now called a bipolar personality. He records symptoms associated with depression: sleeplessness, racing thoughts, nightmares, inability to work. Yet he was remarkably productive, writing compulsively in periods of intense creative inspiration. He had a high sexual drive, often related to manic excitement. He suffered panic attacks; he feared living on a high floor lest he be tempted to throw himself from the window. He idealized his fellow musicians Chopin and Mendelssohn, and he invested his close friends with qualities larger than life. They became characters in a novel, with literary names and personalities. He fell in love with married women, moved on easily to romantic infatuations with more available women, until his attachment to the young Clara Wieck deepened to become the great love of his life.

Schumann's fantasies entered into his music with the creation of the impetuous Florestan and the sensitive Eusebius, Romantic "doubles" of Schumann himself. Florestan and Eusebius are credited as the composers of his early works for piano and the authors of articles for his music journal; it is their names or initials, rather than Schumann's, that appear on his published scores and in the journal. They join commedia dell'arte clowns in his delightful *Carnaval* masquerade; they write variations on themes composed by Clara in dances full of wedding thoughts. Many other elements of Schumann's life play significant roles in his music: his vast reading, his liberal political enthusiasms, his love of games and puzzles.

As he assumed many "masks" in his music, he also had many faces, many selves. He compiled notes for an autobiography at intervals throughout his life, each time stressing selective features of his history. He instinctively presented different aspects of himself to Clara, to Mendelssohn, to close friends and distant acquaintances.

His inmost self is revealed in his music, but that self, too, is multifaceted. In his songs Schumann speaks through the words of his favorite poets. In all his music, the real self, the personal signature, is instantly recognizable but extremely resistant to analysis.

This study of Schumann's life and art is addressed primarily to the general reader, the music lover who may have no specialized musical training. I have tried to avoid technical language, but I hope to convey a sense of the quality and range of Schumann's compositions. In his music he expressed everything that he felt unable to express in words. When he was improvising at the piano or writing at his desk, composing his wonderfully original piano suites, inventing musical settings to love poems and ballads, tackling the larger forms of symphony and chamber music, it was his true self that was speaking. His early works are closely related to his own experiences, his moods, his fantasies, his relationship with Clara, both before and after their marriage. His later works also lend themselves to autobiographical readings. They should be read in terms not only of his life but his world, its politics, its ethos, its dominant themes. He gave musical voice to his imagined *Davidsbund* (Band of David)—his secret society of like-minded friends and artists—and to fellow composers and poets in ways that were as real to him as the spirits who later visited him in Endenich asylum. At the same time, his music is beautifully organized, clear in its structure, reflecting his profound understanding of harmony and counterpoint, his close study of the music of Bach and Mozart, Schubert and Beethoven.

How can one write about music for a reader who has no specialized musical knowledge? Many musicians regard music as a form of storytelling, while musicologists talk about "gestures," or "foreground," "middle ground," "background"—suggestive metaphors useful for pointing out the elements of a work that might otherwise be missed. But music has its own language, and metaphors drawn from literature, mime, or the visual arts are at best approximate. There is no substitute for listening to the music itself, encountering it directly in performance. Schumann believed with his whole being that music could express every human emotion and aspiration, all the manifold "states of the soul." His music speaks with extraordinary power to the imagination of the listener—but what it communicates remains untranslatable.

Fortunately the Internet makes it possible to listen to almost all music composed before the twentieth century. Each work discussed in the following pages can be accessed on the Internet in recordings by the greatest performers. Musical scores are also available on the Internet, and musical analysis ranging from program notes to PhD theses. The curious reader with a beginner's knowledge of musical language can find explanations of tonality, chromaticism, dissonance, modulation, sonata form, the "circle of fifths," and related guides to musical understanding, simply by inserting the term on the search engine of a computer.

I hope in writing about Schumann's life to encourage readers to listen to his music, the major works above all: *Carnaval*, the Fantasie in C, the song cycles, the *Spring* Symphony and the *Rhenish* Symphony, the joyous Piano Concerto, the popular Piano Quintet. I hope that I can also lead readers to the less familiar works: the "secular oratorio" *Paradise and the Peri*, the ambitious *Scenes from Goethe's "Faust,"* and the late fairy tales, some composed for intimate chamber duos, others for grand choral and orchestral forces.

My research has benefited from generous help from the director and staff of the Robert-Schumann-Haus in Zwickau. Their superb ongoing publishing programs have enabled me to present new information about the lives of Schumann and Clara, shedding light on their family background and on Schumann's early sexual experience, including his probable fathering of an illegitimate child. The recently published medical diary by the director of Endenich asylum has made it possible to chart the course and diagnosis of Schumann's final illness and death.

The music is paramount, as all those who love Schumann's music know. His works are constantly being rediscovered, and many have never gone out of fashion. They appeal directly and passionately to performers and listeners. Just as Schumann read his own plots into Schubert's simple dances and Chopin's "Mozart" Variations, artists who study Schumann's works arrive at widely differing views of their meaning. At their best, his works speak directly to the heart. With closer acquaintance the structure of each work becomes clear: the relation of parts to the whole, the melodic, harmonic, and rhythmic continuities and contrasts, the several "voices" speaking separately and together. Schumann's individual musical signature is always unmistakable, his special qualities of tenderness, fantasy, and humor, his emotional extremes and his heroic efforts to resolve them.

I hope the music will be served by my attempt in the following pages to unravel some mysteries of the life, and to convey the joy and the suffering that informed Schumann's musical world.

SCHUMANN

1

CHILDHOOD AND YOUTH

1810–1830

EARLY YEARS
Zwickau, 1810–1827

Schumann's background was middle-class, provincial, unremarkable. The seeds of his development into a great Romantic composer as well as his later crises, emotional and professional, can be traced in the history preserved in the Robert-Schumann-Haus, a beautifully maintained museum reconstructed on the site of the original family home in the town of Zwickau, in Saxony.

He was born on the 8th of June, 1810, the youngest of five children. There were three older brothers and a sister, Emilie, fourteen years older than Robert, who suffered from a severe nervous illness. Robert was petted and adored by his mother, Johanna Christiane, the daughter of Abraham Gottlob Schnabel, the chief surgeon of Zeitz. Johanna was prone to melancholia, and regularly took cures at the famous Bohemian spa of Karlsbad, now Karlovy Vary, fifty-five miles south of Zwickau. She was considered a good singer, with a large repertoire of songs popular at the time.

August Schumann, Robert's father, was the son of a poor country parson from the small town of Endschutz, near Gera. August burned with literary and intellectual ambition but was forced by the family's poverty to leave school at fourteen. He longed to study at the University of Leipzig, and managed a few months there as an auditor. His early life was a series of frustrations and compromises. He was apprenticed to a local merchant, and later worked as a clerk for a bookseller. He set up his own business to convince Johanna's father, with whom he lodged, that he would be able to support a wife. Somehow he preserved his literary ambitions. He wrote and published potboilers, romances of knights and monks in the style of gothic novels, and he founded a circulating library. A few years later he moved with his brother to Zwickau and established a publishing and bookselling firm, the Brothers Schumann. Along with lexicons and commercial handbooks, the firm published inexpensive German translations of the classics and a "Pocket Edition of the most eminent English authors," including novels by Sir Walter Scott and the poems of Lord Byron. August himself translated Byron's comic verse tale *Beppo* and *Childe Harold's Pilgrimage*, Byron's semi-autobiographical verse romance.

August Schumann had a special relationship with his gifted son. He encouraged Robert's literary and musical talents, and was determined to ensure that his son would not have to repeat his own history of frustrated ambition. The boy was always a scribbler, writing poetry, stories, and plays; improvising at the piano, composing ambitious musical scores from an early age. As a fourteen-year-old, Robert helped provide material for his father's publications, including a *Picture Gallery of Famous Men of All Times and Places*—perhaps suggesting to Robert that he, too, could one day achieve great things. August had political as well as literary enthusiasms. He sympathized with the ideals of the French Revolution and regarded Napoleon as a liberator until he assumed the imperial crown and embarked on the conquest of Europe. His father's liberal tastes influenced Robert's lifelong passion for Byron and his sympathy with the revolutions that swept Europe in 1830 and 1848–1849.

August was also a loving and indulgent father. In a letter to his fourteen-year-old son, he writes that he is pleased to learn from Robert's older brother Eduard that the boy is doing well in his studies; he hopes that he will continue to practice on the fine Streicher piano which his father has recently purchased for him. He appreciates Robert's concern about his sister, Emilie, whose condition is not improving under the latest treatment. He proposes that Robert might consider visiting his father in Karlsbad, rather than traveling to Dresden with his teacher, the Zwickau organist Gottfried Kuntsch. He ends with fatherly advice: "Now, Robert dear, live properly, remain cheerful, take care of your health, and either travel with Kuntsch to Dresden or come here. In the second case, I shall await you with heartfelt longing." On an earlier visit to Karlsbad with his mother, Robert heard the great pianist Ignaz Moscheles perform, an inspiration to the youngster, who treasured the program long into his later life.

Emilie died in 1825, aged twenty-eight, officially from "a nervous attack," according to later accounts by drowning herself or throwing herself from a window, in an access of "quiet madness." A year after Emilie's death, August Schumann died suddenly, probably suffering a heart attack, though his death was also attributed to "a long-standing severe nervous illness." He left his wife, three grown sons, who inherited the publishing business, and young Robert, who at sixteen was put under the care of a guardian, Johann Gottlob Rudel. His father's will provided a yearly annuity on condition that Robert pursue a three-year course of university study—his father's unfulfilled ambition. A biography of August, published soon after his death, praised his services as an author and publisher, his selfless devotion to family and friends, and his hope that his talented youngest son might pursue his studies unencumbered by the poverty he himself had experienced as a young man.

These were the first severe shocks in Robert's life. In an early diary, he laments having lost two dear human beings, citing one, his father, as "the dearest of all, forever." One would expect the other loss to be his sister, but the phrase he uses, "one who in a certain view might also be lost to me forever," could plausibly refer to his romantic attachment to a Zwickau sweetheart, Nanni Petsch, who had rejected him. On the anniversary of his father's death, he expressed surprise that he did not feel more distressed. On New Year's Day of 1829, he records reading the "loving letter" of "my wonderful father"—possibly the letter written from Karlsbad to the fourteen-year-old, quoted above. The early losses Robert experienced affected his reactions to the premature deaths of close family and friends during the next decade. His intimate companion the young composer Ludwig Schunke, "a bright star," died of consumption at twenty-four; his beloved sister-in-law Rosalie died at twenty-nine; his close friend and patron Henriette Voigt died at thirty. He also lost all three of his brothers: Julius at twenty-eight, Eduard at forty, and Carl at forty-seven. Death was always close, in real life as in literature.

For his father, and later for Robert, Shakespeare was the first Romantic, and Hamlet's melancholy was its symbol. Madness real and assumed, suicidal urges, the passionate rejection of the hypocrisy of kings and courtiers—all had great appeal for father and son. Their literary interests were European rather than narrowly German, including the Greek and Roman classics, the works of Dante and Petrarch, as well as the writings of Scott and Byron. Edward Young's melancholy *Night Thoughts* was a favorite, as was James Thomson's *The Seasons,* in the German translation set to music so memorably by Haydn. While he was still at school, Robert organized a literary circle which met each week to read the plays of Schiller and other works by German writers.

Wide-ranging as his literary interests were, Robert also retained from his protected childhood its small-town provincial character. In Zwickau, people knew their neighbors and everything there was to know about their business, their income, their personal trials and scandals. Though he attended the Zwickau grammar school, where he learned French, Greek and Latin, and later had some lessons in English and Italian, Schumann was never at ease in other languages. He reveled in his student holiday travel in northern Italy and Switzerland, but he did not travel extensively in later life, apart from six months in Vienna and a disastrous tour of Russia. His real traveling took place in his mind and his music.

At regular intervals throughout his life, Schumann took stock of his achievements and setbacks. These records, meticulously preserved by the family, are a gift to biographers. They are also revealing in ways the writer could not have anticipated.

One of the earliest of these documents, composed in Robert's fifteenth year, describes a cheerful, talented child, eagerly absorbing his school lessons, at eight writing poems to his nine-year-old first love, happiest when wandering alone in the countryside and dreaming. He was already placing himself in the tradition of Goethe's popular novels, *The Sorrows of Young Werther* and *Wilhelm Meister's Apprenticeship*. He was also a gifted mimic, with a keen comic sense. Several themes of his later life are already apparent in this first of several autobiographies, entitled "My Biography, or the Chief Events of my Life."

I was born in Zwickau on the 8th of June, 1810. Until my third year I was a child like any other; but then, because my mother fell ill with a nervous fever and it was feared she might be contagious, I was sent at first for six weeks to the home of the then Burgomaster Ruppius. The weeks flew by; I loved Frau Ruppius, she was my second mother, in short I remained two and a half years under her truly motherly oversight . . . I still remember well that the night before I was to leave this house, I could not sleep and wept all night long . . . I was a good, handsome child. I learned easily and was at six and a half enrolled in a private school in Freiburg . . . In my seventh year I learned Latin, in my eighth French and Greek, and at nine and a half I entered the fourth class of our lyceum. Already in my eighth year—if one can believe it—I learned to know the art of love: I loved in a truly innocent way the daughter of Superintendent Lorenz, by name Emilie . . . My life then began to be less calm; I was no longer so busy with my school work, although I did not lack talent. What I loved best was to go for walks alone and relieve my heart in nature.

After falling in love with young Emilie, who later married his brother Julius, Robert fell in love with Ida Stölzel, for whom he wrote poems, one of which he set to music. His usual pattern thereafter was to fall in love with at least two girls at the same time. His adolescent passions were for Nanni Petsch and Liddy Hempel, one glimpsed at a window, the other sharing a dance—both inspiring an outpouring of longing in his diary.

New Year's Day was always an occasion for Schumann to look back over the past year and to look ahead to the next. His diaries include lists of acquaintances, extracts from his extensive reading, his expenses, and philosophical commentary. Even in his earliest diary he expresses doubt about keeping a record of his life. In true Romantic fashion, he wonders if it might be more authentic to live life intensely than to record it in the cold form of a diary. In the end he embraced the highs and lows of his daily experience and also recorded each day's events, his love life, real and imagined, and his literary and musical projects, some realized, many abandoned. Addicted to the emotional extremes of Romantic fiction, he took note of his own dreams and nightmares and what we would now call panic attacks.

His father would have supported further studies in the arts. But at sixteen, Schumann was subject to the worries of his mother and the guardian appointed to oversee his future. They insisted that he pursue a respectable profession. He agreed to enter the University of Leipzig to study law, hoping to include philosophy and history. It is hard to imagine a less congenial profession for the youth often described as a shy dreamer, lost in his poetic fancies. His brothers were absorbed in running their father's publishing house in Zwickau and a press in nearby Schneeberg, and they left decisions about Robert's future to his mother and his guardian. August Schumann's generous patrimony paid for Robert's music lessons, his law studies, and his holiday travel. But law it must be, first in Leipzig, and a year later in the romantic city of Heidelberg.

STUDENT LIFE
LEIPZIG, 1828–1829; HEIDELBERG 1829–1830

In the pleasant Saxon town of Zwickau, on the banks of the river Mulde, Schumann had known virtually everyone. He was an admired pianist, much in demand at musical evenings of family and friends. Leipzig, forty-three miles north of Zwickau, was the commercial hub of Saxony, with a flourishing book trade, several music publishers, and a bustling economy fueled by semiannual trade fairs. It was bound to offer a very different experience for the sensitive youth. Schumann matriculated at the university in March 1828, and three weeks later traveled with his new friend Gisbert Rosen to Bayreuth, where they paid their respects to the grave of the eccentric writer Johann Paul Richter, known as Jean Paul, and visited the simple room in which he wrote his many novels. They went on to Munich, where they had an introduction to the poet Heinrich Heine. The writer famed for his misanthropy welcomed the young students kindly, took them round to the palace art gallery and invited them afterward to share a game of billiards. In late October Schumann returned to Leipzig, moving into lodgings with his childhood friend Emil Flechsig.

Schumann wrote to his mother that Leipzig was ugly, crowded, and flat; he missed his extended family and the lovely countryside near Zwickau. But while he was a student in Leipzig, ostensibly preparing for a career in law, he had his first piano lessons with the pedagogue and piano dealer Friedrich Wieck, forming a close relationship that was to dominate his life for the next decade and beyond.

Wieck, like Schumann's father, was a self-made man, the son of a poor trader in the small town of Pretzsch, near Wittenberg. Unlike August Schumann, after completing four years at a gymnasium, he entered the University of Wittenberg to study theology. His first sermon was also his last. He was a freethinker, temperamentally unsuited to the church. Instead he took up a post as tutor, first with an aristocratic family, later with a respectable widow. At the age of thirty, with financial support from a friend, he moved to Leipzig, where he established a circulating music library and traded in pianofortes. He married a promising young student from a distinguished musical family, Mariane Tromlitz, and to all intents and purposes prospered, establishing a reputation (or, more likely, promoting himself) as the finest piano teacher in Leipzig. When Schumann met him in 1828, Wieck was living with his second wife, Clementine, and the three children of his marriage to Mariane, from whom he had been divorced in January 1825. Clara, a child prodigy, was nine years old; her younger brothers, Alwin and Gustav, were seven and five. With his usual enthusiasm, Schumann embraced Wieck as his savior and substitute father.

Meanwhile he took his first steps into university life, attended a few lectures, took one fencing lesson, and looked for congenial musical friends. He gave his diaries Romantic titles: *Chronicle of a Youth's Life*; *Hottentottiana*; *Junius Evenings, July Nights*. These literary efforts included sententious reflections, character portraits of his friends, and notes of flirtations, all intended for an extensive romance in the flowing, elaborate style of Jean Paul.

The first volume of *Hottentottiana, The Year of the Fox: A Comic Autobiography,* was dedicated to Emil Flechsig, the friend who shared Schumann's first year of university life. (First-year students were "foxes," and presumably university life was as strange and foreign as the world of the Hottentots.) The project of a romance in several volumes was soon abandoned, and posterity was spared a quantity of florid prose in the style of Schumann's favorite writer.

Although Schumann's literary plans fell away, his diaries contain many of the Romantic themes which were to enter his music, especially *Sehnsucht* (intense longing), usually for an absent beloved, and *Seelenschmerz* (spiritual anguish). He reports on his close friendships with fellow students, and his dislike of the German student clubs (the *Burschenschaften*) and their patriotic excesses. Of his law studies there is little mention. Although he assured his mother that he was spending two hours a day on the dry subject, he told his friend Gisbert Rosen that he never attended any law lectures. Instead he followed his passion for music with like-minded friends and congenial families.

Schumann remained in Leipzig for only one college year, during which his piano lessons with Wieck took their erratic course. He practiced for several hours each morning, "fantasized" (improvised) at the piano he rented, composed a piano quartet, possibly inspired by Mozart's G Minor Piano Quartet, a few bars of which he quotes in his diary. Schubert often appears in his diary ("my only Schubert!"), as does Beethoven, whose complete works he ordered; also Mozart and Haydn, Carl Maria von Weber, Louis Spohr, and many lesser figures—Ignaz Moscheles, Johann Nepomuk Hummel, Ferdinand Ries, virtuoso pianists whose works were studied by every aspiring young soloist. Schumann frequently attended musical evenings at the home of Dr. Ernst August Carus, an eminent physician and a music lover, whose wife, Agnes, was a fine singer. Schumann accompanied her at the piano as she sang Schubert lieder and Beethoven's song cycle, *An die ferne Geliebte* (To the Distant Beloved), which was later to have great importance in Schumann's music. Naturally, Schumann fell more than a little in love with Agnes, who was eight years older than he was and had a young child. He confided to his diary: "I will go to bed and dream of her, of her. *Gute Nacht*, Agnes . . ."—a reference to the song that opens Schubert's song cycle *Winterreise* (Winter Journey).

Despite new friendships and musical pursuits, Schumann found Leipzig oppressive and, inspired by his friend Rosen, he decided to move his virtually nonexistent law studies to the ancient University of Heidelberg. He went to Heidelberg in May, and in late August set off for two months of summer holidays in Switzerland, northern Italy, and the Tyrol. As he explained to his mother and his brother Eduard, pleading for additional funds, holiday travel was part of the education of every student, absolutely necessary if he was to improve his knowledge of life. He prepared for his Italian travels by translating some of Petrarch's sonnets into German. To his friend Rosen and his sister-in-law Therese, he wrote rapturous accounts of his first sight of the Alps and the wonders of Milan's cathedral and opera house. To Rosen he also described romantic dallying with a young English tourist, and in his travel diary he recorded less refined encounters with Italian girls, and at least one sexual overture by a pederast.

Schumann returned to Heidelberg in late October 1829. The historic university town in south Germany, at the confluence of the Necker and the Rhine, was a world away from Leipzig's busy commercial activity. Schumann soon found a congenial circle of friends and fellow musicians. They played a wide range of music together, including Schubert's Piano Trio in E-flat, op. 100, and his duets for four-hand piano. Schumann asked Wieck to send him all of Schubert's works: "Send me . . . everything by Schubert which has appeared since op. 100 (which I learned with you)—do not forget the quintet, which I should very much like to learn."* He added that Wieck should send only the two-hand works, since he had all the four-hand works already. "I have fostered much Schubertianism here, for people hardly even knew his name." He ends his letter with typical hyperbole: "Be assured, honored teacher of my innermost being, of my highest respect, R. Schumann."

Student life in Heidelberg held many attractions. Schumann went drinking with friends at favorite taverns; he flirted with girls, attended masked balls, went to bed late, and recorded his social activities in his diary, sometimes with Romantic embellishments: "This is the most terrible week of my life" repeated three times in the week of February 8, 1830, and on the 15th: "End of the most terrible week, End of the most terrible week. *Ach! Ach!*" There is no further explanation, although wine, beer, and rum are mentioned, and *Katzenjammer* (hangover). He notes seeing the local whores when walking home late at night, possibly soliciting "an innocent"—that is, a virgin (like Robert). His friend Flechsig later described Schumann as "pure and chaste," suggesting that he was different from his fellow students, for whom evenings at the local tavern often ended at the local brothel.

Schumann also reports on events in the larger world, noting with excitement the revolutions which swept European cities in the summer of 1830. He copied out accounts of uprisings in Italy, Spain, the Netherlands, and elsewhere from the liberal English newspaper published in Paris, *Galignani's Messenger,* and he wrote down the whole of the Strasbourg national anthem, which begins: "Mort aux tyrans! Vengeance et liberté!" (Death to tyrans! Vengeance and liberty!)—sentiments that obviously caught his imagination.

---

* Schubert's *Trout* Quintet, for piano, violin, viola, cello, and double bass, was published in 1829.

The professor of jurisprudence at Heidelberg, Anton Justus Thibaut, held weekly choral evenings, featuring works by Handel and the early Italian masters. Schumann often attended these evenings, though he criticized Thibaut's "pedantry" to Wieck. A high point of the year was a visit to Frankfurt with a friend to hear a performance by the wizard of the violin, Paganini. With music taking a central role in his life, Schumann was also composing. He wrote a dozen songs and a set of polonaises modeled on Schubert's polonaises for four-hand piano. He failed to publish these early works, but he reused them in later compositions.

At the end of his year in Heidelberg, before setting out again on holiday travels, this time to Baden-Baden and Strasbourg, he summarized his life in a long, semifictional conclusion to the year's diary. The temperament of "S.," he wrote, was "melancholy." He was sensitive, had more feeling than judgment, was more subjective than objective in his aims and his works. His emotions were stronger than his ambition. He lived a pure life; he knew that he pleased women. The earth was to him not a garden of lust but a holy temple of nature. He was religious without religion—he loved humanity and had no fear of fate. Thus S.—Schumann—on himself, just short of his twentieth birthday.

And here we can detect the dual nature of the young artist. He was already adopting different masks, different ways of presenting himself, to his mother, his teachers, his close friends, his diary. Each self-presentation included imaginative retouching. Writing to his mother and his brother Eduard, he promised to work hard at his studies; he was committed to steady application at the dry study of law. His diaries hint at a riotous student life, including the usual temptations. He records "Attic nights," staying up all night with friends, talking, philosophizing. (The term refers to a popular commonplace book, *Noctes atticae*, by the Latin grammarian Aulus Gellius, containing short pieces on philosophy, history and related subjects, widely available in translation.)

Although he was notionally committed to return to Leipzig for the third year of his law studies, Schumann was reluctant to abandon the pleasures of life in Heidelberg. He confided to his diary:

"How I am loved and honored here! It has never happened to me before ... these good friends with their lovely girlfriends, full of love for me. Must I leave you so soon?"

At the end of his summer holidays, Schumann informed his mother that he had decided he must choose between his passion for music and a career in law. He asked his mother to write to Wieck for a candid assessment of his future possibilities as a musician. Wieck assured Schumann's anxious mother that her son had the making of a first-rate virtuoso. Within three years Wieck could turn him into "one of the greatest living pianists"—if he met certain conditions. Schumann must return to "dry, ugly Leipzig" and take daily piano lessons with Wieck. He must study music theory and submit to its rules and regulations. He must aim for greater precision in his playing. Wieck proposed a six-month trial, after which they would consult again. It was clear that Wieck was not altogether happy with Schumann's love of free improvisation; he intended to tame the wild spirit. Technical skill was the foundation of a virtuoso career. Schumann's mother had little choice but to agree. She knew her son better than Wieck did. Robert was very different from his ambitious, hardworking father. In some ways her beloved youngest son took after her. She feared that he would not easily submit to Wieck's hard conditions.

Schumann was delighted. His future now assured, he wrote to Wieck in high spirits: "I confide entirely in you; take me as I am, and be patient with me in everything ... Most honored sir, take my hand and lead me—I will follow wherever you wish."

A new life was about to begin.

2

LEIPZIG BOOK OF LIFE

Leipzig, 1831–1832

Schumann cheerfully gave up his law studies and returned to Leipzig to study full-time with Wieck. Here his real life began: the deepening complexity of his relationship with his mentor; his uncomplicated relationship with Wieck's daughter, Clara; his first serious love affair; the appearance of Florestan and Eusebius and the invention of the *Davidsbund*. He reveled in Chopin's "Mozart" Variations and reviewed the work for a music journal, breaking into print for the first time. He composed the dance suite *Papillons,* among other works. He injured his right hand by practicing with a mechanical device, ending all prospect of becoming a virtuoso pianist.

These life-changing events were closely interwoven, as Schumann struggled to put his affairs in order, to improve his piano playing, to pursue his passion for literature and music, to give form in words and tones to his chaotic ideas and feelings. Throughout this time, he struggled with his weaknesses—lack of discipline, depression, the cravings of the flesh for drink, for sex. He began to criticize Wieck for his possessive relationship to Clara and his grasping attitude toward money. Clara was taking on increasing importance in Schumann's life as a delightful child companion who was also a mature artist.

The primary sources for these years are Schumann's diaries, supplemented by letters to his family and his intimate friends, including young Clara. He assumes a different guise in each piece of writing, as if a different character were holding the pen. In his diary he gives free rein to his emotional swings, as changeable as the weather. In letters to his mother and his brother Eduard he justifies his perpetual need for funds; he is no different from any other hard-working student, entitled to books, travel, the common pleasures of youth. To his mother he is a loving, if erring, son; to Wieck and his theory teacher Heinrich Dorn he is a serious musician, persisting doggedly with finger exercises (at least two hours daily of scales and arpeggios) and dry theory (harmonizing chorales, plowing through Marpurg's *Theory of Fugue*). To Clara, writing affectionately with his natural charm, he is a playmate and storyteller. His relations with his lover Christel and its consequences, recorded in a private short-hand, appear only in his diary.

He opens his *Leipzig Book of Life* in May 1831 with a promise to write something down every day. The entries which follow set down his chief concerns in no particular order—his miserable headache, Wieck's love of gold, an analysis of the subjective and the objective in works of art, a friend's judgment that Schumann is "an arrogant man who believes that he is a great genius." He dreams of a hundred children crowned with flowery wreaths, dancing around him. All this is in the very first entry. Certain subjects take on greater impor-tance as the diary proceeds. His "sickness" is worrying—a "wound" that "bites and gnaws, like a lion chewing at his meat," which his friend Christian Glock, a medical student, examines, shaking his head over it. Notes on music appear side by side with the course of the illness: Schubert's polonaises for piano four-hands are "the highest Romantic *Schwärmerey*," evoking wild enthusiasm; "May is the natural key of A minor, June blooms forth brightly as C [the rel-ative major of A minor]." Projects for literary or musical treatment are considered and abandoned: the tale of Heloise and Abelard; a "poetic biography" of E. T. A. Hoffmann, the author of "diaboli-cal" tales that open new worlds to the entranced reader. Wieck and Clara become idealized figures in a romance, with new names: Wieck is "Meister Raro," Clara is "Cilia" or "Zilia" (diminutive for St. Cecilia, patron saint of music). Christel enters the romance as "Charitas"—love freely given.

———⁂———

Christel's identity has only recently been discovered. Her name was Christiane Apitzsch, and she was probably a servant in Wieck's house, where Schumann lodged while he was taking piano lessons with Wieck. His sexual encounters with Christel are meticulously recorded in the diary. She does not appear in Schumann's letters, or in his lightly disguised autobiographical writings. Nor does he discuss his "wound" with anyone other than the medical student he consulted. If Wieck had known about Schumann's venereal infection, he would surely have used this shameful fact when he was scheming to prevent his daughter from marrying his former student and protégé.

Christel first appears in the diary when she is summoned to Schumann's rooms after his discovery of a genital chancre. She turns pale when she is told of the infection, and Schumann laments, as if he were a character in Greek tragedy: "Guilt alone brings forth Nemesis." She and Schumann are both treated the next day by his friend Glock. Schumann describes the "frenulum" (the tissue under the foreskin) stinging from "narcissus water"—a traditional treatment for cancer, which could have been used to treat syphilitic lesions. Six weeks later, Christel arrives in the evening with a birthday present for Schumann, and they resume sexual relations *de novo*, confident that the infection has been cured. But a few days later, Schumann confesses to his diary: "I sink, I sink back into the old slime . . . Will no hand come from the clouds to stop me? I myself must be this hand."

Later entries recording Christel's visits alternate with rapturous accounts of Wieck and Clara, whose piano playing far outshines Schumann's. There is also much social activity with friends, often at nearby taverns. For nine days Christel fails to appear, and Schumann congratulates himself on living a pure life.

Their encounters began when Schumann was twenty and Christel was twenty-four. When he moved from Wieck's house to lodgings in Rudolph's Garden, Christel was pleased, "very loving." He reports her conversation on October 31st: "Why don't you write

anymore, dear Robert?" (This suggests that he was no longer composing during his worries about his illness.) "'Robert dear'—no
one else calls you this but your Charitas. She was here yesterday,
full of fire and flame; we drank a lot of Madeira." Schumann imitates her lower-class accent: *"liebe' Robert."* She adores Schumann,
visiting him unannounced at odd times. He sees her at a distance
"behind a bench" in Graf's Garden, where he is dining with Wieck
and Clara; he is embarrassed when his sister-in-law Rosalie visits
him one morning and finds Christel in his rooms. There is no talk of
marriage between them, nor would this be even a remote possibility.
But she loves "liebe' Robert" and understands him. He continues to
record their sexual encounters in his diary, as he was later to tick the
nights when he and his wife, Clara, had intercourse.

His feelings toward "Charitas" were certainly ambivalent. He
was flattered by her passionate caresses (she is "almost like an Italian girl," reads one entry, later crossed out, suggesting that his holiday travel in Italy might not have been altogether chaste). But he
also identified her with the guilty temptations of youth, the shameful abyss of drinking and whoring into which he fell more than once.
He welcomes Christel's visits, only to lament afterwards that he has
succumbed again to his demon, and to pray to his "good Genius"
to save him. One entry records a conversation in which they agree
to end their relations. But he sought out Christel again a few years
later, according to oblique references in his notes for 1836 and 1837.

His diary entries reflect Schumann's deepening relationship
with Wieck, the famous piano teacher whose fame was largely his
own creation; Clara was his one great achievement. Schumann still
admires Wieck but is well aware of his faults: avarice, greed, ambition, arrogance. Clara, on the other hand, is a natural artist, an
entrancing combination of innocence and maturity. Her playing has
the kind of ease Schumann associates with Mozart. Both Schumann
and Clara are working at Chopin's Variations on "Là ci darem la
mano" (the duet in Mozart's *Don Giovanni* with which the amorous
Don attempts to seduce the peasant girl Zerlina). This early work
of Chopin's is extremely difficult for Schumann, who spends hours

struggling to master it. He envies Clara, who easily tosses off the virtuoso passagework.

In July 1831, a full entry is devoted to Clara: "What a creature she is! She speaks more sensibly than any of us. Hardly three feet tall, and her heart is already developed." As so often in Schumann's diary, Shakespeare is close at hand—Clara, like Cleopatra, combines all contraries. One moment she is having a temper tantrum, stamping her feet, tossing her hat away; the next moment she is loving and contrite. "'Ah no, but stories,' she said, 'stories are my life. When I am to go to bed, how I beg to read just one more, then another, just one more, until Mama turns off the light.'" Her understanding is marvelous. "Each word that I have ever spoken, she can repeat to me!" They play charades and riddles, using their own names as challenges, with much gaiety and laughter.

In the young girl's company Schumann was comfortable with himself and the world, free of guilt about his divided nature. It was the happy beginning of the relationship that was to be at the center of his adult life. Wieck was about to take Clara off to Paris on an ambitious concert tour. Before they left, she visited Schumann daily at six p.m. to work together at the Chopin variations. They also sight-read Bach fugues at the piano, as if the keyboard works were written for four-hand piano, like Schubert's sets of four-hand works. The eleven-year-old Clara replaces Christel in the diary as Christel's visits taper off. The innocent pleasures of musical comradeship provided an attractive alternative to a troubled sexual relationship that Schumann was desperate to end.

Wieck and Clara were away from Leipzig for seven months, three of which were spent in Paris. Wieck organized concerts in several towns on the way to Paris and back, starting with Weimar, where Clara played for Goethe. On their return in May 1832, Schumann noted that Clara had grown, was prettier, her piano playing stronger and more skillful. She spoke German with a French accent, which he knew Leipzig would soon finish off.

A few days after Schumann's twenty-first birthday, "two of my best friends, never before seen" appeared in his diary. Their names, soon to enter musical history, were Florestan and Eusebius. The composer had already given Wieck and Clara new identities as Meister Raro and Zilia. A dozen other friends were suitably reinvented, and enlisted as characters in a projected romance. Soon afterwards they became the chief persons of Schumann's imaginary society of artists, the *Davidsbund,* or Band of David.

Florestan and Eusebius, his alter egos, were to figure largely in Schumann's works during the next decade, as "masked" dancers, coauthors, fellow composers, leaders of the *Davidsbund* in its battles against the Philistines ruling the musical establishment. Reading Schumann literally, biographers have assumed that his "doubles" reflect Schumann's split personality, his extrovert and introvert aspects. In his own words, as a young man he was "a hothead" and at the same time shy and tongue-tied. Shortly before his marriage to Clara, he sent her a poem in which he identified himself with "Florestan the wild" and "Eusebius the mild," urging Clara to take both together, uniting joy and sorrow.

The doubles had a conventional literary source in Jean Paul's novels and the tales of the writer who soon joined Jean Paul as a favorite, E. T. A. Hoffmann. In his diary, Schumann lists the "doubles" in several novels by Jean Paul, in which the author portrays himself as two contrasting persons. It was Jean Paul who coined the term *Doppelgänger*, meaning a ghostly "double" or exact image of the self, as in the dark love poem (untitled) in Heine's *Book of Songs* that Schubert set as "Der Doppelgänger."

On a happier note, Schumann played doppelgänger games with Clara: "Tomorrow, at exactly eleven o'clock, I shall play the adagio from Chopin's variations and shall think intensely, exclusively, of you. Now . . . you do the same, so that we may meet and communicate in spirit. The trysting place of our respective doppelgängers will probably be over the St. Thomas gate."

When they entered his diary in 1831, Florestan and Eusebius were far more than Romantic doubles. They *appeared* to him, as real as his student friends, and they took on their own character not only in Schumann's diary but in his music and his essays. In his early piano works, they alternate exuberant and grave sections, in notes of F or F-sharp for Florestan, E or E-flat for Eusebius. Four months after they first appeared, Schumann wrote that Florestan was "the friend of my heart; in the romance he shall be my true 'I.'" It was only when Schumann settled down into married life that he set aside these "best friends." But the musical influences that expressed their contrasting characters continued to dominate his compositions.

Schumann often lists the great past masters from whom every poet of words and tones must learn: among composers, Bach and Mozart; among writers, Shakespeare and Goethe. The quality their works share Schumann calls *Leichtigkeit*—lightness or ease, a natural mastery of art, embodying above all the virtue of clarity. In contrast, for Schumann, Beethoven and Schubert are the first Romantics. They broke all the rules, extending the language of music to realms never before explored. After an excited comment in his diary about Beethoven's *Hammerklavier* sonata, the next entry reads: "Let Mozart and Bach be your models in form, handling, nature, and pure art. But this mighty one [Beethoven] has a magic wand in his hand with which he calls forth a thousand new ideas." Beethoven died in 1827, when Schumann was sixteen; Schubert died a year later. They were Schumann's near contemporaries. He identified not only with their music but with their personalities. Beethoven represented heroic struggle, identified by Schumann as the masculine principle; Schubert represented the feminine principle, sensitivity, yearning, the full range of human emotions. Not long after Florestan and Eusebius appeared to him, fully formed, he wrote in his diary, echoing Aeneas's cry "To Italy!" in book 6 of Virgil's *Aeneid*, "To Vienna! To Vienna—where my Beethoven and Schubert sleep. The die is cast!"

Florestan was the name of the unjustly imprisoned hero of *Fidelio*, Beethoven's only opera, an intensely political work. Schumann had seen a performance and knew the score. He had recently been playing a four-hand piano version of Beethoven's *Eroica* Symphony, dedicated originally to the hero Napoleon. Liberal on principle, Schumann identified with the revolutionary images of freedom and brotherhood in Beethoven's most celebrated works. In *Fidelio*, the political prisoners emerge slowly from darkness into light. Their chorus, "What joy, to breathe freely the air of heaven," starts tentatively, rising to a triumphant cry of "Freedom!" Florestan's aria, praying for freedom while he is chained in the darkness and solitude of the dungeon, spoke to Schumann as it has done to generations ever since. His crime was to tell the truth; his only comfort is that he has been faithful to his conscience. In Beethoven's music, Florestan represented the ideal of "poetry and truth" that Goethe celebrated in his own works, and to which Schumann wholeheartedly subscribed. Schumann also identified with Beethoven's setting in the Ninth Symphony of Schiller's "Ode to Joy," with its stirring affirmation of the brotherhood of man.

For Schumann, passionately committed to individualism and freedom in the arts, these great moments in Beethoven's works fed into the conception of his own Florestan—the leader of the *Davidsbund*, the "friend of my heart," "my 'I.'"

Although Florestan clearly has Beethovenian resonance for Schumann, Eusebius has no obvious counterpart. The only clue Schumann provided came in a later letter to Clara, in which he asks her to look at the calendar dates on either side of her own saint's day, where she will find St. Eusebius. Schumann might have been inspired by Raphael's painting *Eusebius of Cremona Raising Three Men from the Dead*; he was very fond of Raphael and might have seen a copy of the painting, along with other works by Raphael and Michelangelo. He considered these two great artists another example of doubles—Raphael representing the ideal of grace and beauty, Michelangelo the universal human striving toward divinity. It is also possible that Schumann was simply looking for a suitable E to accompany the F of Florestan, and the name struck him as suitably euphonious.

Whatever the origin of the name, as "Eusebius" (known familiarly as "Seb") takes life in Schumann's writings and his music, he seems more and more to be associated with Schubert, the beloved composer whom Schumann regarded as a true soul mate. Schubert's music enters into Schumann's tender, introspective, feminine side, as Beethoven enters into his heroic, declamatory mode. Among Schumann's earliest works were variations on themes by his two musical heroes: the opening bars of the Andante of Beethoven's Seventh Symphony, and Schubert's "Sehnsucht" Waltz (Waltz of Longing). His musical tributes to both composers can be traced throughout his works. Florestan and Eusebius, with their links to Beethoven and Schubert, take major roles in Schumann's music throughout the next few years, until in his late revision of the piano works he removed all printed references to his youthful companions.

Schumann was as eager to welcome his contemporaries as he was to learn from his predecessors. To his credit, Schumann recognized Chopin's extraordinary qualities at once when he acquired a copy of Chopin's "Mozart" Variations. "I cannot describe how I feel about Chopin," he wrote. "I embrace him with a thousand arms . . . Between seven and ten, I study Chopin alone, with my hand as steady as possible." Shortly afterwards: "Chopin is going well—today is the fifth day that I've worked at it four hours each day." His famous review of the Chopin Variations, which he was studying at the time, described Eusebius entering the rooms of "Julius," where Florestan is seated at the piano. Eusebius greets his friends thus: "Off with your hats, gentlemen—a genius!" Florestan later describes each variation in rhapsodic terms: "The first variation expresses a kind of coquettish courteousness . . . the second is at once comic, confidential, disputatious, as though two lovers were chasing each other, and laughing more than usual about it."

Wieck sent the review to Chopin, who mercilessly parodied it in a letter to his friend Tytus Woyciechowski. In their piano works, Chopin and Schumann complemented each other in their originality and expressiveness. In most other ways they were polar opposites. Chopin was intensely private, scornful of the Parisian society to which he conformed so meticulously, with his seven pairs of white gloves, dove-gray trousers, private valet and hairdresser. He was comfortable only with his Polish compatriots in exile. Schumann was gregarious, eager for praise, an unabashed Romantic. They were to meet a few years later, when they exchanged compositions, to Schumann's delight. According to his students, Chopin took no interest whatever in the compositions that Schumann regularly sent to him. Fortunately, the larger world was eventually to embrace the music of both composers as defining works of nineteenth-century Romanticism.

Papillons, op. 2

Schumann's own op. 2, *Papillons*, published in April 1832, was composed in stages between 1829 and 1831. It is original in conception, fresh and delightful in performance. Unlike many of the virtuoso works so popular at the time, it was playable even by amateurs. The *Papillons* (Butterflies) are short dances, loosely linked by key, rhythm, and common motifs. The entire work could be imagined as a sequence of dances at a ball. This is exactly how Schumann explained *Papillons* to his family, friends, and critics. He told them that it was a musical representation of the masquerade ball that ends Jean Paul's novel *Flegeljahre* (Fledgling Years), in which the chief characters, the twins Walt and Vult, are both in love with the heroine, Wina, and take turns wooing her under their masquerade disguises. When Schumann sent the newly published work to his mother and sisters-in-law, he begged them to read the scene in *Flegeljahre* "as soon as possible," hoping they would discover in the music reflections of "Wina's angelic love, Walt's poetical nature, [and] Vult's sparkling intellect."

One wonders if they made the attempt, or were simply puzzled by the composer's literary fancies. Even if they had had access to Schumann's copy of *Flegeljahre*, in which he underlined and numbered several passages in the relevant chapter, they would have remained mystified. The first piece after the Introduzione, a rapid rising and descending scale in octaves, supposedly corresponds to Walt in his miner's costume, setting forth "like a hero, thirsty for fame," to fight for Wina's love. But when the same motif returns in the Finale, fading away in the distance, it refers not to the honest Walt but to his brother, Vult, who has won Wina by deception. In Schumann's autograph of the musical score, he included a reference to the scene: "Wult, enraptured, listened to the fleeing tones [of Vult's flute] as they resounded upward from the street." Before publication, Schumann removed the sentence, the only key to the link with *Flegeljahre*. He liberated his *Papillons* so that they could take their course unencumbered by clues to extramusical meaning.

Yet he was still reluctant to abandon the literary source. He wrote to the critic Ludwig Rellstab: "You may remember the last scenes in the *Flegeljahre*, with the *Larventanz* [masked ball] . . . I often turned to the last page, for the end seemed like a fresh beginning, and almost unconsciously I found myself at the piano, and thus one *Papillon* after another came into existence." His account suggests Schumann's typical way of composing. He is the passive recipient of musical thoughts which "come into existence," much as Florestan and Eusebius had appeared to him, without conscious effort on his part. What is essential to Schumann is heightened receptiveness, sensitivity to the worlds of nature, books, emotions, and to the music with which his head was filled. But *Papillons* also shows the artist's shaping hand at work, his love of patterns, interlinked motifs, his ability to frame and organize his composition.

The immediate musical influences on *Papillons* were Schubert's waltzes and his polonaises for four-hand piano—charming sets of dances, often quite slight, varied by changes in rhythm and melody. Schumann turns his own sequence of dances into character sketches. Each dance is introduced by a flourish, as if to announce the next figure in a carnival procession. The Finale combines the opening motif with the "Grandfather's Dance" which traditionally serves as the penultimate dance at a German ball. The dances evoke the dancers, each one making his or her entrance, stomping or pirouetting gracefully, flirting, joining forces, disappearing as the clock strikes six.

Schumann was fond of the title *Papillons*, which appears several times in his diary, as a new *Papillon* flutters into his mind. The image suggests that each short dance represents the brief, evanescent life of a butterfly, a moment of beauty caught only to vanish. On the published score, the title *Papillons* is adorned with butterflies of different sizes, shapes, and patterns, some with wings closed, others with wings extended. Like butterflies, the contrasting dances of the masked ball—waltzes, ländler, polonaises—are symmetrical in their structure and motifs. The opening dance best illustrates the butterfly-like symmetry of construction: a palindromic rising and falling motif, developed in a rhythmical four-bar pattern and repeated, followed by an answering four-bar pattern, repeated. The musical *Papillon* could represent the matching wings of a butterfly, the upper two halves symmetrical, with the two lower halves also matching.

Traditionally, the butterfly is identified with the soul, the winged Psyche. The chief function of art, and especially of music, according to Jean Paul, is the portrayal of the various "states of the soul"—the full range of human passions. Schumann adopted the idea enthusiastically. This is how he understood the music of his beloved Schubert. His later review of Schubert's German Dances could be a description of his own *Papillons:* "An entire carnival dances through the German Dances, op. 33 . . . no. 1 in A minor, a crowd of masks, drums, trumpets . . . 2, a comic figure scratching its ear and whispering psst, psst . . . 3, Harlequin, with his hand on his hip, turns a somersault out of doors; 4, two stiff, polite masks dancing and conversing very little with each other; 5, a slender cavalier following a mask." Schumann was convinced that music had the same power of description as a novel or a short story. Yet he also insisted that music must stand on its own, free of any program. Everything feeds into the composer's imagination, but at a decisive point the craftsman takes over, the dedicated artist, who creates a unified work which communicates in its own language to a receptive listener.

Papillons followed Schumann's op. 1, a set of Variations on the Name Abegg, dedicated to "Mademoiselle Pauline, Comtesse d'Abegg." Schumann sent the work out widely to friends and relatives, with the hope of coming before the great world with this first publication. Both the title and the dedication reflect Schumann's whimsical love of games. The theme was made up of the musical equivalents of the letters A, B [B-flat], E, G, G. The "countess" was invented as a joke; Schumann might have known a "Pauline," but there was no "Comtesse d'Abegg." The variations are charming but conventionally virtuosic, and they are quite frequently performed today. Similar works were composed soon after *Papillons*: a set of six

Etudes after Paganini's Caprices, six Intermezzi which Schumann called "longer *Papillons*," and twelve Impromptus on a Theme by Clara Wieck. The latter have a special interest, since they reflect Schumann's admiration for Clara not only as a pianist but as a composer, and because they link Clara with Beethoven. Schumann notes in his diary the sudden appearance of a theme of descending fifths: C-F-G-C—a variation of Beethoven's *Eroica* theme. He uses the notes as a bass line against which Clara's theme is set, in variations that show close familiarity with Beethoven's *Eroica* Variations. The published work must have been extremely flattering for the young prodigy, who was already including Beethoven sonatas in her concert programs.

Schumann's most ambitious work during these early years was a symphony in G minor, with three movements sketched, elaborated, and revised over several months, and a final movement contemplated but unwritten. The first movement was performed at a concert in Zwickau in November 1832, at which Clara performed virtuoso variations by Henri Herz, one of the popular composers scorned by Schumann. Wieck commented that Schumann's symphony was inventive but too thinly orchestrated—probably a just criticism. A revised version was presented a year later at Schneeberg, and again in Leipzig, after which it lapsed into obscurity.

Throughout this time, Schumann was combining his activities as a composer with intensive practice at the piano. Mechanical aids for strengthening the fingers were widely available, often prescribed by teachers, and probably sold by Wieck himself. The "chiroplast" was a contraption attached to the piano, in which one finger at a time was inserted and held still, while the others practiced finger exercises. Schumann first noted that a finger was "stiff" in late January of 1830, probably because of excessive practice. When he was living with Wieck, Schumann decided to improve his manual dexterity with an invention of his own, immobilizing the middle fingers on his right hand one at a time so that the neighboring weak fingers would be strengthened. In his diary he refers to the invention as his "cigar mechanism." He was a dedicated cigar smoker, and it is possible that he made use of the stiff tubular packaging of each cigar to immobilize his fingers. Whatever his invention was, it had the unintended consequence of paralyzing his middle fingers. He tried every measure available to him to restore mobility to his fingers—electric shocks, homeopathy, bathing his hand in the hot entrails of a recently slaughtered animal. Nothing helped; his fingers were worse after each treatment. Eventually all three middle fingers seemed to be paralyzed.

Although Schumann continued to improvise at the piano, his virtuoso career was finished. He could not possibly earn a living through concertizing, which meant that he would have to find another source of livelihood. There was no point to continuing his piano lessons with Wieck, although he continued his study of theory and counterpoint with Heinrich Dorn. He tried valiantly to get through the theory textbooks, but always fell back on his love of the great masters for his understanding of musical composition. He was studying Bach's *Well-Tempered Clavier*, all forty-eight preludes and fugues—the work that was to sustain him in all the crises of his life. Bach was the source of all music, all art. In an echo of Hamlet praising the late king, his father ("He was a man, take him for all in all"), Schumann wrote of Bach: "He was a man through and through; his works were for all time."

By the end of 1832, having by his own ill-conceived efforts thwarted his dream of becoming a great pianist, Schumann was ready, aged twenty-two, to embrace his destiny as a serious composer.

3

REVERSALS, RENEWALS

Leipzig, 1833–1834

His diary notes for 1832–1833 suggest that Schumann was suffering from one of the bouts of melancholy that frequently afflicted him: "Why can I write nothing when life streams over me, why do I turn to you, my Book of Life, when everything is quiet and lifeless? . . . And how much more truly and richly imagination speaks, when it comes from life!" He was reading Heine's poems, planning to study classical piano works from Mozart on, refining an exercise in double notes, an early version of his fiendishly difficult Toccata op. 7. Shakespeare often appears in his diary. He lists the female characters in each play; he writes a "sinfonia" which might form an introduction to a *Hamlet* opera or symphony. The relationship between words and music continually absorbed him. The poet and the composer are closely allied, but music, he believed, was the highest form of poetry.

In October 1833, Schumann's restlessness reached a point of crisis. "The night of 17–18 October," he wrote later, was "the most terrible of my life . . . I was seized by an idée fixe of going mad." This terrible night immediately followed the death of his beloved sister-in-law Rosalie, his brother Carl's wife. He described his symptoms and his slow recovery in a letter to his mother: "I was hardly more than a statue, neither cold nor hot. Life gradually returned when I resumed my usual work. But I am now so fearful and timid that I cannot sleep alone, and so I've taken a good-natured man to live with me, whom I can educate, which pleases me." At his worst, he told his mother, he suffered from "congestion of the blood, unspeakable anxiety, breathlessness, dizziness." The symptoms are typical of a panic attack, which could have been triggered by news of Rosalie's death. Schumann's brother Julius had died of tuberculosis in August, which also contributed to Schumann's terror.

His breakdown of mental and physical health at this time was to affect Schumann's later life and his music in incalculable ways. The fear of recurrence never left him. His mental state remained fragile, and he was careful to avoid anything that could trigger a repeat of the horrors of that night. He moved from the upper floor of his lodgings to the first floor; he dreaded the sight of a nearby mental asylum. His mother was told to spare him from details of any other family catastrophes.

Schumann described the year that followed his breakdown, 1834, as "the most significant of my life." The reasons were in part personal, but also professional. In 1834 he realized his dream of founding a music journal in which he and his friends—real and invented members of the *Davidsbund*—would take arms against the Philistines ruling the European musical establishment.*

The first issue of the *Neue Zeitschrift für Musik* (*New Journal for Music*) was published in April 1834 in four closely-printed pages. The masthead boasted a motto by Shakespeare from the prologue to *King Henry VIII* (also known as *All Is True*):

---

* The *Davidsbund,* or Band of David, was inspired by the biblical figure of David, the young shepherd summoned to heal the black moods of King Saul by playing his harp, the poet-singer of the Psalms. Schumann might have had the added inspiration of Michelangelo's famous sculpture of the heroic youth, armed only with his sling, his foot on the head of the slain Philistine giant Goliath. (Schumann probably knew the sculpture from the many copies circulating in Germany.) In exile, David gathers a band of comrades who rout the Philistines, and he forms a loving friendship with Saul's son, Jonathan. (Schumann's friend Ludwig Schunke was given the pseudonym "Jonathan" in his writings for the *New Journal for Music*.) Schumann adapted the biblical associations that suited the needs of his own "Band of David," with Florestan as its leader in battle against the Philistines of the musical world.

Only they
That come to hear a merry, bawdy play,
A noise of targets, or to see a fellow
In a long motley coat guarded with yellow,
Will be deceived.

The *New Journal for Music*, unlike the established music journals published in Leipzig and other European cities, was to be devoted to truth telling. It had a "weighty and serious" purpose which the editors were eager to explain.

"Our basic policy was clear from the start," Schumann wrote in his New Year's editorial for 1835. "It was simple: to pay close attention to past times and their works, and to insist that only from such a pure source can the best new art be created; to oppose as inartistic the mere virtuosity which has become so fashionable; and finally to hasten and help to promote a new poetic era."

The journal started as a collaborative venture by "an Association of Musicians and Friends of Music." Schumann and Wieck, his former teacher, were copartners. They had two coeditors, Ludwig Schunke and Julius Knorr, comrades in the *Davidsbund*. (Knorr was "Julius" in Schumann's review of Chopin's "Mozart" Variations.) Schumann wrote to leading musical figures across Europe, inviting them to report on musical life in Paris, Vienna, Berlin, Hamburg, London, Edinburgh, Petersburg, and Moscow. The journal was conceived as a forum for battle, as Schumann made clear in letters to potential correspondents. To Franz Otto in Hamburg: "My dear friend, accept this letter as the beginning of a rapid and regular correspondence . . . Take it as the herald of a brighter musical future . . . Come and strike a blow with us. A new musical periodical is arising, which is to be the representative of poetry and will mercilessly attack all the weaknesses of the age." The journal was to be international, progressive, a voice for the highest artistic principles.

Schumann urged his friends to write in a light-hearted style, with the imaginative musical writings of E. T. A. Hoffmann in mind. Along with "Raro" (Wieck), Eusebius and Florestan contributed aphorisms about music similar to the "random thoughts" of Hoffmann's Kapellmeister Kreisler. Essays in Romantic style, usually signed by Eusebius or Florestan, fictionalized Leipzig's musical life. Eusebius wrote "Letters from an Enthusiast" in "Firlenz" (Leipzig) to Chiara (Clara) in Milan, a city she had never visited. (Clara was extremely offended by the portrait of "Beda," another musical pseudonym for her, in one of the letters.)

In the course of his ten-year editorship, Schumann enlisted over a hundred contributors, each assigned a number or letter as pseudonym. Twice-weekly numbers followed the precedent set by the first issue, with the masthead featuring quotations about the true function of art by Goethe, Schiller, Shakespeare, Jean Paul, and other favorite writers. The first issues reprinted excerpts from the recently published correspondence of Goethe and his friend Carl Friedrich Zelter, director of the Singakademie (the choral society) in Berlin. A "Letter from England" carried on for several issues, maintaining the international character of the journal, along with notes of musical life in several European cities. Even with contributions from friends, Schumann's hand was increasingly in evidence. Ludwig Schunke, a gifted young composer, had arrived in Leipzig at the end of 1833, and they roomed together briefly. But Schunke was already suffering from tuberculosis and died in December 1834. Wieck, Schumann's ostensible partner, was abroad much of the time, expanding his business, buying and selling pianos, taking Clara on concert tours. By the beginning of 1835, Schumann was de facto owner and editor-in-chief of the journal, with his name alone appearing on the masthead. The journal occupied much of his time; he neglected his diary and for a while ceased composing.

Despite his best intentions, the first issues of the *New Journal for Music* showed few signs of the battle against "all the weaknesses of the age" promised by the editor. The most significant piece Schumann wrote for the *Journal* was a serious analysis in five parts of the *Symphonie fantastique* by Hector Berlioz—an extraordinary work that defied all the classical conventions, meeting at first with general incomprehension. Schumann was responding to a negative review by Gottfried Fink, the editor of the conservative *Allgemeine musicalische Zeitung* of Leipzig. Berlioz had attached a specific program to the symphony as the story of an artist who is enmeshed in a tragic love affair. Schumann, with only Liszt's piano reduction of the orchestral score, analyzed it as a serious work of music, recognizing its bold originality and the astonishing genius of the young composer.

It was not until 1837 that Schumann engaged in deliberate controversy, in a long article contrasting Meyerbeer's opera *Les Huguenots* with Mendelssohn's oratorio *St. Paul*. He introduced his essay with these words: "I feel today like a brave young warrior who draws his sword for the first time in a great cause." Armed with his strong convictions, Schumann attacked Meyerbeer's popular opera for vulgarity, superficiality, and immorality, and praised Mendelssohn for writing "a work of pure art, the creation of peace and love." Journalists in Paris, Hamburg, and elsewhere seized on the review to attack Schumann, which he took as vindication of the journal's high purpose.

The excitement of founding his journal coincided with new developments in Schumann's personal life. Ernestine von Fricken was the daughter of a wealthy baron and landowner from Asch, on the border of what is now the Czech Republic, a day's journey south of Leipzig. In April of 1834 she came to live in Wieck's house as his student. Ernestine was seventeen, Clara fourteen, and the two girls soon became close friends, though Clara was whisked away by her father for a month's study in Dresden and a short concert tour of German cities. Although Schumann was no longer studying with Wieck, he was a regular visitor at Wieck's house. He was likely to meet Ernestine there or at Henriette Voigt's regular musical evenings. Biographers assume that he was soon smitten with Ernestine. What is certain is that she was infatuated with Schumann. Her innocent adoration was flattering to the twenty-four-year-old composer, who was also attracted by the prospect of entree into an aristocratic world. Baron von Fricken was married to the countess of Zedtwitz, whose family had long controlled the Bohemian region of Asch. As the baron's only child, Ernestine would be assured a substantial income—or so Schumann believed.

By the summer they had become secretly engaged. Schumann's friend and patron Henriette Voigt became their go-between. Clara suffered torments as the romance proceeded. In her later letters to Schumann, she reproached him for ignoring her, treating her like a child, talking only to Ernestine when they went on country walks together. Even more distressing for Clara, Wieck invited Schumann and Ernestine to be joint godparents to Clara's new half-sister, Cäcilie. Evidently Wieck looked kindly on the romance, perhaps hoping that he too might benefit from closer contact with the rich baron.

Carnaval; Études symphoniques

Most significant for posterity are the compositions inspired by Schumann's engagement to Ernestine: the masquerade of *Carnaval* and the variations on a theme composed by Ernestine's father, which became the *Études symphoniques*. Both works demonstrate the ways in which extramusical inspiration fed Schumann's imagination. The years of failed attempts proved extremely useful. Schumann could now manage the structure of a long work without suppressing his natural inventiveness, tempering his first inspired thoughts by serious revision. Both *Carnaval* and the *Études symphoniques* took shape over a period of months, with new episodes included, reworked, omitted, or reinstated.

Easily the most frequently performed and recorded of Schumann's piano suites, *Carnaval* is a musical version of Schumann's earlier plan of a *Davidsbündler* novel, in which his alter egos Florestan and Eusebius were to feature, along with Wieck, Clara, and the master magician Paganini. *Carnaval* took form as a masquerade in which the *Davidsbündler* join the traditional commedia dell'arte "masks" in a series of comic pranks. Each "mask" is characterized in music rather than words in a way that was to become one of Schumann's most distinctive art forms.

The decisive impetus for the composition was the prospective union of Schumann and Ernestine. In a letter to Henriette Voigt

Schumann explained his idea of the work that was to become *Carnaval* as a series of "scenes" held together by Schubert's "Sehnsucht" Waltz. Schumann had made the astonishing discovery that the "musical" letters of Ernestine's birthplace, ASCH, were also the musical notes in his own name: SCHumAnn. In German notation ASCH would be A, Es (E-flat), C, H (B); SCHA would be the same letters in a different order. And so he combined the idea of masquerade scenes, as in a carnival procession, with puns on a musical name. Each scene was to open with the notes of the musical letters, as if the character were offering a toast to the composer and his bride. But Schumann did not want the linking theme to be too obvious. With great ingenuity, he varied the rhythm of the musical letters introducing each new "mask" so cleverly that the resemblance is almost impossible to detect, until the four notes are spelled out loud and clear at the end of the piece he called "Florestan."

Perhaps sensing that these rhythmical disguises were working too well, at the halfway point of *Carnaval* Schumann inserted three sets of notes spelling out ASCH-SCHA in an imitation of antique score which he called "Sphinxes," or riddles. The Sphinxes were

Sphinxes.

meant to be silent, not to be played aloud—revealing but also preserving the mystery. The second Sphinx notates yet another form of ASCH, as AsCH (A-flat, C, B), the sequence that dominates the second half of the work. A dance that follows soon after the Sphinxes adds another dimension to the game. Entitled "A.S.C.H.—S.C.H.A. (Lettres dansantes)," it challenges the performer (or the reader of the printed score) to discover the "letters" as they appear dancing about in the piece. ASCH opens the piece in the Sphinx form A-flat, C, B, and if one catches the dancing letters out of sequence, including bass as well as treble notes, the Sphinx spelling SCHA (Sphinx No. 1) can also be detected.

Carnival masquerades appealed to Schumann as an infinitely

suggestive meeting of music and literature, literature and life. The masked commedia dell'arte characters, pictured in the celebrated caricatures by Jacques Callot and beloved by Jean Paul and E. T. A. Hoffmann, are in their nature transgressive, comic parodies of romantic love and seduction. Schumann had personal experience of masquerades; he was a good dancer in his student years, and he boasted of his carnival role as an old woman in a student masquerade in Heidelberg. A series of masked characters perfectly suited his genius for imitating voices, a natural gift exercised to the amusement of fellow pupils in his schooldays.

Carnival meant freedom from all restrictive rules and conventions that "masks" offered to students, artisans, servants, persons high and low. In Goethe's account of the Roman carnival, young men dress in the holiday finery of "women of the lowest classes" (a euphemism for prostitutes), women dress as men, life is turned upside down, and the spirit of anarchy levels all social hierarchies. In post-1815 Europe, with the feudal system in large part restored, the aristocracy newly empowered and the churches reinstated, carnival took on political as well as social resonance. It meant licensed revelry, freedom of expression, the celebration of a classless world in which commoners could be kings. Schumann's early liberal sympathies were deepened by his love of Jean Paul and Hoffmann, Beethoven, and Schubert—free spirits all, if not in their lives, most compellingly in their works.

Schumann's earlier attempt at depicting a masked ball, *Papillons,* had failed to convey its meaning to listeners. Schumann reluctantly agreed with the first critics of *Papillons* that the short episodes succeeded one another too rapidly to be comprehensible, and only those who knew the work's source in Jean Paul's novel would realize that it was meant to represent a masquerade ball. Determined to give the clearest possible expression to his theme, he supplied a full range of clues to the extramusical meaning of *Carnaval.*

The title page of *Carnaval* spells out its design: "Scènes mignonnes composées pour le pianoforte sur quatre notes." In an earlier draft in German, "Scènes mignonnes" are *Schwänke,* or pranks, best translated as "comic vignettes." Opening with a grand

Schubertian flourish, the "Préambule" introduces several themes that appear later and are recapitulated in the concluding "Marche," providing a frame for the loosely linked scenes, each of which opens with a version of the four notes promised on the title page. The traditional commedia dell' arte clowns, the melancholy Pierrot and the mischievous Arlequin, are first to appear. After a pause for a "Valse noble," Eusebius and Florestan introduce themselves in turn. Eusebius speaks sotto voce in a meditative adagio piece in E-flat; the notes that spell ASCH are shared by bass and treble in the opening two measures. His tender voice is evenly spaced in long phrases that override the bar lines. He remains modestly within the span of a single octave until a middle section of his "scene," marked *molto teneramente*, is broadened by rolled chords in the bass and octaves in the treble. Florestan follows Eusebius in a contrasting *appassionato* style, dancing up and down the keyboard in strongly accented rhythms. He identifies himself with a *sforzando* F-sharp, after which he recalls us to his earlier incarnation as Wult in *Papillons* (setting off for the ball "like a hero dressed for battle") by a memory of the opening theme of *Papillons*. At the end of Florestan's scene, the notes spelling ASCH are given full weight for the first time. These lead into an extended flirtation in two parts, "Coquette" and "Réplique," the lovers not yet identified, although two young women in the composer's life are soon to appear.

"Chiarina" is a portrait of Clara at the piano, both hands in total command, performing fortissimo octaves at speed with bravura confidence. Like Florestan's, her voice is *appassionato,* as she exuberantly demonstrates her natural mastery of the keyboard. Her musical portrait conveys Schumann's delight in her artistry, compared with that of another young pianist, Anna de Belleville, who had been on tour in Leipzig: "Belleville's playing is technically the finer; Clara's is more impassioned. Belleville's tone flatters but does not penetrate the ear; Clara's tone reaches the heart. Anna is a poetess; Clara is poetry itself."

Ernestine is masked as "Estrella," suggesting "star." Her dance officially confirms her as a member of the *Davidsbund,* inviting her to promenade with the others and to join the march against the Philistines that ends the carnival. She takes her place in a confident, strongly accented waltz, suggesting grace and well-bred restraint. A *piano* interval, faster and *molto espressivo*, hints at a childlike delight in play, the masked young woman leaping about before returning to the decorous dance style of the opening. The instruction *con affetto*—with feeling and tenderness, with love—suggests a love affair. But it is hard to get a clear sense of Ernestine's character from her scene. Before starting work on *Carnaval*, Schumann had described Ernestine to his mother as "a noble, pure, childlike spirit, tender and sensitive, with the deepest love for me and for all artistic endeavor." He added that if he were to think of the perfect wife, it could well be "this one." Hence the contrasting sections of "Estrella," which reflect not only Ernestine's aristocratic parentage but her innocent character.

Two admired artists appear as guest members of the *Davidsbund*: Chopin and Paganini, speaking in their own styles, cleverly imitated. Schumann recognized in Chopin's music a fellow spirit, subject to no rules, giving free rein to his genius. "Chopin" suggests in its lovely free-floating melody and arpeggiated accompaniment one of Chopin's own nocturnes. "Paganini" cavorts unstoppably in rapid presto leaps. Schumann had heard Paganini perform, and thought of him as a magician bursting upon the tired scene of European music and transforming it forever.

Additional scenes probably conceal hidden messages for Ernestine. "Reconnaissance" suggests lovers recognizing the faces behind the masks; and "Aveu" (confession) marked *appassionato,* could be read as a confession of love. A penultimate "Promenade" brings together all the carnival revelers, and the final "Marche des Davids-bündler contre les Philistins" provides a grand conclusion.

As the full cast triumphantly recall the carnival themes of the "Préambule," the "Marche" takes on political meaning. Florestan, the leader of the *Davidsbund*, represents not only his namesake, Beethoven's imprisoned patriot, but David, enemy of the Philistines. The traditional "Grandfather's Dance" of *Papillons* reappears in the "Marche" as "Theme from the 17th century." Asserting the continued power of the past, it is imitated, parodied, and roundly defeated by the *Davidsbündler*—youth triumphing over age, the united forces of the new artistic age claiming their rights against the tired conventions of the Philistine bourgeoisie.

Carnaval captivated audiences from the start. It inspired one of Mikhail Fokine's most magical ballets, in which each scene is acted out by dancers appearing and reappearing in new combinations as the music moves to its climactic end. Fokine also turned *Papillons* into a ballet. The great Russian choreographer had a perfect understanding of the short dances which puzzled their first listeners.

The *Études symphoniques*, like *Carnaval*, were originally composed as a tribute to Schumann's prospective union with Ernestine's family. Her father visited Leipzig in the summer of 1834 to assess Schumann's suitability as a husband and to rescue Ernestine from danger, taking her home with him to Asch. On her departure Schumann gave Ernestine his portrait and a ring, signs of serious commitment. His parting letter to her is singularly formal, opening thus: "If I dared to speak as I would like to, I would first thank the good Genius who permitted me to get to know you, my honored friend." Wieck, observing his protégé with his usual cynicism, wrote to Ernestine's father that the infatuated couple had not yet exchanged a kiss.

In a sign of good will, the baron had presented the would-be fiancé with his own set of variations for flute. Schumann then took the flute melody as the theme for his *Études symphoniques*, which he acknowledged in the first edition with a footnote in small print: "Les notes de la mélodie sont de la Composition d'un Amateur," a note omitted in the revised edition of 1852. When he sent a copy of the work to the baron, Schumann suggested that Ernestine play it for him. Evidently he had great confidence in her musical ability, since the *Études* posed extremely difficult challenges for the pianist.

Carnaval is essentially a merry work, romantic and tender, made of games, pranks, disguises, secret love messages. The *Études symphoniques* are *serioso*, the theme marked *grave* in an early draft, and the title suggesting a grander style than the piano alone could provide. Schumann set the baron's melody to an accompaniment of full chords, suggesting a funeral march—an odd choice for a love gift. But the solemn theme is enlivened in the variations by upbeat counterthemes and tender lyrical meditations, with markings that suggest increasing excitement: *un poco più vivo, vivace, vivacissimo, agitato, scherzando, presto possibile*, and in the grand Finale, *allegro brillante*. No fun-and-games here, but the *Études* form a worthy contrast to *Carnaval*, with a much wider emotional and compositional range than the variations Schumann had composed previously. In the Finale he reaches new heights of expressiveness and drama. No doubt the passionate quality of the work has to do with Ernestine. His feelings were evidently very strong at the time of writing both *Carnaval* and the *Études symphoniques*. He wrote to Henriette Voigt, sending a message for Ernestine as she was leaving for Asch: "Tell her that if she should not get a letter from me for some time, she is never to be in doubt about my feelings . . . It is my Ernestine whom I love so immeasurably, and yourself, Henriette, my beloved friend."

The publisher's advertisement of the *Études* in Schumann's *New Journal* attributes the work to "Florestan and Eusebius," and it is possible to hear their joint authorship, with the left hand and the right speaking in counterpoint, often in different rhythmic patterns, sometimes in unison. Some variations could conceivably be in the voice of one or the other, Florestan speaking with strongly accented passion, Eusebius more tenderly. Schumann plays with each element of the baron's theme and his own accompaniment as the source of new subjects. A countertheme holds a conversation with the original melody when it makes a late entry; the heavy accompaniment is turned into sharp staccato chords chasing each other in canon; the theme appears *forte* in the bass, with ornamented *pianissimo* arpeggios floating above it.

While Schubert is the presiding spirit of *Carnaval,* the *Études* suggest Schumann's close knowledge of Beethoven's works, especially the *Eroica* Variations and the most romantic piano sonatas, the *Pathétique* and the *Appassionata*. The symphonic character of the *Études* reflects Schumann's study of Beethoven's symphonies and his admiration of Beethoven's "heroic" style. He adapts Beethoven's characteristic mode of development, breaking up an initial theme into its constituent elements, using these to initiate new motifs or counterthemes, and bringing them together dramatically in counterpoint. With his imagination working at full stretch, he breaks up the baron's simple melody, varies it rhythmically, takes a single element, like the opening interval of a descending fourth, and uses it to initiate what seems to be an entirely new motif. The listener might wonder what has happened to the first theme until it suddenly reappears, disguised at first in the bass, or almost suppressed by an elaborate accompaniment, only to emerge at last in full strength, working perfectly in counterpoint against the new subject. The pleasure for performer and listener lies in the transformation of the theme and its sudden full-blown reappearance, along with the unexpected way all the elements work together. Each sequence sounds like Schumann—the driving rhythms, the sustained harmonies, the long-delayed resolution. But the spirit of Beethoven is speaking through Schumann's voice.

As with the final version of *Carnaval*, several variations were considered and later rejected. These are mainly Eusebian in style, lyrical and reflective rather than dramatic. Later published in Clara Schumann's edition, they are often included in modern performances.

Carnaval and the *Études symphoniques*, composed at the same time in response to a love affair, in different ways announce Schumann's fully formed style and signature. They mark a dramatic extension of his powers of invention and his control of structure. Everything he has done up to this time contributes to a new freedom and mastery: his lessons in counterpoint, his intensive study of Bach's *Well-Tempered Clavier*, his familiarity with Schubert's published works and the complete works of Beethoven. His own earlier efforts, too, published and unpublished, constituted excellent preparation: the masquerade of *Papillons*, the brilliant Toccata, the early unpublished variations on Schubert's "Sehnsucht" Waltz and on Beethoven's Seventh Symphony; the published sets of variations, intermezzi, and impromptus. True to his conviction of his own ability and his impatience with conventional instruction, his real masters in the craft were not the textbooks recommended by his teachers, but Bach and Mozart, Beethoven and Schubert.

By the time *Carnaval* and the *Études symphoniques* appeared in print in 1837, their original impetus had long been displaced. Although the baron would probably have agreed to her marriage to Schumann, he kept Ernestine safely at home in Asch after his visit to Leipzig. Schumann visited the Bohemian town in October and again in December. In the summer of 1835, Ernestine confessed to Schumann that she was not the baron's daughter but the illegitimate child of his wife's sister, Countess Caroline Ernestine Louise von Zedtwitz. Her father was a man identified only as a *Handwerker* (craftsman or artisan) and by his surname, Lindauer. Some documents suggest that he was a factory owner, probably married. The baron and his wife were childless, and brought up Caroline's child as their own. After Schumann's December visit, the baron formally adopted Ernestine. But in addition to her illegitimate birth, she confessed to Schumann that she was poor. According to one account, the baron had decided not to make her his heir or to provide a dowry. More likely, the baron was not as rich as had been assumed; his property was probably entailed and his income compromised. Whatever the reasons, Schumann's passion cooled when he learned that the young woman he had sworn to marry was neither noble nor rich. Within a few months, the engagement was terminated. According to Schumann's diary: "Summer of 1835: cut loose from Ernestine—*ach!*" and, at the end of 1835, "broke formally with Ernestine."

During Ernestine's absence from Leipzig, Schumann was in frequent company with Clara, and by the autumn of 1835 she had supplanted Ernestine in his affections. It was to be a far more serious love affair, transforming Schumann's life and his music.

4

AN EVEN MORE IMPORTANT YEAR

Leipzig, 1835

Schumann described the year 1835 as "even more important [than 1834] in its consequences." Central to this year was his new relationship with Clara, which developed during the spring and summer, reaching a climax after Clara's sixteenth birthday on September 13. Of great importance, too, were the other key events of September: Mendelssohn's arrival in Leipzig as music director of the Gewandhaus Orchestra and the visit soon afterwards of Chopin, Schumann's idol.

MENDELSSOHN

At twenty-six, a year older than Schumann, Mendelssohn was an international celebrity when he took up his post in Leipzig. He was famous throughout Europe for organizing the first performance of Bach's *St. Matthew Passion* in Berlin. His early Octet for Strings, composed when he was only sixteen, and his Overture to *A Midsummer Night's Dream*, composed a year later, were as original and perfectly formed as his later works. He was already making a brilliant career as a composer and a virtuoso pianist.

Mendelssohn's grandfather was the philosopher Moses Mendelssohn, a good friend of the playwright Gotthold Ephraim Lessing and the model for the hero of Lessing's play *Nathan the Wise*. Mendelssohn's family on both his mother's and father's sides were wealthy bankers in Hamburg and Berlin. They were Jews of the highest cultivation, patrons of the arts with a strong dedication to service. Many family members converted to Lutheranism, including Mendelssohn's father, Abraham, who had Felix baptized at the age of seven, partly for prudential reasons, since many professions were legally closed to Jews. But Abraham considered Christianity a far more enlightened religion than Judaism, as he carefully explained to Felix and his sister Fanny when they were confirmed.

During two years of European travel, Mendelssohn had met leading musical figures in Vienna, Rome, London, and other major cities. In Paris he became friends with Chopin, Liszt, and the composer Ferdinand Hiller, who later chronicled their youthful escapades, describing Mendelssohn turning cartwheels as they walked home one evening. Although Mendelssohn continued to have close relations with musical circles in London, with many of his works commissioned and first performed in England, he chose to make his career in Germany, avoiding his family home of Berlin, which he knew too well as a center of political and artistic conservatism.

He was a young man of extraordinary gifts and immense personal charm. He drew beautifully, he was an expert gymnast, he knew several languages. He was slim, boyish, with dark curly hair, bright eyes, a ready smile. Wherever he went, all doors were open to him. He remained modest, devoted to his family, and determined to use his phenomenal gifts in the service of humanity and of music, which he, like Schumann, considered the noblest of the arts.

He was offered the post of municipal music director at Düsseldorf, where he remained for only two years. Then Leipzig beckoned, with its higher musical standards and a unique musical tradition. Johann Sebastian Bach had served as cantor of St. Thomas Church in Leipzig until his death in 1750; he composed many of his greatest works in the Saxon town. The offer from the Gewandhaus Orchestra left Mendelssohn free to travel and to compose for several months of the year. He arrived in September 1835, eager to take charge of the subscription concerts. He soon transformed the city's musical life, replacing virtuoso showpieces with serious works by Bach and

Handel, Mozart and Beethoven, and performing new works by the best living composers.

Before taking up his position, he visited Leipzig briefly in August and met Henriette Voigt, who presented Mendelssohn with Schumann's recently published Impromptus on a Theme by Clara Wieck. Mendelssohn wrote to Henriette, praising some parts, especially no. 11 (later omitted by Schumann), and expressing reservations about others. When Mendelssohn arrived in Leipzig in September, Schumann told him that he knew all his music well. The young men soon discovered that they shared many of the same passions—reverence for Bach, love of Mozart and Beethoven, enthusiasm for the novels of Jean Paul. Schumann was enraptured by Mendelssohn, writing to his sister-in-law Therese: "I look up to him as to a high mountain. He is a true God." In his diary he recorded Mendelssohn's conversation, impressed by his general intelligence, his high ideals, his literary and artistic culture. He reveled in Mendelssohn's companionship and their games of chess and billiards. Yet, inevitably, aware of his own deficiencies, he felt a certain envy of Mendelssohn's privileged background. He wrote to Clara later: "I know I could learn from him for years; but he too could learn some things from me."

Possibly Schumann thought that his example might encourage Mendelssohn to be more daring, less perfect, less puritanical. He commented on Mendelssohn's joy at his engagement to Cécile Jeanrenaud, the daughter of a Huguenot pastor, with the amused response of one who, unlike Mendelssohn, was sexually experienced. Though awkward in his manners, ill at ease in society, Schumann knew more about ordinary life than the man whom he held in such esteem.

In their frequent social meetings, often with others of the *Davidsbund* circle, Mendelssohn was naturally the center of attention, with Schumann an admiring listener, secretly including Mendelssohn in the *Davidsbund* as "Felix Meritis." Mendelssohn described Schumann to his mother as "introverted, but a very good man." Mendelssohn despised journalism, having been annoyed by hostile comments in the Berlin newspapers. When Schumann asked if Mendelssohn would send him a review of the Lower Rhine Festival, where Mendelssohn was conducting Beethoven's Ninth Symphony, Mendelssohn sought all possible reasons to decline, suggesting that someone else would be far more qualified. After long delays and with many apologies, he finally sent Schumann a new composition—his "Pagenlied"—for a special feature of the *Journal,* a supplement featuring new work. It was not until he conducted Schumann's *Spring* Symphony in 1841 that he recognized Schumann's genius as a composer. Apart from his early comments on the Impromptus, he seems to have been unimpressed by the piano works, several of which he heard Clara perform.

The only contemporary musician to appreciate Schumann's piano suites with real enthusiasm was the Hungarian pianist Franz Liszt, who used his own fame to present *Carnaval* and other works to audiences in Vienna and Paris. With prescient judgment, Liszt found Chopin and Schumann the two most interesting young composers of the time.

CHOPIN

Chopin himself did not share Liszt's view of Schumann's works. The composers met for the first time in September 1835, when Chopin stopped briefly in Leipzig, at Wieck's invitation. Wieck had met Chopin in Paris in 1832, when Clara played Chopin's compositions "like a witch," Chopin told a friend. Chopin had presented Clara with a copy of his First Piano Concerto, writing in French: "I look forward greatly to hear it performed by such an outstanding talent."

Wieck, the great impresario, behaved with typical arrogance, insisting that Clara make Chopin wait for an hour at their house before presenting herself. She then entertained Chopin with the final movement of her own piano concerto, Schumann's Sonata op. 11, and two of Chopin's études. Later that night, at Mendelssohn's lodgings, Mendelssohn played through the whole of his new oratorio, *St. Paul,* while Chopin, to Mendelssohn's amusement, played two new études and his own new piano concerto between parts one and two of the oratorio. Schumann was an enthralled listener.

Chopin's brief visit inspired a joint letter from Mendelssohn, writing in French, and Schumann, writing in German, urging Chopin to join them the following Easter at the Lower Rhine Festival in Düsseldorf. No answer came, but Schumann wrote to Chopin again a few months later, with typical enthusiasm:

> Dear and Honored Sir, You need only write the one word "Yes" . . . in answer to the question whether, as I have just heard, you are in Dresden or not. Being on the point of returning home via Dresden, I would never forgive myself if I had been anywhere near Your Magnificence without giving a sign of my love and respect. I beg you most longingly to say Yes . . . Your devoted Robert Schumann

Two weeks later Schumann wrote to his former theory teacher Heinrich Dorn:

> Just as I received your letter two days ago . . . who should walk in but Chopin! We spent a wonderful day together . . . He gave me a new Ballade in G Minor, it seems to me his most inspired work . . . Besides that he played a whole number of new études, nocturnes, and mazurkas—everything incomparably. Just to see him sitting at the piano is affecting . . . Try to conceive such perfection, a mastery that seems unconscious of itself.

Schumann rewrote his encounter with Chopin for his *New Journal* in a piece by Florestan, who tells "Beda" (Clara), enraptured by Chopin's music, that he has actually met the great man:

> I told her what an unforgettable sight it was to see him at the piano, like a dreaming seer, and how, as he played, one became identified in one's own mind with his dream, and

how he had a nervous habit, at the end of each piece, of running a finger from one end of the keyboard to the other in a glissando, as if to break the spell, and how he had to spare himself because of his delicate health.

Schumann's half-fictional account shows the insight of a fellow composer who, like Chopin, started life as an aspiring piano virtuoso. He knew that Chopin's music reflected his special relationship with the instrument.

Chopin inscribed his G Minor Ballade "to my friend R. Schuhmann [sic]." But he was unsympathetic to the high Romanticism that Schumann espoused so enthusiastically. Chopin scorned the very idea of literary titles for music; he believed that music should speak for itself. He was a remarkably original composer, but he deliberately adopted traditional conventions, naming his pieces études, preludes, nocturnes, waltzes, even while turning the conventions upside down. The titles some of his works soon acquired—the "Raindrop" Prelude, the "Revolutionary" Étude—would have appalled him. He had very little interest in the works of his contemporaries. He used Mendelssohn's early *Songs Without Words* in his teaching, but he resented Mendelssohn's fame. He hated the way his friend Liszt reinterpreted his works, adding ornaments of his own. His only comments about Schumann, as reported by his students, referred to the elaborate frontispiece of *Carnaval*: "The Germans know how to do these things." About *Kreisleriana*, which Schumann dedicated to him, he said that it was not music as he understood music.

Schumann remained happily ignorant of Chopin's negative views, and he continued to review Chopin's works with high praise. He thought of Chopin as a fellow Romantic; he learned from Chopin's chromaticism, his free use of dissonance, the passionate feelings expressed in his works even when they were presented as technical studies. He understood Chopin's political passion. In a famous review of Chopin's piano concertos, he wrote: "If the powerful autocratic Monarch of the North [the Russian tsar] knew what a dangerous enemy threatens him in Chopin's works, in the simple melodies of his mazurkas, he would ban all music. Chopin's works are cannons buried under flowers." Occasionally he offered advice; he thought that Chopin was in danger of being corrupted by shallow Parisian values. He found Chopin's Sonata in B-flat formless: "four of his maddest children" yoked together. He agreed with Mendelssohn that Chopin's second subjects in his sonatas tended to be weak. Schumann and Mendelssohn were receptive to everything new and original, but they both believed in the necessity of structure and clear organization.

CLARA AT SIXTEEN

As Schumann was gaining recognition from his weekly articles for the *Journal* and published compositions, his private life entered a new phase. After Ernestine confessed her illegitimacy, between her poverty and her sentimental letters, written frequently during her absence from Leipzig, Schumann's ardor significantly cooled. He spent much of his spare time with Clara throughout the spring and summer of 1835. She presented him with a watchband for his birthday on June 8th, accompanied by a charming letter, which he answered in turn. The tone of the exchange suggests that behind their long-standing friendship, deeper bonds were taking shape. He released himself from his ties with Ernestine in the summer, emotionally if not formally. After Clara's sixteenth birthday in September, celebrated by Schumann with Mendelssohn and other friends (the *Davidsbündler* presented Clara with a gold watch), he records a dawning realization of Clara's new being. Her attachment to him had a different coloring; her eyes were shining with love. Their first kiss, in November, marked a defining stage in their relations. Clara told Schumann afterwards that she thought she would faint when he kissed her.

They both recalled these events in their correspondence, delighting in the details of their early friendship—with Clara reproaching Schumann for his evident preference of Ernestine. Schumann: "My earliest memory of you goes back to summer 1828: you were painting letters and trying to write, while I was studying [Hummel's] A

Minor Concerto, and I often looked round at you. I remember it as though it were today." Clara: "How clearly I remember that first afternoon after we got back from Hamburg, when you came into the room and scarcely even said hello; so I went off to Auguste, who was with us then, and said through my tears, 'Oh, I don't love anyone the way I do him; and he wouldn't even look at me!'"

Clara was not only prodigiously gifted but remarkably independent. She was her own person, free from the usual restraints suffered by young girls. She was already acclaimed as an artist; she moved in sophisticated circles in Paris and Vienna. As a child, she was passionate and willful, with a wild temper and strong opinions.

She adored her father and could not bear her stepmother, Clementine. Schumann was her favorite companion. She looked after him, skipped ahead of him to pick up pebbles in the road, worried that he would stumble over them in his usual absentminded way. She was sure that she alone knew the real "Herr Schumann" whom nobody else understood—the delightful playmate, an endless source of charades, puzzles, ghost stories. The child prodigy and the aspiring young composer exchanged compositions, shared musical motifs, criticized one another's works as if on equal terms.

When Clara turned sixteen in September, Schumann recognized the love that Clara had never tried to disguise, and he responded in kind. Soon they were secretly affianced. Each element of their earlier relationship carried over into their relations as lovers, eventually as husband and wife. Clara continued to protect her Robert; she remained the one person who understood him. They continued to share their lives as fellow artists—with a significant difference. By 1835, Clara was recognized in the major European capitals as a brilliantly gifted pianist. Schumann was better known as a journalist than as a composer. Although he had a strong inner belief in his abilities, apart from Liszt only Clara recognized the originality of his early piano works. But even she found them awkward and difficult. Wieck, in his letter to Schumann's mother, predicted that his best prospect of earning a livelihood would be as a teacher, like Wieck himself. Schumann's friends regarded him affectionately and with amusement as a Romantic enthusiast.

But Schumann had vast ambitions, and Clara knew that she alone had the power to make his works known to the larger world. They continued to share their compositions, but for Clara, Schumann's genius was primary. Meeting incomprehension from audiences, she begged him to write in a more accessible way. At every stage of their shared life, she used her fame to promote his works. Although it has been fashionable to consider her a victim of contemporary attitudes toward women composers, it was her own decision to put Schumann's needs as both a man and an artist ahead of her own. She was always the stronger of the two, and her fame as the greatest woman pianist in Europe far outshone Schumann's uncertain reputation as a difficult, obscure Romantic composer, working in the shadow of Mendelssohn and Chopin.

In his diary summary of 1838, Schumann charted the course of their love. The brief record is supported by his letters to his sister-in-law Therese, Eduard's wife, who had taken Rosalie's place as his confidante, and by his letters to Clara. The letter Clara sent with her birthday gift of a watchband could be read as a confession of love. Their "doubles" were still meeting as they had done when Clara was thirteen. To Clara, he was still "Herr Robert Schumann," and she signed herself "Your friend Clara Wieck. Clara Wieck, *Doppelgänger*." To Schumann she was "clarissima Cara, cara Clarissima!"—affectionate puns that could be read in more than one way.

There was another exchange of letters in August 1835, when Schumann was visiting his family in Zwickau. Clara wrote from Leipzig on September 1st:

Just as I was wending my way like a worm through your [F-sharp Minor] Sonata, which two gentlemen from Hanover wished very much to hear, a letter came to me, and from where? thought I. Then I read—Zwickau. I was very much surprised, since when you left here, you did not give me much hope of such a letter. I have studied it for two hours, and there are still several words that I cannot make out. What has happened to me, don't blame me for this, is that the Rosenthal [the garden where they often met] has been completely neglected since you have been gone. The reason is my great industry. You will smile, but it is true. 1. I've finished my "parts" [for her concerto]. 2. The voices have all been written out, in two days. 3. I've written out my Variations in F clearly for the printer, also my "Dance of Phantoms" and "A Sabbath Night." I've begun to orchestrate the concerto, but not yet written it out. I've changed the tutti a little . . . Greet both the Graces whom you have described to me so poetically, especially Therese . . . The *Davidsbündlerschen Florestanschen* Sonata pleased [the gentlemen from Hanover] a lot.

In December, Schumann notes "engagement—happy hours in her arms at Wieck's house in the evening." A mature professional artist, Clara was also a sensual being in a way probably unknown to Ernestine—though Ernestine later wrote to Clara that she had been hopelessly in love with Schumann. The relationship that both Schumann and Clara believed to be destined was about to take its natural course.

The "happy hours in her arms" coincided with the death of Schumann's mother, who had been ill for some time. She had in effect given her blessing to their love in December, when Clara performed at a concert in Zwickau. Schumann followed her there, and they spent some time with his mother. Now Wieck had taken Clara to Dresden, having sensed a change in her relations with Schumann. In early February, Wieck left Dresden for a few days on business, leaving Clara behind. Schumann rushed to Dresden before going to Zwickau, therefore missing his mother's funeral. The letter he wrote to Clara from the coach, as he left Zwickau to return to Leipzig, expresses his love as poetically as his music was to do during the following months and years:

At the Zwickau post office, in the evening about 10 o'clock [13 February 1836]

My eyes are heavy with sleep . . . How you stand before me, my beloved, beloved Clara, ah, it seems as if you are so close to me that I could embrace you. Once I could put my feelings into words, however strong they were; now I can no longer do so. And if you didn't know how much I love you, I wouldn't be able to tell you . . . Do you hear, only love me well in return . . . Today many things happened—the opening of my mother's will, accounts of her death. Behind all the darkness your bright image gleams and I can bear everything more easily. I must tell you that my future now looks much more certain. But I mustn't let my hands lie idle and must work hard . . . to win what you see each time you happen to pass by a mirror . . . You too must remain an artist . . . that is, you will bear with me, work with me, share all joys and sorrows with me. Write to me about this.

In Leipzig my first task will be to put all my affairs in order—with my inner being I am at peace . . . Perhaps your father will not hold back his hand when I ask him for his blessing . . . I trust to our good genius. We have been destined by fate for each other—I have known this for a long time, but I was never confident enough to tell you before, nor could you have understood me.

What I'm writing to you briefly and in haste, I'll explain more clearly for you later . . . Know only that I love you unspeakably. It is growing dark in the room. Passengers sleep near me. Outside it is gusty and snowing. But I will bury myself deeply in a corner with my head on a cushion and will think only of you. Farewell, my Clara. Your Robert . . .

P.S. Write to me often, every day.

FRIEDRICH WIECK, PATERFAMILIAS

What followed was a blow that shattered their hopes and dominated the struggles of the next four years. Schumann had every reason to expect Clara's father to share in the lovers' happiness. He was twenty-five years old, owner and editor-in-chief of a serious music journal with a European circulation of over three hundred subscribers. His annual income included the interest on his father's legacy, increased by his mother's recent death. His published works were receiving performances and critical acclaim.

Wieck was his "honored master," his teacher and friend, his close associate in the *New Journal*. In effect he was a foster father to the youth, who had lost his own father at the age of sixteen. There was not yet any talk of marriage, although there was a "kiss of engagement" in February. Mainly there was simply a shared love which had its roots in the companionship which Wieck had always encouraged.

But Wieck behaved like a comic caricature of the enraged paterfamilias. Schumann had betrayed the man who had done so much to promote his career, entrapping Wieck's gifted daughter in a doomed romance. Her father had very different plans for her. How dare a man of no consequence aspire to the hand of an artist who had already conquered Paris and was soon to make her name in Vienna? Schumann drank too much; he was hardly able to speak in company; he stuttered; his handwriting was illegible; his compositions, according to many eminent musicians, were incomprehensible. And what about Ernestine von Fricken, the young woman whom Schumann had only recently wooed and won? Wieck refused absolutely to countenance any talk of love or marriage. Within days he removed Clara from Leipzig and forbade her to meet Schumann or write to him.

At sixteen, Clara had to obey her father. She was Wieck's child, in thrall to his will, and she loved him. She had been motherless in all but name from the age of five. Wieck was father and mother to her, one moment stern and demanding, the next moment loving and indulgent. She could not believe that his rage would last; in time he would come round. She could only grieve in private, and counsel patience to herself and to her beloved Robert.

Schumann's outrage at Wieck's treatment was fueled by his sense of undeserved rejection. Yet, like Clara, he believed secretly that Wieck was bound to relent. His relations with Wieck went back to his first piano lessons in Leipzig. He had been eighteen years old, a reluctant law student with a passionate desire to pursue his true vocation as a musician. Wieck made it possible for him to abandon law for the piano, writing to Schumann's mother that he was convinced Schumann would do well under his own expert tuition. Wieck was central to his entire career, with all its ups and downs—his enthusiastic studies of piano technique and composition, his experiments with mechanical aids for dexterity, the crippling of his right hand, his deepening companionship with a circle of musical friends, with Wieck and Clara at its heart. As recently as a year before, Wieck had been his partner in the founding of the *New Journal for Music*. His veneration for his "honored master" is evident in his diaries and letters throughout this period: his gratitude to Wieck for introducing him to the Schubert E-flat Piano Trio, his assiduous work on technique, Wieck's evident acceptance of the disaster of his lamed finger. Their continued friendship was the source of Schumann's social and musical life; they met daily at cafés or beer cellars, frequently at musical evenings at Wieck's house. Schumann had eagerly dedicated his Impromptus on a Theme of Clara Wieck to her father, moving heaven and earth to have the published work ready to present to Wieck on his birthday. He continued to regard Wieck as a counselor. As "Raro," Wieck was a wise figure who was able to resolve differences between the impetuous Florestan and the more cautious Eusebius. Despite his diary complaints about Wieck's arrogance, his materialism and greed, Schumann continued to take Wieck's affection and interest for granted. To have Wieck turn against him so violently was a wrenching blow to his judgment and his self-esteem as well as to his prospects in life.

Clara could not understand her father's implacable hostility to her Robert. She remained convinced that he would change his mind. She knew that Schumann had certain faults. But that these should weigh at all against their love for each other was inconceivable.

Behind Wieck's enraged response to Schumann lay the disaster of his divorce from Clara's mother, Mariane Tromlitz. Despite his insistence that Clara's success as a pianist was entirely due to his teaching, Wieck must have known that her talent came from her mother, a gifted singer and pianist. Mariane's family included several accomplished musicians; her father was a cantor, her grandfather a well-known flautist.

The bare facts of her mother's departure from the family home are set down in Clara's diary, dictated by Wieck: "In Easter 1821 my parents moved to Kupfers House in Salzgässchen, and it was here that I would lose my mother. That is, she left my father on the 12th of May 1824 to go to Plauen until their divorce."

Mariane left Leipzig with the four-year-old Clara and the infant Victor, born the previous February and registered as the child of Wieck and Mariane. She took refuge in her parents' home in Plauen, a small town about sixty miles south of Leipzig. Clara was returned to Wieck just after her fifth birthday, as required by Saxon law, which gave the father rights over the child from the age of five. In a heartfelt letter, Mariane begged Wieck to allow her to accompany Clara to Leipzig. Wieck, responding with the self-righteous coldness of an injured husband, insisted on having his maid Johanna Strobel meet Mariane halfway, in Altenburg, where Mariane and her mother handed over the child. The couple were granted a divorce in January, and a few months later Mariane married Adolf Bargiel, a friend and colleague of Wieck's.

Mariane and Bargiel lived together in Leipzig for a year, during which time Clara was permitted to visit her mother. Wieck's letter to Mariane is typical of the man, and also hints at the circumstances behind their divorce:

> Madam! I send you here the dearest thing I have left in my life, on condition that where possible you remain silent about everything that has happened, or explain matters so simply and truthfully that this innocent, harmless, and entirely natural creature shall hear nothing that causes her any suspicions. Above all make sure that she has few pastries and do not overlook any bad manners, as happened in Plauen. When she plays, do not let her rush. I expect you to follow my wishes to the letter, or I shall become very angry.

A year later, Bargiel was offered a post in Berlin at an institute for teaching music students the Logier method, based on mechanical aids like the one which Schumann used so disastrously. The family moved to Berlin with one-year-old Victor. Clara saw her mother in Berlin a few years later, when she was briefly on tour there with Wieck. A few letters to her mother survive, written in a formal tone that suggests Wieck's guidance and his determination to stamp out any remaining affection on Clara's part.

Until recently, biographers have been unable to explain the divorce beyond speculating on its possible causes. Wieck must have been difficult to live with; he was a severe taskmaster, and kept Mariane working as a concert performer and a teacher on a rigorous schedule. But the fact that she gave birth to five infants in less than eight years suggests that the marriage was reasonably stable. (The first child, a girl, Adelheid, died nine months after birth; next came Clara, then the boys Alwin and Gustav and Victor). Wieck would not have considered the radical step of divorce unless compelled to do so. Unsurprisingly, a third person was involved.

Wieck had become friends with Adolf Bargiel in his early days as a tutor in an aristocratic household, where the young Bargiel was employed in a similar capacity. Bargiel followed Wieck to Leipzig, and it is possible that Wieck invited Bargiel to lodge with him, at least at first, and to help with Wieck's expanding music business. Wieck was often absent on travels to Vienna and other musical centers to purchase instruments. Although Victor was registered as his child, Wieck must have discovered soon afterwards that the father was in fact Bargiel. There is no evidence that Wieck took any interest in the child or made any claim for his return. Victor survived for only three years.

A hitherto unpublished letter to Wieck by Mariane's father, Georg Christian Tromlitz, makes plain the facts behind the divorce:

Never would I have believed that Mariane could sink so low . . . and I cannot understand even now how she can have become what she now is. My God! Must I and my dear wife in our old age live through such disgrace from a child whom I raised with so much care, and for whom I and her mother have sacrificed everything? You as her husband must know your wife best, and must know best whether she deserves your forgiveness or not; for I hardly know her now, since at least toward her parents she has changed entirely.

He tells Wieck that whatever course matters take, Mariane cannot depend on her parents to support her, for he has hardly any income from teaching; besides, should she return to her parents, their town is too small for the reason for her presence to remain hidden. He goes into some detail about how poor he has become. And he must think about her younger sister, Emilie, too. These are the reasons why he cannot do anything more for Mariane. And for whom should he be doing this?

> For an ingrate, who is making her parents, her husband, her children and herself unhappy. And if she does not give up her love for this scoundrel, then let her go and beg! God in heaven, this breaks our hearts! Ach—the unhappy Mariane! . . . I think you yourself must be guilty of your wife's straying—you should have stayed with her and forbidden all opportunity for her to spend time with Bargiel. How could you leave these two people alone so often and for such a long time? . . . God give you patience and Mariane good sense!

It seems clear that even if Wieck decided to "forgive" Mariane, she refused to give up her lover. Hence her departure from Leipzig with three-month-old Victor and Clara, taking refuge with her parents. By the following September, Tromlitz was writing to Bargiel as "my dearest friend," thanking him for his loving letter to Mariane, asking for help with various personal chores (a request for five yards of cloth, unavailable in Plauen, for his overcoat), sending warm regards from himself and his wife, asking Bargiel to write to them again very soon, and signing himself "your true friend."

When Wieck learned that Clara was virtually affianced to Schumann, it must have triggered the rage that he still cherished toward Mariane. He had made sure that Clara understood how wicked her mother was to abandon husband and children. Was it possible that Clara, his darling, his creature, had inherited her mother's low character? He could not bear the thought that having lost her mother, he would now lose his daughter—his pride, his source of income—to a man with no real prospect of fame or fortune, a drinker (as Wieck knew from their shared evenings at local taverns), eccentric, awkward. His feelings toward Clara's mother remained bitter and unforgiving. He was equally unforgiving toward Schumann, a man who had betrayed his hospitality by stealing the one precious thing left in his life—his daughter.

Schumann's life for the next three years was dominated by Wieck's furious reaction to what he saw as Schumann's betrayal and Clara's foolishness. He threatened to shoot Schumann; he banned all communication between the lovers. He took Clara away on tour, and he insisted that she return Schumann's letters. The lovers were not to meet again for eighteen months.

5

WIECK ON THE WARPATH

Leipzig, 1836

"A DARK YEAR"

The "dark year" of 1836 signaled what Schumann feared was a complete break with Clara. He sank into depression and sought diversion with his former lover Christel. Yet it was also a period of intense work, compositions completed and published, and new work begun, expressing his love and his despair—the complementary emotions which characterize his greatest work.

There are two diary sources for this troubled period: Schumann's summary of the years from 1834 onward, written in Vienna in 1838, and his day-to-day record from July 28, 1836, to October 28, 1837. In his 1838 summary, Schumann notes cryptically that in 1836 he sought out "Charitas" (Christel, real name Christiane Apitzsch) and that "consequences" followed in January 1837. Schumann also mentions encounters with "La Faneuse," a slang term for a whore, literally "one who makes hay," which suggests that he had another sexual relationship during this period. After her first mention, the diary notes "former thoughts of *Faneuse* entirely laid aside"; and just before August 1837: "angry encounter with the *Faneuse*—and discovery in the beer *Keller*." The relationship, if there was one, was finished.

A note in Schumann's diary for January 1837 reads "A little girl, (on the 5th, I think)." According to local records, an illegitimate child was born to Christiane Apitzsch in St. Jacob's Hospital, Leipzig, on the 2nd of January, 1837. The infant was baptised four days later as "Louise Ernestine," and the father was named as "David Veit, Caretaker." No other record survives of a "David Veit." The name might well have referred to Schumann's *Davidsbund*, of which "Charitas" had been a secret member. As a servant in Leipzig, probably in Wieck's house, Christiane would also have known about Ernestine von Fricken. There seems little doubt that Schumann was the father of "Louise Ernestine," who was sent at once to Christiane's parents. Nothing further is known of her fate. In November 1837, Schumann records paying two thalers to "C" as a present; another two thalers were paid in December "to Charitas for Christmas." Christiane Apitzsch (that is, Charitas, otherwise Christel) died of typhus the following year.

Despite his sexual adventures, Schumann's chief concern during this time was his passionate, tormented relationship to Clara. He was banned from communicating with her, but when she returned to Leipzig in April, he saw her at least twice "from afar." The autumn of 1836 was darkened by Clara's letter breaking off their relations "by her own decision." Then at the second Gewandhaus concert, on October 9, he noted in his diary, turning to French for his private thoughts: *"A la sortie les yeux de C."* A month later, at the Gewandhaus concert on November 3, Schumann and Clara heard Mendelssohn play Beethoven's G Major Piano Concerto, a work they both loved. Schumann noted: "C. very sad and lovely." A week later he wrote to his sister-in-law Therese: "C[lara] loves me as much as ever, but I have quite given up hope."

Unhappy though he was, Schumann continued to have an active social life. His professional life prospered with the publication of his F-sharp Minor Sonata, op. 11, and the first version of his *Concert sans orchestre*, in three movements (suitable for a concerto) rather than the five originally composed. The *Davidsbund* circle expanded to include visiting musicians from London, Paris, Poland, and Italy. There were regular musical evenings at Henriette Voigt's house and in Schumann's lodgings, where friends read through Beethoven's last string quartets, with Mendelssohn often taking the part of second violin or viola. A morning musicale in Schumann's lodgings included Beethoven's String Quartet op. 130, Mendelssohn's A Minor String Quartet, and four-hand music played by Schumann himself with Ferdinand David, who was a pianist as well as violinist and composer. Schumann had thoughts of a "quintet for strings and piano four hands," possibly the germ of the lovely Andante and Variations for horn, two cellos, and two pianos, or the famous Piano Quintet, both composed a few years later. In September Schumann noted: "Idea about a contribution for Beethoven"—the first mention of what was to become the three-movement Fantasie in C, op. 17.

On Chopin's second visit to Leipzig, on September 12th, Schumann spent time alone with him before accompanying him to the door of Wieck's house, joining him again at the Voigts' for dinner. Chopin played several new works for Mendelssohn and Schumann: etudes, the F Major Ballade, a nocturne. They talked about Liszt and his phenomenal powers of invention, which were not altogether to Chopin's taste. The visit ended with an exchange of new works. Schumann gave Chopin his F-sharp Minor Sonata and his *Études symphoniques;* Chopin gave Schumann a copy of his G Minor Ballade.

Special musical events are noted in the diary: Mendelssohn and friends playing Schubert's B-flat Major Trio at sight, Bach sonatas, Schubert's Divertissement for four hands. Schumann improvises at the piano, sometimes playing *Carnaval* to new acquaintances. In spite of his finger injury, he was able to sit at the piano for hours. On December 16th he notes that the "sonata for Beethoven" has been virtually finished.

In late December he recorded his hope of a better life: "Plans. Tears, dreams, work . . . Awakening." He congratulated himself in February 1837 on having lived well, which suggests that he curbed his drinking. He copied out Bach's *Art of Fugue.* Clara left for Berlin and he saw her for the last time at a morning musicale in the Hotel de Pologne. In late March he heard the great singer Wilhelmine Schröder-Devrient as Leonore in Beethoven's *Fidelio.*

In the "dark summer" of 1836, when on her father's orders Clara had returned Schumann's letters, he oscillated between *Seelen-*

schmerz and the conviction that Clara still loved him. He poured out his feelings in two major works, the F Minor Piano Sonata, op. 14 (first published as *Concert sans orchestre*), and the Fantasie in C—works of extraordinary passion, both of which far transcend their autobiographical origin.

Virtually all the piano works of the years 1835–1839 were dominated by Schumann's struggle to win Clara as his bride, his despair at her father's intransigence, his doubts, his resurgent hopes. They are Schumann's most original and idiosyncratic works, equaled only by his song cycles of 1840, composed in a joyful riot of inspiration during the months before their marriage.

Schumann's use of Clara's themes goes back to his earliest works, starting in 1833 with the Impromptus on a Theme by Clara Wieck, which takes the theme from her *Romance Variée,* op. 3, composed in 1831, as the subject of a set of Schumann's own free variations. It was a compliment not only to the young composer but to Wieck, to whom the Impromptus were dedicated. A year later, *Carnaval* includes a portrait of Clara as Chiarina, promenading alongside Florestan and Eusebius, Chopin and Paganini, as a cherished member of the *Davidsbund*. She was a central presence in the works that followed, identifiable in the liberal use of her themes, acknowledged and unacknowledged, and above all in the three piano sonatas composed during these years.

Despite his erratic studies of compositional technique, Schumann was determined to produce major works in the classical style: sonatas and symphonies. To make his name, a young composer had to master the traditional forms, following the supreme examples of Haydn, Mozart, and Beethoven. Schumann was encouraged by the performances of a movement of his early G Minor Symphony in Zwickau and Schneeberg, and finally in Leipzig. But no further performances were scheduled, and no additional movements composed.

A classical sonata or symphony called for at least three movements, sometimes four: a substantial opening movement setting out the composer's claim to serious attention, a lyrical slow movement, and a brilliant finale drawing the work to a grand conclusion. A lighthearted scherzo or minuet might be included on either side of the slow movement.

Unlike the long-established form of "theme and variations" which Schumann found so congenial, the opening movement of a sonata, or "sonata allegro," had evolved into a distinct pattern, described in contemporary manuals: an *exposition* of the basic musical material, usually two themes in contrasting keys, stated clearly and explored separately and together; a middle section of *development*, in which the themes are broken up into their elements, varied and combined; and a *recapitulation* of the opening section, restating themes in the home key, thus concluding the "argument."

Beethoven had stretched the form to its limit in his late sonatas. And it was Beethoven who loomed largest as Schumann tackled the classical form. Schumann had written at age twenty-one: "Beethoven is not only the means to the goal; he is the goal itself!" How could a young composer possibly aspire to the heights occupied by the great ones? "Study the masters" was Schumann's advice to others, a principle he followed himself. But he was in no danger of simply imitating his models. His natural inclination was to take his own way.

Three Piano Sonatas; Fantasie in C

Schumann's three piano sonatas were composed during the same years that he was writing sets of variations and creating his own form of piano cycle, from *Papillons* in 1832 to the major works of 1837–1839, *Davidsbündlertänze, Kreisleriana,* the *Novelletten, Kinderszenen,* and *Humoreske.* Sonatas no. 1 in F-sharp Minor and no. 2 in G Minor both date in large part from 1832 and 1833, the Sonata no. 3 in F Minor from 1836. All three sonatas show Schumann struggling to express his Romantic nature as the impassioned Florestan and the gentle Eusebius while conforming as best he can to classical sonata form.

Even today, Schumann's sonatas present problems for performer and listener. There is some feeling that the F-sharp Minor and F Minor Sonatas are too repetitive, especially in the passagework of the first and final movements. Schumann himself proposed remov-

ing at least one repeat from the F Minor Sonata. The G Minor
Sonata, the earliest in its conception, is most traditional in its structure and in the relative simplicity of its harmonies. But this early
sonata, too, seems to announce a new Romanticism, with its surging
passion, the irresistible momentum carrying along composer, performer, and listener in its rushing sequences. The tempo markings
are deliberately challenging: *as fast as possible, faster,* and *even faster*
in the first movement; *presto* and *prestissimo* in the final Rondo. The
slow movement is based on a song, "An Anna," which Schumann
composed in 1828, one of a group of six he sent to the songwriter
Gottlob Wiedebein. He had introduced himself to Wiedebein as "a
youth who, uninitiated in the mysteries of sound, [is] yet inspired
to try his untrained hand at original composition." He explained
ingenuously, after receiving a kind but critical response: "I know
nothing whatever of harmony, thorough bass, or counterpoint, but
am Nature's pupil pure and simple." (Wiedebein had written that
the songs showed poetic feeling, but could use more "calm and critical Reason to curb sacred inspiration.") The song sets a despairing
love poem by Justinus Kerner, a prolific poet for whom Schumann
felt a special affinity; he later set a cycle of twelve Kerner poems as
his op. 35. Recast note for note as the second movement of a classical sonata, the song forms a tender, lyrical contrast to the stormy
opening movement.

Clara was especially fond of the G Minor Sonata. "I love it as I
love you; your whole being expresses itself so clearly in it," she wrote
to Schumann, adding "and it's not too incomprehensible." On her
urging, he composed a more accessible final Rondo, a mirror image
of the opening movement, recalling its motifs in reverse direction
and order. The G Minor Sonata remains a favorite with students and
performers.

The F-sharp Minor and F Minor Sonatas, with all their difficulties, have devoted advocates. The F-sharp Minor Sonata was
begun in 1833, with substantial debt to a "Fandango" Schumann
composed in 1832. It was completed almost in full in 1834, alongside *Carnaval.* But it was not published until 1836, when the florid
title page proclaimed the secret relations of the *Davidsbund* artists.

A winged angel holds a framed placard proclaiming in bold letters: "PIANOFORTE-SONATE, CLARA zugeeignet von FLORESTAN und EUSEBIUS"—dedicated to Clara by Florestan and Eusebius. Schumann's name does not appear anywhere in the published score.

Composed when Clara was barely fifteen, the sonata incorporates themes from her early compositions in an extended compliment to the young prodigy. The work reflects the relations of Florestan, Eusebius, and Chiarina in *Carnaval* rather than the mature relationship of lovers. The three *Davidsbündler* are portrayed in purely musical terms, with Florestan and Eusebius transforming Clara's simple themes into impassioned Romantic motifs. It is as if the twenty-four-year-old Schumann, delighting in the musical accomplishments of the gifted child, anticipated his later, mature relationship to her. His letters suggest that he always knew they were meant for each other, although a few other relationships intervened. But in retrospect, the engagement to Ernestine, the sexual liaison with Christel, the romantic attachments to older married women—Agnes Carus and Henriette Voigt—and to his sisters-in-law Rosalie and Therese, like the early infatuations with Liddy Hempel and Nanni Petsch, lost the power they had had at the time. Clara too dallied with possible suitors when it seemed that Schumann was lost to her. It was all very natural—flirtations, spasms of intense jealousy, the flickering of the flame. But Schumann's music told the true story, in which—so the music proclaims—the union of these artist-lovers was destined by fate.

In both *Carnaval* and the F-sharp Minor Sonata, Florestan and Eusebius speak in their identifying notes and keys, F-sharp and F for Florestan, E-flat and E for Eusebius. In Florestan's vehement dissonance, in Eusebius's gentle chromaticism, in the youthful exuberance and passion each character expresses, classical balance moves irresistibly toward Schumann's distinctive musical Romanticism.

His invented doubles take on transformative power in music. The contrasting characters of Florestan and Eusebius lend themselves naturally to the dramatic contrasts of the traditional forms which Schumann developed in his own way: variations on a theme, dances

and dance suites, classical sonatas. Sometimes Florestan and Eusebius speak in sequence (Allegro—Adagio—Presto); sometimes they
interrupt each other; often they seem to be having a conversation.
It hardly matters whether performers or listeners are aware of their
presence, so well do their identities—their varied "masks"—project
the music. But for Schumann they had an uncanny reality, allowing
him to express the full range of his thoughts and feelings.

Florestan introduces the F-sharp Minor Sonata with a slow
but passionate motif, a dotted rhythm in the treble against a slow,
widely spread arpeggio in the bass, his keynote of F-sharp prominent in both treble and bass. Eusebius follows sotto voce with a tender theme opening on his key note of E, over an A-major arpeggio.

Clara enters the sonata in the Allegro vivace immediately following the Introduzione, with a quotation from her early composition
published as "Le Ballet des Revenants"—one of her party pieces,
probably composed in 1832 and shared with Schumann in manuscript. Clara played Schumann's F-sharp Minor Sonata for Chopin
when he visited Leipzig in October 1835; she also played it for Ignaz
Moscheles, the eminent pianist who was a close friend of Mendelssohn's. Moscheles found it "very recherché, complex and rather
confused, but interesting." Schumann reprinted a long letter from
Moscheles in his *New Journal*, welcoming the sonata as "a genuine
sign of the Romanticism that has been awakened in our day." Liszt
reviewed the sonata for the *Paris Revue et Gazette musicale* in 1837,
praising the "simple and mournful solemnity of the beginning,
the powerful style and density of ideas in the Allegro." He thought
the second movement "one of the most perfect ideas" he had come
across and praised the "great originality" of the last movement.
Years later, Clara described playing the sonata for friends, writing
that she thought it "one of Robert's most beautiful works."

Not only is it a beautiful work, it is a remarkably original expansion of sonata form as Schumann understood it from his study
of Beethoven's sonatas. He might have had the structure and the
emotional gravity of Beethoven's *Pathétique* Sonata in mind in the
opening movement. As in the *Pathétique*, the slow Introduzione
announces a deeply serious, meaningful subject, with Florestan

speaking in the expressive left-hand accompaniment as well as the tragic motif that it supports. The Allegro brightens the mood with its "fandango" rhythms. But the Florestanian motif interrupts the dance twice, reminding the listener of the underlying gravity of the musical argument. When the Allegro makes way for the song-like Aria—marked *senza passione, ma espressivo*—the melody recalls note-for-note the Eusebian motif of the Introduzione.

If Eusebius is responsible for the tenderness of the Aria (with brief comments by Florestan in the bass), Florestan is at his most exuberant in the leaps and bounds of the Scherzo which follows the Aria and the burlesque Intermezzo attached to it. The Finale: Allegro un poco maestoso, with its driving sequences and its pauses for reflection, is a joint composition by the two *Davidsbündler*. It recalls virtually all the earlier themes, with suggestive markings: *quasi improvisato* for a recall of the Florestanian Scherzo, *delicato* and *espressivo* for a Eusebian motif; *brillante e veloce* for a thundering Florestanian chord sequence; *ad libitum ma semplice* for another Eusebian repeat.

In the revised second edition of 1840, Florestan and Eusebius disappeared from the title page, where the composer is identified properly as Robert Schumann. But even without its *Davidsbündler* element, the sonata is so dissonant, so free in its chromaticism, and rhythmically so driven, so generous in its multiple motifs, that it seems to announce a new musical form—part sonata, part fantasy, part something entirely new, for which there is not yet a term.

Although Beethoven stands behind the sonata, the work sounds entirely like Schumann in his dual personality, impassioned and lyrical by turns. This is also true of the Sonata no. 3 in F Minor, in which the presence of Beethoven's late *Hammerklavier* Sonata, one of Schumann's favorites, can be sensed. It was completed in June 1836 and published the following September in the novel form of a *Concert sans orchestre*, the title signifying the orchestral expansiveness of the writing.

Clara is present in the F Minor Sonata in the third movement, a set of variations on an unpublished "Andantino by Clara Wieck." The theme is typical of her style, a melody based on the first five notes of a descending scale, conventionally harmonized. But the simple motif is a note-for-note recall of the opening theme of the first movement, where it thunders forth in Florestan's F-minor style, impassioned, bravura, unresolved. The dates confirm that the sonata reflects the new relationship of Schumann and Clara. It was a lonely cry from the composer's heart, he later told Clara, expressing his love and the anguish of their separation. His variations on Clara's Andantino portray the troubled course of their love, moving from a gentle Eusebian accompaniment to the driven rhythms of an impassioned final Florestanian variation.

In its musical and its emotional expressiveness, the sonata is close to the first movement of the C Major Fantasie, composed in the summer of 1836. Schumann later wrote to Clara that the first movement of the Fantasie was "the most passionate thing I have ever written—a profound lament for you." His despair at Wieck's rejection, his grief at Clara's acceptance of her father's demands, his faith in their eventual union—all are expressed in the musical language closest to his heart and mind. Even without its autobiographical resonance, the Fantasie would stand as the crowning summit of Schumann's struggle with sonata form, a defining work of the new Romanticism.

Like the F Minor Sonata, the Fantasie opens with a passionate descending-scale motif which forms the basis of the entire work. The first movement is driven by Florestanian passion, with the gentle Eusebius responding in turn, sometimes echoing his friend's notes, sometimes offering his own variation on them or a new thought of his own. Both the F Minor Sonata and the Fantasie move toward an image of Clara, revealed as if in response to the composer's passionate longing. In the F Minor Sonata she appears as her own Andantino theme. In the final movement of the Fantasie, she appears in her defining key of C major, transfigured by the composer's love and his faith in her love for him.

Schumann composed what became the first movement of the Fantasie during his most despairing time, when he feared Clara was lost to him. The movement was written to stand on its own and was given a title in French: "Fantasie: Ruines." But in September of 1836, Schumann thought of offering a substantial work as a contribution to a planned monument for Beethoven in his native city, Bonn. The idea of the monument had been widely advertised, with a notice in Schumann's journal, alongside a piece by "Florestan and Eusebius" discussing the merits of such a monument. Schumann composed two more movements, a heroic March in E-flat and a serene final movement in C. In mid-December he offered the work to Friedrich Kistner, the Leipzig publisher who had already published Schumann's F-sharp Minor Sonata. He wrote to Kistner: "Florestan and Eusebius would be very happy to do something for Beethoven's memorial, and for this purpose have written something with the title of *Ruins—Trophies—Palms*: Grand Sonata for the Pianoforte for Beethoven's Memorial." Kistner turned down Schumann's offer, and when Breitkopf & Härtel accepted the work a year later, the title became simply Fantasie, with no mention of the Beethoven memorial. The completed Fantasie was dedicated to Liszt, in the hope that he would be able to perform the difficult work at sight. There was no concession to sonata form, as Schumann had struggled with it in his three piano sonatas. No changes were made to the original Fantasie, and each of the new movements provided a satisfying contrast to its improvisatory, rhapsodic character.

From the start, Schumann had the text of Beethoven's song cycle, *An die ferne Geliebte,* in mind. The words, probably commissioned by Beethoven, were written by a little-known young poet and physician, Alois Jeitteles. It is not known whether the text had special meaning for Beethoven. But for Schumann, Beethoven's song cycle—the first of its kind—had uncanny resonance. The songs are sung by the poet to his beloved, who is separated from him by insurmountable obstacles. She cannot see his gaze or hear his sighs, but she can sing his songs, and the singer's longing can overcome the mountains and valleys separating "two loving hearts."

The poet speaks to her in the opening song of Beethoven's cycle: "I sit on the hill, gazing into the wide misty heavens, seeking where I can find you, my beloved." Leipzig is flat, with not a hill in sight. Clara had returned from her tour and lived only twenty minutes' walk from Schumann's lodgings. But he had sent his "songs" to her—his F-sharp Minor Sonata—and he could stand outside the family house while she played his notes. And so it was appropriate for Beethoven's songs to enter Schumann's Fantasie, in phrases recurring at intervals throughout the opening movement, all hinting at the melody and words of the final song.

Rather than introducing the full quotation first, as in a theme and variations, Schumann uses a truncated version of Beethoven's phrase as a motif on its own, so that when the full quotation, slightly varied from Beethoven's original, appears at the end, it reflects back on the entire movement. The Beethoven quotations were a message for Clara. She was also meant to understand the verse by Schlegel which Schumann inserted on the score when the Fantasie was finally published: "Through all the tones in this colorful earthly dream, a soft note sounds for one who listens in secret."

By common consent, the Fantasie is the masterpiece of these years of piano cycles and sonatas, all with intense personal meaning for Schumann. His struggles with sonata form, in the shadow of Beethoven, gave him the confidence to compose with complete freedom. He expresses his Romantic personality, his longing, his despair, his dreams, in his own distinctive musical language, breaking all the rules or disregarding them with impunity, creating his own structure, his own way of unifying his unique work.

The Fantasie opens with the instruction "To be performed throughout with imagination and passion." Like the early G Minor Sonata, the work begins with a rapid arpeggiated bass, above which a descending scale motif thunders in Florestan's most declamatory style. But in contrast to the lyrical opening of the G Minor Sonata, both the arpeggiated bass and the scale motif are dissonant, one echoing the other, chromatic, unresolved, suspending any resolution into a home key. This is new, extreme, emotional—and the contrasting Eusebian motif which appears later, marked *piano*, is equally passionate, with repeated trills echoing the dissonance of the opening sequences.

The storm continues with only momentary relief, until an *adagio* pause introduces a brief motif which anticipates another phrase in the Beethoven song cycle, from the setting of the words "and a loving heart is reached by what a loving heart has consecrated." The words seem to apply directly to a contrasting *piano* section in Euse-bius's characteristic key of E-flat: *Im Legendenton* (in the style of a legend), as if a story is being told, an old tale familiar to listeners. Different as the theme and the mood are, there are connections to the first section: the bass quietly echoes the descending scale of the opening, while the evenly spaced theme in the treble echoes the rising fourth of an earlier motif. After a flourish, a pause introduces a brief allusion to yet another Beethoven quotation, setting the words "For what separates us yields before these songs." The opening theme then returns in C minor, eventually resuming its home key of C major in a final recapitulation, now moving toward the full Beethoven quotation, repeated twice, as if to ensure that the meaning is clear: "Then take these songs which I sang to you, beloved." A long, tender cadence follows, affirming C major as its inevitable destiny.

Despite all these signs of close construction, Schumann is composing with wonderful spontaneity, in his own harmonic language, conveying "the finest shades of passion, the deepest feelings of the soul."

The movement could have been complete on its own, with its Beethoven allusions, its secret messages to Clara. But the hope of contributing to the Beethoven monument inspired two further movements, evolving into Schumann's own form of "Sonata cum Fantasie." Throughout the three movements, Clara is present, seen through the anguish of the lover denied communication with his beloved except through his music. A heroic Beethovenian second movement, similar in its propulsive rhythms to the March movement of Beethoven's Sonata op. 101, affirms the composer's confidence in his eventual union with his beloved. As in the *Im Legendenton* section of the first movement, motifs developed earlier—the descending scale in the bass, the rising fourth in the middle voice—are recalled and varied throughout the triumphant march.

Most remarkable is the final movement, an Adagio in C major, a radiant transfiguration of Clara herself. Florestan and Eusebius make brief appearances, but the C-major Clara presence is always felt, in the gentle stretched arpeggios of the opening, the serene harmonic changes. There are three motifs, hardly motifs, recognizable only when they are repeated with added emphasis and linked in the most subtle way, barely audible on first hearing but unmistakable on closer study. All three motifs recur, intertwined, moving through a series of unexpected, unprepared key changes toward Clara's defining home key of C, when the opening arpeggios are given their own dramatic development, moving "more and more quickly" to a final adagio cadence, and a repeated C-major chord in the bass. Schumann considered including the entire Beethoven quotation at the end—the notes setting the words "Then take these songs which I sang to you"—and some pianists still include the phrase. But the final published score omits the quotation, leaving the gentle adagio cadence to speak for itself.

If the F Minor Sonata is indebted to Beethoven's *Hammerklavier* Sonata, Schumann might have found a precedent for the unusual form of the Fantasie in Beethoven's final piano sonata, op. 111, also in C and in two movements only—the first movement, in C minor, passionate and dissonant, the second, in C major, a radiant Arietta marked *Adagio molto semplice e cantabile.*

Schumann was inspired, too, by Beethoven's late string quartets. He was fascinated by their profound poetic feeling and their intricate construction of overlapping motifs. He developed the technique of linking motifs, deconstructing and varying them, in his own large-scale compositions, from the early piano works to virtually all his major projects. Form and poetic feeling were his guiding principles, complementary and transformative, informing works that were driven always by his own powerful imagination.

In 1842, Pietro Mechetti of Vienna published a *Beethoven Album* as a contribution to the Beethoven monument in Bonn. The album included Mendelssohn's *Variations sérieuses,* two preludes by Chopin, and works by Liszt, Moscheles, Thalberg, and other major European composers. Schumann's name was not among them. The monument, a large bronze statue of Beethoven, was erected in 1845 in Bonn's Münsterplatz, in front of the great cathedral. Ten years later, a portly gentleman could be seen standing before the statue in meditative pose, hands clasped behind his back. When he was incarcerated in Endenich asylum, Schumann would frequently walk to Bonn with his attendant, determined despite his ailing body and mind to pay homage to the Master whom he held in such great reverence, and from whom he had learned so much.

6

LOVE CONFIRMED

Leipzig, May 1837–September 1837

Their eighteen-month separation was intolerable for both Schumann and Clara. Sooner or later they would have to make peace, if not with Wieck, then most certainly with each other. Clara returned to Leipzig in May 1837, still banned by her father from seeing Schumann or writing to him. In August she sent word to Schumann by way of a good friend, Ernst Becker, of her forthcoming concert at a morning musicale in the Buchhändlerborse (Booksellers Market). She had bravely decided to include three of Schumann's *Études symphoniques* in her program. At the concert, Schumann stood in a dark corner, listening in anguish, separated from Clara as if by the far mountains concealing Beethoven's "distant beloved." He saw her as she was leaving the hall with Wieck and others, and was unable to speak to her. She wrote to him later: "Did you not know that I was playing for you, because I knew no other way of showing you all that was in my heart? I could not tell you in secret, and so I did so in public. Did you not realize how I was trembling?"

Later that day Schumann wrote to Clara, asking in his most eloquent, impassioned manner if she still loved him. Most dramatically, the envelope was enclosed in another short letter reading thus: "After many days of silence full of pain, hope, and doubt, may these lines be received with the former love. If this is no longer so, then I ask you to return this letter to me unopened. Robert Schumann." The enclosed letter had no salutation, only the date.

13 August 37. Are you still true and *firm*? As indestructibly as I believe in you, even the strongest spirit loses hope when nothing is heard from the one who to him is dearest in the world. I have thought it over a thousand times and everything tells me: *it must be, if we will it and act.* Write to me only a simple "yes," if you are willing to give your father a letter from me on your birthday, on the 13th of September . . . He seems well disposed to me now, and will not reject me if you plead for me.

Clara wrote back at once, echoing their shared love of Beethoven's *Fidelio* and the faithful Leonore, as well as Beethoven's String Quartet op. 132 with its motto "It must be": "All you need is a simple 'yes'? Such a little word—and so important! Should not a heart so full of inexpressible love as mine say this little word with my whole soul? I do so, and whisper it to you from my deepest self *forever* . . . I too have felt for a long time 'It must be'—nothing in the world can change me, and I will show my father that one so young can also be steadfast."

Meetings followed in which the lovers affirmed their union "unto death" with words, embraces, and a solemn exchange of rings and portraits. Schumann wrote formally to Wieck, asking for his blessing. In the past two years, Schumann's position had improved significantly. He was recognized as a critic and a composer, with an assured income from the *New Journal for Music* and, increasingly, from his compositions. He also received interest on his father's legacy and investments in his brothers' publishing business.

He began his letter by presenting himself in his most optimistic aspect: "Today I am able to face the future—I am assured, in all probability, against want, full of pleasant projects, able to champion any noble cause with youthful enthusiasm, capable of work and conscious of great opportunities, strong in the hope of using my talents to the full, and rich in esteem and affection."

Clara would be eighteen in September. She was confident that her father would relent, given his love not only of his daughter but (at least in the past) of Schumann. With Clara's approval, Schumann delivered his letter on her birthday, September 13th, with a note to Clara's stepmother, Clementine, pleading for her support.

Wieck's response, Schumann told their friend Becker, was incomprehensible. "The meeting with your father was horrible," Schumann wrote to Clara. "This coldness, this ill will, this confusion, these contradictions—he has a new way of destroying one, he has mastered the art of stabbing one in the heart, dagger and hilt . . . That my devotion, my long service, should count for so little! And now, my beloved Clara, what shall we do? . . . Above all, stay firm—do not let him sell you to a rich banker."

This was a real fear for Schumann. He knew that Wieck's authority over Clara was still strong. He could imagine that she might submit to a rich suitor who would ensure her continued career, with Wieck still in charge. For Clara, a marriage to anyone else was inconceivable. She had no intention at any point of giving up her Robert, her adored childhood mentor, now her betrothed, whom she had sworn to love forever. But she still hoped to reconcile her father to her marriage. She was willing to make almost any compromise if she could win him over. He was already making conditions: she could meet Schumann only in public; they could write to each other only when Clara was on tour.

Schumann saw each compromise as a betrayal. Taking elaborate precautions to avoid discovery, with the help of Clara's faithful maid Nanni, they managed to meet in private. They exchanged letters, using secret codes, ABCD for Clara, FGHI for Schumann. Steeped in the Romantic language of Schumann's favorite writers, their letters dramatized the perils of their situation as they vowed eternal love: "Before I take farewell from you today, my beloved girl, swear yet again by your future happiness that you have the courage to meet the trials that hang over us, as I too swear, holding up these two fingers of my right hand: I shall never let you go—and you must never let me go! And so help me God I shall remain forever Your Robert." To which Clara answered, echoing Shakespeare's Cleopatra as she chides Antony: "Do you still doubt me? I forgive you, for I am still a weak girl! Weak, yes—but I have a strong soul, a heart which is firm and unchangeable." She told Schumann that she had promised her father to be more cheerful and to practice her art for a few more years, out in the world. If Robert did not hear from her, he must remember that everything she did was for him. Should he waver, he would have broken a heart that could love only once.

Schumann reaffirmed his faith in her strength and her love. He asked only that she would address him with the sign of their love, the intimate "Du," before she left on tour with her father. She was his passionately beloved bride—and he sealed his letter with "one last kiss." They agreed to think of each other every night at nine, echoing the meetings of their *Doppelgänger* years before, when they played Chopin's Variations at eleven a.m. on Thursdays and met in spirit at St. Thomas's gate.

Before Clara left Leipzig for an extended concert tour, Schumann sent her the manuscript of the *Davidsbündlertänze*. They contained every strange and lovely thought that came to him, he told her, and his pride and joy in their renewed love. But Wieck's malice cast a dark shadow over their future.

> Today I could think of nothing but you and your father . . . Like you I spring from laughter to tears. How terrible last night was. How my head burned, how my imagination led me from abyss to abyss, so that I wanted to hurl myself down—I reproach myself for my discontent—haven't you assured me of everything, have I not the word of a noble, strong girl?— but yet the pain of not being able to see you, our best years of youth to be spent apart—that torments me so . . . I am weaker than I thought.

Two days later he wrote: "If I improvise at the piano, everything I write turns to chorales; if I write, it is without any ideas—I can paint only one thought with capital letters and chords: CLARA."

He urged her to take his *Davidsbündlertänze* with her on tour. But in a final twist of the knife, Wieck refused to let her take the manuscript. Schumann sent her the dances again when the work was published the following February.

He had said farewell to Ernestine in early August, in person, breaking with her formally in December. He records in his diary "the most blissful and purest days of my life from 12th August to 13th September"—that is, from the date of Clara's concert to her birthday. He promised himself that he would long for one woman only—that is, for Clara.

At the same time that Schumann was writing these words, he gave himself firm instructions: "Be moderate, industrious, and sober." He summarized his life thus: "New striving, new relationships . . . past love, former hearts, wild fantasies, belief in [Clara's] steadfastness . . . How will everything end?" He was exhilarated, happy, convinced that all would be well. From the diary, after meeting Mendelssohn on the street and keeping him company for a while: "In the afternoon, Mendelssohn by the hand, in the evening Clara on my heart—do I deserve this?"

Schumann was to spend the next two and a half years defending himself against Wieck's calumnies. Again and again he sought to prove himself as a future husband for Clara. To each appeal, Wieck found new objections, sabotaging every effort Schumann made to prove his financial and emotional stability. He started his campaign even before he took Clara away on tour, following Schumann for two weeks to see if he was keeping his promise to remain sober. Could it be true, as her father reported, that Schumann had gone one night to Nohr's Hotel garni, on Nicholaistrasse? She refused to believe that Schumann would break his solemn promise to fight against temptation—but if he had broken faith, she would still remain true to him; she was his wife, if not in this life, then in the next.

Clara matched Robert in the vividness of her hope and despair. During their separation, each lover had an uncanny power of summoning the other. Schumann's preferred way of communicating with Clara was through his music—writing her name in letters and chords, incorporating themes from her compositions, creating her image, her looks, her love in one work after another.

Fantasiestücke, op. 12; Davidsbündlertänze, op. 6
In response to the turbulent summer of 1837 Schumann composed two substantial works for piano—a set of *Fantasiestücke* (Fantasy

Pieces) inspired by the Leipzig visit in early July of an eighteen-year-old British pianist, Anna Robena Laidlaw; and the *Davidsbündlertänze*, begun in late August, after the lovers confirmed their vows.

With their extramusical inspiration completely transformed, both works are wonderfully inventive. The *Fantasiestücke* are divided into two books of four pieces each, in related keys and closely related in their motifs. Each piece has a suggestive title, with only a casual relationship to the others, as if they are separate episodes loosely arranged in a single work. Book 1 opens with "Des Abends" (In the Evening), a tender Eusebian piece in five flats, played mainly on the black keys, like Chopin's first nocturne, which inspired his portrait in *Carnaval*. Marked "to be played very intimately," *piano* throughout, ending *pianissimo*, the piece is an even sequence of falling and rising notes in a rippling rhythm of three against two, repeated throughout with subtle variations. Halfway through, the sequence is raised three half-tones—a Schubertian effect, as is appropriate for Eusebius.

All four *Fantasiestücke* of book 1 are played mainly on the black keys, in D-flat or F minor, with closely overlapping themes but changing rhythm and dynamics, as if composed alternately by Eusebius and Florestan. The second piece, "Aufschwung" (Soaring), marked *very fast*, is dramatic, impassioned, Florestan leaping about the piano, *forte* with *sforzando* accents, interrupted twice by a soft Eusebian interlude which recalls the opening piece. Next comes the simple "Warum?" (Why?), Eusebius again, asking an unanswerable question, *slowly and tenderly*, *piano* fading away to *pianissimo*, with a troubled *sforzando* accent midway, as the question takes on a more anguished character. The final piece of the four is "Grillen" (Whims; Capricious Thoughts), Florestan in burlesque, humorous form, with stomping chord sequences, sharply accented.

The pieces of book 2 are longer, in contrasting keys, less obviously related to one another. The first, "In der Nacht" (In the Night), was Schumann's favorite, which he thought Clara might include on its own in concerts. After it had been composed, he told her that he could see the entire story of Hero and Leander portrayed in the piece.

> When I am playing "Night," I cannot get rid of the idea; first he throws himself into the sea; she calls him; he answers; he battles with the waves and reaches land in safety. Then the cantilena, when they are clasped in one another's arms, until they have to part again, and he cannot tear himself away until night wraps everything in darkness once more. Of course, I imagine Hero to be just like you, and if you were sitting in a lighthouse, I would probably learn how to swim too.

The letter was written many months after the piece was composed, and the story of Hero and Leander played no part in it originally. But Schumann projected his own drama into the music, including his recurring fantasy of throwing himself into a river. It was yet another message to Clara, perhaps a warning.

The three remaining pieces of book 2 suggest a general literary character: "Fabel" (Fable), "Traumes Wirren" (Troubled Dreams), "Ende vom Lied" (End of the Song). Their specific literary meaning is left to the imagination of the listener. It has been plausibly suggested that the titles, and the work as a whole, can be linked to Hoffmann's *Fantasiestücke* and the most famous story in the collection, *Der goldne Topf* (*The Golden Pot*). The hero of Hoffmann's tale, the young student Anselmus, has a strange experience "one evening" as he is sitting under an elder bush, and looks up to see three green and golden snakes slithering up and down. The intrepid Veronika, who loves him, has a terrifying experience "in the night" when she is subjected to a witch's spells in a dark forest. Unanswered questions, sudden winged flight, whims and dream visions also enter into the tale, as does a fabulous allegory. Schumann loved Hoffmann's tales, and took his figure of the Kapellmeister Johannes Kreisler as the key to a work he composed later that year, *Kreisleriana*. Slithering snakes, a witches' cauldron, young love rapturous, impossible, suicidal—all are part of the Romantic imagery of the time, with

Hoffmann one of their most popular literary sources and Schumann a fervent admirer. *The Golden Pot* ends with two marriages, one in the fabled Atlantis, the other in bourgeois Dresden. Schumann provided a more personal clue to "End of the Song" in a letter to Clara: "I meant, in the end, all to resolve in a merry wedding, but in the final bars the painful longing for you returned, and now it sounds like the intermingling of a wedding and a funeral."

The *Fantasiestücke* are Schumann's personal variation on music-as-poetry, a theme found in so much of the music he loved: Schubert's *Moments musicaux* and *Impromptus,* Mendelssohn's *Songs Without Words,* Chopin's first two *Ballades,* which the composer himself had played for Schumann, and his untitled but romantically suggestive nocturnes and études. These works, composed for piano alone, the most intimate of instruments, were intrinsically poetic but free from a specific literary program. With or without titles, they invite the imagination of pianist and listener to roam freely, responding to the emotion expressed, the varying moods portrayed—passionate, wistful, dramatic, tender, humorous. Often there is the suggestion of a tale being told: "in the style of a legend" in the Fantasie, "in the mode of a ballad" in the *Davidsbündlertänze*; in the unspecified plots of the *Novelletten* composed later that year. Schumann claimed that he thought of his titles after he wrote the pieces, and he was very good at improvising plots for works by other composers, like Schubert's German Dances, reviewed in the *Journal* with a fantastic scene imagined for each dance. When he invited Clara to share his interpretation of "In der Nacht" as the story of Hero and Leander, it was a private reading, not meant for others.

He published the two books of *Fantasiestücke* as a sequence of related pieces, and they are closely linked, especially in book 1. But he was happy for the pieces to stand on their own, and he suggested that Clara might perform one or two in public, "In der Nacht" or "Traumes Wirren." The full set when published was dedicated not to Clara but to Anna Robena Laidlaw, with whom Schumann had become good friends. In his diary he records "the good Laidlaw and quick understanding between us; farewell taken from her with sorrow." Like *Carnaval,* with which they have much in common, the *Fantasiestücke* were rapturously received and became among Schumann's most popular works, performed by Clara and other pianists at the time and later.

The *Davidsbündlertänze* mark a return to Schumann's favorite form, a variety of dances on a common theme, like *Carnaval*—this time not a carnival masquerade but a wedding party. They were a direct response to the lovers' vows of August, a joyful celebration of their reunion. With links to *Papillons* and *Carnaval*, they celebrate the new relations of the chief persons in the *Davidsbund*: Florestan and Eusebius as composers and Clara as dedicatee. A verse quatrain is inscribed above the title, called an "Old Saying," although it also refers to Klärchen's song in Beethoven's incidental music to *Egmont*, "Freudvoll und leidvoll" (In joy and sorrow): "In all times joy and grief are intertwined; be sober in joy and face grief with courage."

Schumann told Clara that the dances were full of "wedding thoughts." In their structure and substance, he united his music with Clara's themes in a way that beautifully represents the joy of their love and its anticipated consummation. With typical disregard for posterity, he concealed the secret meaning of the *Davidsbündlertänze* from all but his bride. And it is not even clear that she read his messages in each of their ingenious disguises.

Davidsbündlertänze opens with a short "Motto by C.W." taken note for note from the opening bars of Clara's Mazurka in G, published in 1836 in her *Soirées musicales,* op. 6—and the dances, too, were to be Schumann's op. 6. The "Motto" leads to a series of variations by "F" and "E," speaking together (in the first dance of book 1 and no. 6 of book 2) or separately, in the character first expressed musically in their keynote pieces in *Carnaval*. There Eusebius is *teneramente*, Florestan *passionato*. In the *Davidsbündlertänze* Eusebius speaks "expressively," is "simple"; Florestan speaks "with humor," is "jocose," "passionate," "wild and cheerful." As if to embody Schumann's love of puns and anagrams, letters as notes, the doubles take ingenious musical form, dancing around their key letters, as in *Carnaval* and the F-sharp Minor Sonata. In the first two contrasting dances, Eusebius signals his authorship by a prominent E-natural in the bass, Florestan by a sudden intrusion of accented

F-sharps (recalling a sequence characterising *Carnaval*'s Arlequin, with whom Florestan has much in common). The pattern continues, with Eusebius speaking in E minor or E-flat, Florestan in insistent Fs or F-sharps. They sign each dance with their initials (removed in the revised version of 1850–1851). The final piece in each book is announced in words by one of the lovers, introducing the last dance in Clara's key of C. In book 1, a superscription above the final piece reads: "Here Florestan stopped and his lips trembled with sorrow," followed by a lively C-major dance recalling Clara's portrait in *Carnaval* as Chiarina. In book 2, the final dance is introduced by the words: "Superfluously, Eusebius added the following, and his eyes shone with great happiness." What he adds is a *pianissimo* arpeggio in the dominant (G7), leading to a wistful waltz in C, composed as if it is Clara herself who is speaking.

Schumann was particularly eager for Clara to understand the *Davidsbündlertänze*. All the variations express the love of "F" and "E," taking the smallest elements of Clara's short motto as the kernel of their improvisations—an open fifth, a falling second, a dotted rhythm. The dances of book 1 remain close to the opening motto. Book 2 is freer, with the motto virtually disappearing at times. But Clara appears in more substantial form in two dances that include full quotations from the two pieces Schumann told her were his favorites: the Trio of her Toccatina and the Notturno, both from her *Soirées musicales*, op. 6. Schumann treats Clara's themes in a subtly erotic way, incorporating elements of the earlier dances by "E," with Clara's theme and Eusebius's accompaniment intertwined, exchanging places, conversing, making love. A third dance is marked "as if from afar," suggesting a love message coming from a distance—presumably from Clara. She is present throughout the work, in her motto and the variations played on its constituent elements by "F" and "E," in the themes of her own pieces, and in the concluding C-major dance of each book. There are also links both to *Carnaval* and *Papillons*, in brief allusions. A coda to no. 5 of book 2, with its long quotation from Clara's Toccatina, refers note for note to the slow movement of Beethoven's *Pathétique* Sonata—linking Clara with Beethoven's most romantic work.

The *Davidsbündlertänze* were intensely personal, not designed to achieve the popularity of the *Fantasiestücke* or *Carnaval*. They do not separate into individual, self-contained pieces, and the entire work is much longer than *Carnaval*, ending not with a grand finale but with a quiet fading away. Although there are bravura sections, the work lacks the character of a showpiece. But the *Davidsbündlertänze* are always being rediscovered by pianists, attracted by their poetry, their charm and inventiveness—even though some of the secret messages remain hidden.

Schumann was initially disappointed by Clara's reaction to the work when he sent her the published edition in February 1838. She thought the new cycle was too much like *Carnaval*, her favorite among all his works. He begged her to play the dances again, telling her they were written in his happiest time.

He also told Clara that the *Davidsbündlertänze* were the "faces" as opposed to the "masks" of *Carnaval*. In *Carnaval*, Florestan and Eusebius, masked like all the carnival revelers, lead the assembled members of the *Davidsbund*, including the young Chiarina, in a triumphant march against the Philistines. In the dances, Florestan and Eusebius, in their "real" persons, are making love to Clara in music, playing variations on her motto, quoting her longer pieces, entwining her themes with their own accompaniment, and giving her the final piece in each set of nine.

Even if "F" and "E" have removed the masks assumed for a carnival, they are still only representatives of the "real" composer—his alter egos, the characters his imagination produced to speak for him. There are different levels of reality in Schumann's music, where the substance of each work is determined not only by its literary or personal inspiration but by the demands of form and structure, harmonic relationships, thematic and rhythmic continuity and variety. The miracle of Schumann's art lies in his mastery of these elements to convey his own unique poetry of love and longing. The "faces" that speak in his music are intimate, revealing but also self-dramatizing, humorous, teasing, confessional, and subject always to his poetic imagination.

In real life, still deeper levels remained, the face of Schumann himself, exposed in his most intimate letters to Clara. In an ecstasy of love he wrote to her:

Who ordered you to love me—who ordered me to love you? Who can be held to account—yes, Clara, I loved you then, I love you now and will love you forever . . . But truly it is *you*, you angel of joy, who hold me under your wings. And if you left me I would sink back down into desolation and darkness. But you would never do that, you would never leave me, truly? You once wrote to me, "If you ever fail me, you'll have broken a heart"—You would do more than that, you would break my spirit into pieces, until I lost my mind.

Even in these letters, with their confessions about his earlier life, his fear of losing his reason, his thoughts of doing away with himself, not everything was told. He confessed his faults, his drinking, his overuse of cigars, his "bad manners"—that is, remaining silent in company, his difficulty in expressing his real feelings, his lapses of taste, his general awkwardness. But dark secrets remained untold or disguised by euphemisms. Under no circumstances could he have told Clara about his relations with "Charitas" or "La Faneuse." Despite his desire to share everything with his muse, his guardian angel, he could never tell her that he had been with servants and prostitutes and that he had been infected with syphilis. Yet these events were to have the most terrible consequences not only for Schumann but for Clara, and they contributed to the fears that continued to haunt him.

NEW WORLDS

Leipzig, October 1837–October 1838

On October 13, 1837, Clara left Leipzig with Wieck for an ambitious concert tour, stopping first in Dresden, where she performed *Carnaval*. They went on to Prague and arrived at last in Vienna, where they remained for over six months, returning to Leipzig in late May 1838.

Now began an extraordinary exchange of intimate letters, in which the lovers bared their hearts to each other, reaffirming their vows of love even as Schumann was assailed by doubts of Clara's steadiness, and of his own capacity to survive the continuing strain of Wieck's enmity. In their letters they tell and retell the story of their romance: their first meetings when Clara was a child, their country walks to Gohlis and Connewitz, the interruptions and obstacles to their love. They rehearse the details of Schumann's engagement to Ernestine and Clara's flirtation with admirers. They write to each other under the shadow cast by Wieck's contradictory claims and charges, his attacks on Schumann's character, his insistence on Clara's need for an income far beyond Schumann's means, his determination to poison the lovers' lives.

Clara's letter writing was surrounded by difficulties. Her father was at her side, controlling her life during almost every minute, each day. The only time she had for herself was late at night, after returning exhausted from an evening soirée, when she could write a few lines to Schumann, standing at her bureau. The next day she would contrive to send her letter to the post without her father's knowledge. She knew he had no compunction about reading her correspondence. She invented elaborate ruses to ensure secrecy, matched in turn by Schumann, desperate for his letters to her to arrive unobserved.

Their first exchange began with mutual recriminations. First letter from Clara: "Friday 3 Nov. 1837, 9 in the evening—Why your long silence? I have heard nothing from you for three weeks . . . Father says I will forget you—forget? The word makes me shudder! He has no idea of the strength of a loving heart." Wieck had written secretly to Schumann, vowing that before he would permit two such artists to live a mean bourgeois life together, he would marry Clara off to a rich man who could support her in style, and it would be entirely Robert's fault.

Schumann wrote back to Clara: "Never would I have thought you could remain silent for so long . . . I cannot tell you what I have suffered in the last few days." She could always write to him; he had no way of writing to her, no address. He described her father's letter as that of a shopkeeper. If Clara had any doubts about marrying him, he would send back her ring. But if she still loved him, with all his faults, all his awkwardness, then let them stay true to each other. He loved her idea of thinking of each other at nine at night—he had the most wonderful feeling of being close to her at that time. She could continue to love her father, and also to love him, Robert. But she must not let herself be married off to someone else. "Ach! If only I had you here with me for a moment."

The theme recurs through all their letters—if only they could be present to each other! In his Christmas letter to Clara, Schumann conjures up a meeting.

In the midst of a thousand voices which joyfully call to you, do you also perhaps hear one which softly calls you by name—you look about—and it is I. "Are you here, Robert?" you ask me. Why not,—am I not by your side, following you everywhere, even when you do not see me? On New Year's Day, on your birthday and also on mine, I will appear to you, always more clearly and more lovingly, so that nothing can come between the kiss of our former love, except for a look, a sigh, or a "*Du*"—And the figure fades away. But love and truth remain as before.—With these lines I remind my beloved Bride of her Robert.

Schumann promised more than once to tell Clara the truth about his earlier life. Finally, in a long letter of February 11, 1838, he put together yet another version of his history.

Come and sit beside me, my dear, sweet girl . . . and let me talk to you a little. I am going to lay bare my inmost soul to you, as I never did to any living being. You, my dearest on earth, shall know all. My real life began at the point when I arrived at a clear conception of myself and my talent, and by choosing art marked out a definite course . . . This was in 1830. You were then an odd little girl, with strong views, beautiful eyes, and a weakness for cherries. I had no one else but my dear [sister-in-law] Rosalie. A few years passed. As early as 1833 a certain melancholy made itself felt, which I regarded merely as the discouragement experienced by every artist when results are not achieved with the speed he expected. I received little recognition; and I lost the use of my right hand for playing . . . The idea that you might one day be my wife occurred to me even then, but it all lay in the too distant future . . . My love for Rosalie was very different. We were the same age. She was more than a sister to me, but of course, actual love was out of the question. She looked after me, gave me good advice, encouraged me, and expected great things of me . . . This was in the summer of 1833. But I was seldom happy . . . The death of a dear brother [Julius, in August 1833] threw me into a state of melancholy, which increased more and more. The news of Rosalie's death found me in this condition . . . In the night between the 17th and 18th of October I was seized with the worst fear a man can have, the worst blow heaven can inflict—the fear of losing one's reason . . . Terror drove me from place to place. My breath failed me as I imagined my brain paralyzed. Ah, Clara! no one can know the suffering, the sickness, the despair of this state, except those who have once been so crushed. In my terrible agitation I went to a doctor and told him everything—how my senses often failed me so that I did not know where I was, how I was tempted to take my own life. Do not be horrified, my angel from heaven, but listen—the doctor comforted me kindly and finally said: "Medicine is of no use here. Look for a wife [*eine Frau*]—she will cure you right away."

Schumann offers the doctor's diagnosis as the reason for his courtship of Ernestine von Fricken. A full story, but not the whole truth. *Eine Frau* could mean either "a wife" or "a woman." The kindly doctor probably shared the common belief that chastity, the withholding of vital fluids, caused melancholy, even madness. While Clara knew all about Ernestine, Schumann could not tell her about his actual sexual experience.

Their letters chart their emotional swings in sharp detail, their crises of doubt, their repeated vows. But it is in Schumann's works that the most intimate record of their love is inscribed. Again and again he summons Clara, longing for her physical presence, often using themes from her own compositions—messages heard only by "the one who listens in secret." She was his chief subject, sometimes his only subject. But many other elements entered into his compositions.

Everything that goes on in the world affects me, politics, literature, people—I think about everything in my own way, and I have to express my feelings, and then I find an outlet in music. That's why many of my compositions are so difficult to understand; they relate to distant, often significant concerns because all the strange things of the time touch me, and I must express them musically.

Novelletten; Kreisleriana; Kinderszenen

In a happy mood, he wrote that he had composed a "shocking" number of things for Clara in three weeks of February 1838: "humorous things, Egmont stories, family scenes with fathers, a wedding—I've called the whole thing *Novelletten* because your name is Clara, and *Wiecketten* doesn't sound good enough"—a teasing remark guaranteed to annoy Clara. (Clara Novello was a gifted young English singer, daughter of a well-known London publisher, who was creating a sensation in Leipzig.) To a fellow composer, Hermann Hirschbach, he described the *Novelletten* as "intimately connected, written with great pleasure, on the whole light and cheerful, apart from one or two where I sank to the depths." An additional clue to their meaning appears in a letter to Schumann's former theory teacher and friend Heinrich Dorn: "Much of the battle which Clara cost me is contained in my music . . . it was virtually she alone who inspired the *Concert sans orchestre* (the F Minor Sonata), the F-sharp Minor Sonata, the *Davidsbündlertänze, Kreisleriana,* and the *Novelletten.*"

The eight *Novelletten* were published as four books, most of the pieces in the cheerful key of D major, with overlapping themes running all the way through. Like the *Fantasiestücke* composed the year before, they tell stories in music—but without titles or other clues in the printed texts. No. 2 was sent to Liszt as "The Saracen," a reference to the "Suleika" love poems in Goethe's *West-Eastern Divan*, set by Schubert and later by Schumann. Presumably the Saracen appears in the outer sections of no. 2, to be played "extremely fast and with spirit," with his lover, Suleika, represented in the Intermezzo, a tender song set above a rippling accompaniment which suggests an oriental lute. "Family scenes with fathers" was meant for Clara: probably Wieck was satirized in no. 6, marked "very light and humorous." Schumann published the Intermezzo of no. 3 in the *New Journal* supplement with a quotation from Shakespeare's *Macbeth*: "When shall we three meet again / In thunder, lightning, or in rain?" and he refers elsewhere to one of the *Novelletten* as "Macbeth," which must be no. 3. The "quick and wild" music of the Intermezzo, sharply accented dancing chords marked *forte* and *sforzando*, suggests the witches plotting mischief as they stir the cauldron. The "*Egmont* stories" must refer to Count Egmont's splendid military presence as he seeks freedom for the Netherlands, his love for the simple Klärchen, and her devotion and sacrifice. Schumann had recently attended a performance of Beethoven's incidental music to Goethe's play, and he told Clara he had never been so moved; he had reread the play at once. No. 1 seems a likely choice: the martial frame is suitably heroic (like Klärchen's first song celebrating Egmont's appearance in armor, and her desire to join him as a fellow soldier), while the reprise at the end could represent Liberty appearing to Egmont in prison, assuring him of the eventual triumph of freedom. The intervening Trio represents the loving Klärchen and her song, "Joyful and sorrowful," merging with the real Clara in her typical descending theme. The musical portraits of Egmont and Klärchen, Suleika and the Saracen, refer not only to their particular love stories but also to Schumann and Clara.

The final piece, no. 8, opens with an anguished sequence in F-sharp minor, repeated in each register, similar in its unresolved pain to the opening measures of the C Major Fantasie. It is here that Schumann "sank to the depths." Halfway through this novelette, Clara's Notturno theme is quoted at length as a "voice from afar," which initiates a drama realized poetically in the sections that follow. On first hearing, the "voice" is barely audible, as if whispered from the distance, a soft message of love set above a rhythmic Florestanian bass which has been well established beforehand. It is immediately restated as a simple song in Eusebian mode (with his signature note of E emphasized), and at last, after an interval, in Florestanian thundering octaves, note for note as in Clara's Notturno, set against her lover's theme in the bass, expressing his unbearable longing for her. Then, suddenly and briefly, it resolves joyfully into Clara's own keynote of C, with a sustained bass octave supporting the tender melody, marked by Eusebius's characteristic *innig* or *con sentimento*.

There is no way of knowing whether Clara heard the drama as it unfolded. When she included pieces from *Novelletten* in her own programs, they were from the cheerful early sections, with "Suleika" a favorite—never the impassioned final piece, with its intertwined motifs representing Florestan, Eusebius, and Clara.

The tales of *Novelletten* were followed by *Kinderszenen* (Scenes of Childhood), several deceptively simple pieces to which Schumann assigned titles referring to a game or a childhood activity. He chose only twelve pieces for the published set. Before publication he added a thirteenth, a coda to the entire set, which he called "Der Dichter spricht" (The Poet Speaks), in which the author himself comes out from behind the curtain. The pieces go together beautifully, opening and closing in G major, with pieces shifting from major to minor, connected often by repeating their opening notes in a new rhythm, all in similar eight-bar sequences, like Schubert dances or the movements of baroque suites. Each is charming in itself, often serving pianists as an encore piece. "Träumerei" (Dreaming) was a favorite encore of the great Russian pianist Vladimir Horowitz. The collection is even more satisfying as a loosely organized sequence, linked by related keys, with contrasting tempi and rhythms. The final piece ties the set together, as "the poet speaks" with calm tenderness, pausing for a solo aria, freely improvised, then returning to earth—all in Schumann's preferred language of feeling. It is a perfect conclusion to the collection, touching on each of the twelve notes constituting G major. Similarly, Bach touches on all twelve notes of C major in the opening Prelude of *The Well-Tempered Clavier*. But unlike Bach, who establishes C major in his first four bars, Schumann delays resolving the harmony to G until the final cadence—a favorite device of his, with its own special Romantic effect.

Kreisleriana, composed soon after *Kinderszenen*, was Schumann's favorite of all his works of this period. He wrote to Clara that she herself and one of her ideas played a central role, and he begged her to play the work often: "There's a very wild love in some movements, and your life and mine and many of your glances." The title points to E. T. A. Hoffmann's *Kreisleriana*, the most extensive work in Hoffmann's *Fantasiestücke*, the popular collection that inspired the title of Schumann's earlier *Fantasiestücke*. Hoffmann's *Kreisleriana* features the tragicomic history of the eccentric Kapellmeister Johannes

Kreisler, a true artist forced to entertain at his employer's tea parties. Kreisler is devoted to Bach's *Goldberg* Variations and despises the frivolous dance music so popular at the time. He is also maddened by a hopeless attraction to his employer's niece. His musical passions and his unspoken love are ignored by the philistines, and his fate is mysterious—he simply disappears.

Schumann obviously felt great sympathy for the abused musician, a figure widely known across Europe, since French and English translations quickly followed the early editions of Hoffmann's *Fantasiestücke*. Schumann's musical response, in eight linked "Kreisler pieces," is a portrait of the "eccentric, wild, witty" Kapellmeister (Schumann's description), and a protest against the incomprehension with which the bourgeois world regards him. Kreisler himself, in Hoffmann's words, "tossed back and forth by his inner visions and dreams as though on an eternally stormy sea," his devoted admirer (and "double") Baron Wallborn, and the landlord's cat, "caterwauling up and down the chromatic scale," also enter into the contrasting sections of Schumann's work, speaking in their own voices like the masked revelers in *Carnaval* and "F" and "E" in the *Davidsbündlertänze*. Kreisler's beloved Bach is a felt presence, as is Beethoven. Schumann was studying *The Well-Tempered Clavier* during this period of frenzied composition, and his *Kreisleriana* reflects the love of Bach that he shared with the fictional Kreisler. Schumann's delight in counterpoint and its expressive potential is evident in each section of *Kreisleriana*, with the interplay of two or often three voices driving each climax.

Like all his music of this time, *Kreisleriana* also portrays Schumann's longing for Clara and his hopes for their future. He wrote to Clara that she would smile when she recognized herself in the work. Yet it is quite possible that she missed her own portrait, since it is subtle, reflecting Schumann's love of puzzles and conundrums. Like the "Andantino by Clara Wieck" in the F Minor Sonata and the opening theme of the C Major Fantasie, Clara's theme is a simple descending scale, closest to her Notturno theme which appears as the "voice from afar" in *Novellette* no. 8 and in no. 6, book 2, of the *Davidsbündlertänze*. The descending scale is tacked on to the end of the theme that opens no. 2 of *Kreisleriana*; it appears more recognizably in no. 4, when it includes the turn that Clara uses in her Notturno, and again in yet another form in no. 6. Schumann's "mad love" for Clara is portrayed in several linked episodes, in which unresolved ascending sequences suggest the anguish of prolonged separation and the lover's intense longing for consummation.

Schumann's diary indicates that *Kreisleriana* was first composed as six "Kreisler pieces," starting with no. 2, a slow piece to which Clara is central, with intervening episodes spoken in part by the landlord's cat, marked by light staccato sequences. Nos. 2, 4, and 6 are closely related, as are nos. 3, 5, and 7. No. 7 is a true tour de force. A simple but dramatic short sequence opens the piece. Strongly accented chords and arpeggios in contrary motion, Beethovenian in character, echo the opening theme of no. 3 and an episode in no. 5. The sequence is transformed in passionate episodes of increasing intensity, concluding with a soft chorale version of the opening motif—a portrait of the demented Kapellmeister in all his moods, improvising wildly on a common theme.

Nos. 1 and 8 were composed two or three weeks later, framing the work. No. 1 is a portrait of the Kapellmeister at his most tortured, with a dissonant version of a Bach prelude followed by an episode in reasonably authentic Bach style, returning to the tortured Kreisler as he improvises recklessly for a vanishing audience. The Presto of no. 8 functions like a coda, with a light staccato imitation of the cat racing up and down the piano, leading seamlessly into fiery episodes suggesting Kreisler's (and the composer's) wild passion.

Schumann wanted to dedicate *Kreisleriana* to Clara. She begged him not to do so, since it would only enrage her father, making it difficult for her to perform the work. Schumann instructed his publisher to change the title page, dedicating *Kreisleriana* instead to "his friend Herr F. Chopin." Schumann must have hoped that Chopin would sympathize with the portrait of Kreisler, given Chopin's love of Bach and his contempt for salon music. But there is no record of Chopin responding positively to *Kreisleriana* or to any other works by Schumann. It must have been soon after he received the work that Chopin instructed his publisher to dedicate his second *Ballade* to

"Monsieur Robert Schumann " (no "friend" included). By this time Chopin's life had changed radically. He was part of George Sand's literary and political circle, and his Leipzig visits belonged to the past. Schumann was delighted by the printed dedication, which, he said, made him happier than a royal decoration.

Novelletten, Kinderszenen, and *Kreisleriana* were all composed within a few weeks. Extramusical inspirations played a role—*Egmont* stories, Hoffmann's *Kreisleriana,* Schumann's longing for Clara. But the forms these inspirations took were new, original, ambitious far beyond Schumann's comments to Clara and to fellow musicians. He had found his own way of organizing material, with overarching harmonic development of a highly personal kind, subtle thematic links, and new ways of expressing his own emotional states. He employs the most dissonant chromaticism, suspending resolution as long as possible, so that when it finally occurs, it expresses over-whelming joy and relief—although it also contains the memory of earlier pain. Schumann was deliberately exploring the contrasting elements he believed to be essential to art, which he called *Witz* and *Gemütlichkeit,* sometimes *Geist*—roughly translatable as intellect (wit or humor would be the closest English equivalents) and spiritual depth; the joint faculties of mind and heart. He found these qualities combined in Beethoven, a composer whose feet were firmly planted on the earth even as he reached to the heights. Florestan and Eusebius exemplified the double strand in their musical debut in *Carnaval,* the impetuous Florestan capering about, turning somersaults in Harlequin fashion, mocking the Philistines, while the sensitive Eusebius was quietly meditating, expressing his inmost feelings. The "doubles" take on added depth in the sonatas, the Fantasie, and the *Davidsbündlertänze,* and in the later piano works, although their signatures there are not so obvious or explicit. Perhaps Schumann had less need for the "masks" at this point. He was finally happy to appear on his own, as the true composer—often in a serene adagio cadence toward the end of a turbulent episode, much like the final piece of *Kinderszenen,* in which "the poet speaks."

When Schumann was seized by musical inspiration, writing joy-fully to Clara as if he were simply the scribe, he also knew that he was discovering a new way of composing. As he refined his craft, creating new forms of canon and counterpoint, experimenting with inner voices, moving farther and farther away from classical models, he was realizing in his own compositions the founding aim of his *New Journal*: to build on the great masters of the past in order to create something entirely new, expressing the artistic, personal, and political sensibilities of his own time. He aspired to the highest artistic standards even as he was expressing his most intimate feelings. His liberal political sympathies were embodied in his portrait of the heroic Count Egmont, in the rage of the worthy Kapellmeister against bourgeois frivolity, in his tributes to the Romantic writers he admired so enthusiastically, Jean Paul and E. T. A. Hoffmann.

He could not review his own compositions in the *New Journal*, but he hoped fervently that others would recognize his achievement. He wanted Clara above all to understand his music. When she was less than enthusiastic, he was bitterly disappointed. Much as she loved him, she did not always appreciate the extraordinary qualities of these later piano works. Her reaction to *Kreisleriana* was an exception. She told him that it was so original, so new, that it frightened her to think the composer was to be her husband. She wanted to reassure him that she loved his music, especially *Carnaval* and the G Minor Sonata. But she urged him repeatedly to write music she could play in public.

Franz Liszt understood Schumann's piano works as only a generous fellow pianist could, performing them privately and in public. But most music critics, and even sympathetic friends like Ignaz Moscheles, found Schumann's music difficult, obscure, if not incomprehensible.

Clara knew Schumann's works would never appeal to a public used to tuneful melodies and virtuoso showpieces. Chopin should have been a fellow spirit for Schumann; he was equally original and daring. At the same time that Schumann was creating his piano cycles, Chopin was remaking the traditional forms of étude, waltz, polonaise, impromptu, ballade, and prelude, extending and developing them beyond recognition. But Chopin was also very good at providing memorable tunes and dazzling showpieces. His works were published simultaneously in Paris, London, and Vienna. He was recognized everywhere as a master, as he had been by Schumann and Mendelssohn when they first met the frail composer, with his remarkable touch at the piano, his enchanting nocturnes and mazurkas, a creature from another world. Schumann had to wait far longer for recognition.

Mendelssohn, who was fond of Schumann, and who consulted him about his own Six Preludes and Fugues, thought of him mainly as the editor of the *New Journal*, which Mendelssohn read only when he was feeling too exhausted or ill to compose. He shared with Schumann a profound understanding of Bach and Beethoven, although they disagreed about the fast tempo at which Mendelssohn took the Ninth Symphony. (Schumann was so greatly offended that he walked out of the concert.) Mendelssohn, who had his own distinctive musical language, was continuing the great traditions, building upon them rather than breaking free. He had heard Clara perform Schumann's piano works, which were so different from his own *Songs Without Words* and his rather conventional sonatas and fantasies; he received presentation copies of each new publication by Schumann. But he seems not to have shared Schumann's belief that he was creating something entirely new.

In his diary, Schumann refers to "new worlds" that were opening up before him, and which his works were exploring. One element these works have in common is a daring reversal of common practice stretching from Bach to Beethoven, in which a major work, a set of variations or the first movement of a sonata, announces its subject at the start in the home key, develops, deconstructs, and varies the themes, and recapitulates them at the end. This is the pattern Schumann follows in his earliest works: the *"Abegg"* Variations, the Impromptus on a Theme by Clara Wieck, the dance suites *Papillons* and *Carnaval*. In the extraordinary piano works of 1836–1839, Schumann typically leaves the full statement of the major theme for the end, anticipating its elements along the way, so that when the theme appears in full, it comes as a revelation, casting light on everything that has come before. This procedure has often been noticed in the C Major Fantasie, in which the theme from Beethoven's song cycle, *An die ferne Geliebte,* appears in its entirety only at the end of the first movement. It is also true of the F Minor Sonata, in which the serene "Andantino by Clara Wieck," the theme of the third movement, is anticipated in the stormy Florestanian opening bars of the first movement. In the F-sharp Minor Sonata, too, the slow Aria is anticipated in the Eusebian theme of the opening movement, but only heard in full in the Aria.

In the *Davidsbündlertänze, Novelletten,* and *Kreisleriana,* Schumann experiments with similar strategies, different ways of subverting classical structure, while quoting from the great masters allusively, incorporating their themes into his own Romantic textures, using them to express the poetry of feeling that is at the heart of his music.

CLARA IN VIENNA

While Schumann was entering "new worlds" of composition in *Novelletten* and *Kreisleriana,* Clara was conquering Vienna with performances of the kind of works Schumann considered purely virtuosic, mediocre, and outdated. She was competing with the Austrian pianist Sigismond Thalberg, whose virtuoso brilliance appealed to Viennese musical taste. Clara, the young prodigy, a slight figure in a modest white voile dress, her dark hair pulled back and tied with a golden bow, her expression serious and thoughtful, far outshone the veteran musician with her impeccable, effortless technique, her innate musical feeling. Pastry shops sold *torte à la Wieck* in her honor, a "feather-light confection," she told Schumann. After the huge success of her first concerts, she took the brave step of performing Beethoven's *Appassionata* Sonata for the fashionable Viennese audience. The famous Austrian poet Franz Grillparzer praised her in his poem "Clara Wieck and Beethoven," picturing her as "a shepherd maiden" who has discovered the lost key to the Master's music. She was in demand at private houses and at court, where she was awarded the title of "Royal and Imperial Chamber Virtuosa"—which is how Schumann addressed her henceforth in his weekly letters. In private, for the cognoscenti, she played Schumann's *Carnaval,* which fellow musicians enjoyed, and his F-sharp Minor Sonata, which listeners found difficult. She told Robert that she was baffled by her phenomenal success. Schumann was immensely proud of her, but his pride was tinged with jealousy, which he tried valiantly to suppress. He wrote to Clara:

> First of all, congratulations to my dear, loyal love on her latest honor . . . But you'll still love your poor artist as you did, won't you? I spent three empty-headed days celebrating after your elevation, and dreamt of Royal Musicians and Kings, but eventually I retreated into my own simple heart and looked around and saw that it was all right, and that you will stay true to me even as I am. Clara, my heart, oldest love of my soul . . . you turn me into a child—I wander among men like one in bliss—often I press my heart against the cold wall, in the evening, when I come back home—if you could only see what is in my eyes—how I love you, how I weep for happiness.

He pictured their married bliss. They would live in a simple cottage, three rooms below and three above:

> One room dreamily dark, with flowers in the window, another light blue, with the piano, and prints on the walls—we will love one another well and stay true . . . You will gently guide me where I need it, and tell me if I have failed and if I have made something beautiful—you'll love Bach in me, and I Bellini in you—we'll often play four-hand music. In the evenings I'll improvise for you in the twilight, and sometimes you'll sing softly—and then you'll fall happily onto my breast and say "I never thought it would be so lovely."

He imagined them living a private life just outside Leipzig, with flowers in every room, sharing their music. If Clara really wanted to continue her career as a concert artist, they might consider spending three months abroad, in Paris or London. She assured him that she wanted nothing more than to share their love of music in private; she would even learn to cook. But she also wrote that after careful consideration she realized that as an artist she would need a more substantial income than Schumann could provide. She could easily meet the increased expenses by her own efforts. Schumann took this as a threat to end everything on which they had solemnly agreed, with so many vows, so many promises, so many kisses. He wrote indignantly that he could see her father holding the pen as she wrote.

To Wieck's delight, the Vienna tour was a great financial success. Audiences fought for tickets to Clara's six public concerts. Clara realized that if she continued to concertize, she would be able to secure her financial future with Schumann, thus answering her father's objections. She was torn between her love for Schumann and her loyalty as a dutiful daughter. She told Schumann that she still loved her father, much as she resented his crude attacks on her beloved. Wieck was unrelenting. He made it clear to Clara that he would never tolerate their married life anywhere in Saxony. In the unlikely case that the marriage eventually took place, he had to be spared the sight of a union he found so odious. In another twist of the knife, he insisted that she pass on the profits of any concert tour to her younger brothers, whom he intended to send out from the family home to earn their living as they might.

As she was about to leave Vienna, Clara wrote joyfully to Schumann that her father had at last consented to their marriage, on condition that they agreed to live in Vienna. He had written the words in her diary. Schumann was skeptical. He asked Clara several times to tell him Wieck's precise words. But they agreed that Vienna would be their goal. It was, after all, the home of Beethoven and Schubert, the European capital of music. Clara was already known and admired in the Austrian city. She would give one concert a year and weekly lessons, which would pay for her share of their living expenses. Gone was Schumann's dream of a simple cottage in the country, with Clara playing for him alone, or for a few friends and family. He decided to go to Vienna, to try to establish his *Journal* there, and to plan for their marriage by Easter 1840.

Clara returned to Leipzig from her Vienna tour as a European star, at eighteen no longer a child prodigy. Much as the lovers longed to meet, to embrace, to spend hours and days together, Schumann was seized by fear. He was unable to face the thought of pretending that he and Clara were strangers. Clara, too, worried about their first meeting. She told Schumann that her father said he would be welcome to visit "as a friend of the family." Schumann saw the invitation as a deliberate insult. He thought he might go to Paris or hike in the mountains, anything to postpone confrontation.

When Clara arrived at the rather grand new family home on Nicolaistrasse, the lovers resorted to letters, as in the past. Schumann confided to his diary that it had all begun badly—he had thought himself more manly. "Now let my pride give me strength!" He saw Clara for the first time at a concert devoted to Schubert's music. "Is it possible? Am I alive?" He spoke briefly with Wieck, though not with Clara, and the next day Wieck visited him in his "little room near the park," on the Ritterstrasse. Though he was surprised to find his former affection for "the old scoundrel" coming back, his pride would not let him return the visit. Instead, he stood outside Clara's house, listening for the piano—perhaps she would be playing one of the works he had composed for her. Often she walked back and forth outside Schumann's lodgings, hoping to see him at the window. He saw Clara in the distance at an evening musical soiree, then met her by chance one afternoon. "She was my Clara!" And again on a walk to Lützschena: "Do I live or dream?" A day later: "By good chance in the evening I see Clara, we speak and kiss." Meanwhile their letters went back and forth. From Clara: "I thought I saw you pass by at Felsche's . . . but you didn't notice, and I was trembling from joy and grief and almost ran after you—I felt as if I were about to faint . . . It is almost more than I can bear." From Robert: "I am so desperate to see you, to press you to my heart . . . I see you everywhere; you walk back and forth with me in my room; you lie in my arms, and nothing, nothing is true . . . Each minute later is like dying. I can't endure this much longer."

As Schumann's birthday approached, it was clear that the lovers had to meet properly. It was Clara who took the initiative: "Be at our window at nine sharp. If I signal with a white handkerchief, walk slowly toward the old Neumarkt. I will follow then and go with you." The story continues in Schumann's diary: "My twenty-eighth birthday—never one happier, more peaceful." In the evening, he had a few drinks with friends at Auerbach's Keller: "And then, and then—I met my girl and took her home with me—we played like children—too great a happiness—this girl—tears of love came to my eyes—for the first time, the *Du* spoken often and from a full heart—*Never forget what Clara has endured for you.*"

To refer to Schumann and Clara as "lovers" is not to suggest that they were lovers in the sense that Liszt and Marie d'Agoult, or Chopin and George Sand, were lovers. They had the rights and privileges of engaged couples in the bourgeois society of the time. They could meet in private without chaperones, they could embrace, they could walk arm in arm in public. Clara was still a noble priestess to Schumann, the ideal of love and fidelity. Sexual love waited upon marriage, although when it seemed that Wieck might force them to postpone their marriage for another five years, Clara told Schumann that she was ready to fly to him at any time. Meanwhile, they were lovers in the sense that they were engaged to marry and had solemnly sworn to love each other for all eternity.

They decided that Schumann would go to Vienna in October to prepare for their new life together. Another long separation loomed, but now there was the prospect of marriage at Easter, 1840. Their letters during this period take on a new character. Supremely confident in their love, they now had a definite plan, which they both were determined to follow. Schumann thought that Clara might join him in Vienna at Christmas rather than waiting for Easter. "Imagine when I can walk with you on my arm—when you can wish me 'Good morning' each day—when we can walk together through forests and meadows for entire days—when you only need to call me to have me with you." He promised never to tell Clara an untruth—even if the truth would hurt her. "The great comfort is that we know each other and that nothing in the world, no slander, no tricks the world can play on us, can separate me from you."

Yet he still led a disorderly life; he drank too much and suffered *Katzenjammer* the next day. That he had been chaste during this time, although true, was not something he could tell Clara in so many words. He suffered a crisis of anxiety in late July, "the most frightful night of my life," he wrote in his diary. He thought he must explode from terror. A letter from Clara was of no help. He was assailed by everything at once—the approaching separation, fear about whether he could carry out his aims, the thought of being alone in Vienna.

Even if Clara's letter was no help, her actual presence dispelled his fears. As she was to be throughout their married life, she was his rock, his support against his crippling anxiety attacks and his enemies. She returned to Leipzig from a visit to Dresden on August 8th, and they arranged to meet at the old Wieck family house on August 14th, Eusebius's Saint's Day, the first anniversary of their engagement. Clara proposed further meetings: "Can't we speak to each other on Saturday? I long for you so much I can't stand it anymore." On the 30th of August: "About Friday night, I thought it would be too frightening in the [old] house, and I suggest that if you want to see me, walk along the little alley at eleven o'clock on Saturday, Tuesday, or Thursday. I'll be walking down there each day, but do not go too far, because there are two paths, and we could miss each other." From Schumann, after another precious meeting: "I hardly know what to do for joy, I am so happy to have you, you true-hearted girl. How you were the other evening, so tender, so lovable, so much yourself! And this morning you stand before me so poetically, and I am unworthy of you. Now we have only three more weeks together. There are many things that I must discuss with my future wife calmly and properly."

They had to discuss Schumann's departure for Vienna, letters to friends and publishers in the Austrian capital, his arrangements for the *Journal* in his absence. He suggested, only half in jest, that Clara might hide him in the lodger's room at her house. "If only I could speak to you and embrace you safely and undisturbed for

half an hour!" Clara gave a concert on the 9th of September, playing a movement of Chopin's E Minor Piano Concerto and one
each of his mazurkas and études, Liszt's piano arrangements of
two Schubert songs, her own new Scherzo, and works by Henselt
and Thalberg—but nothing by Schumann. She still wanted to
keep their relations secret, and she also feared a negative reaction
from the audience. Two days later, they had a "blissful half-hour"
in the public gardens. On September 13th Clara turned nineteen,
and Schumann saw her and kissed her in the morning. They made
elaborate plans for a farewell meeting before Schumann left for
Vienna. Wieck was going to Dresden, where he maintained a branch
of his piano business. They decided that Schumann would travel
to Zwickau and return secretly to Leipzig after Wieck had left. It
all happened as planned. They met, enjoyed private time together,
talked about their future. Schumann's parting words were: "Let us
live together and die together"—a solemn promise, as unrealistic as
many of their best-laid plans.

At this time Wieck was writing to everyone he knew in Vienna,
warning them against helping Schumann, insisting that he was
unstable and financially irresponsible. He included Clara in his
rage, writing what she described as a "terrible" letter to her from
Dresden. She had told him that she planned to marry Schumann at
Easter 1840 and to live with him in Vienna. He wrote that he would
never consent to their marriage; she must dismiss the good Nanni,
their courier; and there would be no more piano lessons, no more
touring.

"I have to go away from here, and I *will* leave, heaven will protect
me," she wrote to Schumann:

Oh, Robert, where will all this lead! Father won't have anything more to do with me, and I have only one hope, one
protector—you, my sweet Robert! . . . Oh, I think of you so
often! I almost didn't sleep at all Thursday night, you were
always standing before me! Now I am so miserable, so many
worries, and where shall I go? My longing for you is inde-
scribable, beyond imagining. Only stay true to me, as I am

to you. Your words last time—"We shall live together and die together"—were also said from my whole being; yes, my Robert, that is what we shall do, and we shall be happy.

Secretly pleased that matters had reached a critical point, Schumann urged Clara to leave Leipzig as soon as possible. Where should she go? Ideally to his sister-in-law Therese in Zwickau, or to Clara's friends in Maxen, Major Friedrich Serre and his wife, or to Prague, to continue her theory studies, a possibility they had already considered. By the time Clara received Schumann's letter, Wieck had made his peace with his favorite child. He proposed a short tour from Leipzig to Dresden, then perhaps to Munich, and afterwards he might go with her to Paris. She knew there was no point in arguing. At heart nothing had changed; she was committed to Schumann as firmly as ever. They had sworn to live together and die together. But difficult as her life had become, she decided to stay with her father for another year and a half. Schumann told her that she and her father were like children: he would rage, she would cry, they would make up, and it would start all over again.

8

TOWARD THE FUTURE

October 1838–May 1839

SCHUMANN IN VIENNA

Schumann arrived in Vienna in early October. He was delighted at first by the beauty of the city and its surroundings, the carefree atmosphere, the hospitality, the warm memories many people had of Clara. But he soon realized that he would face huge obstacles in moving the *New Journal* to Vienna. He would need official permission from the authorities; he might even have to become an Austrian citizen. He struggled with bureaucratic delays, canceled meetings. Important officials were unavailable for weeks at a time. His cherished copies of works by Jean Paul and Byron were confiscated when his goods arrived from Leipzig; they were revolutionary writers, proscribed in Metternich's Vienna. The publishers he managed to approach were reluctant to assume responsibility for the *New Journal for Music*. Schumann also feared for its quality under Austrian censorship. He told Clara: "From everything I've experienced up to now and seen with my own eyes, it is hardly possible, because of the pressure from above, for anything imaginative, open-minded, or spirited to come about here."

His melancholy was exacerbated by his loneliness. He arrived at a low point in December, writing to Clara:

The past two weeks were the most terrible; everything looked black or blood-stained around me; I thought I'd have to take my own life; evil spirits took hold of me . . . I was overcome by one thing after another: the distance from you, your father's malicious actions, the slow progress of my affairs here . . . I imagined death would be easy and thought, "Then come." But truly, Clara, believe me, among all these unhappy thoughts a heavenly vision often arose, an image of faithfulness and love; that is what you are to me, and you stood before me in your noble simplicity . . . I'll whisper once again to the person who closes my eyes, "Only one person held sway over my life so completely and drew me so completely into her innermost being, and I've always adored and loved that person above all else."

The black clouds lifted, and he composed a set of "little verses to Clara," rhyming couplets celebrating their future life together.

If Florestan storms,
Nestle close to Eusebius.
Florestan the wild,
Eusebius the mild,
Tears and flames,
Take them together,
Both are within me,
The pain and the joy!

The verses continue with the image of Clara led to the altar by two figures—the intimate comrades who appeared to Schumann in 1831 and who were still signing articles in the *Journal* and informing the contrasting moods of his music. Clara was central to the fantasy, as Chiara or Zilia in the *Journal*, Chiarina in *Carnaval*, as Egmont's lover, Klärchen. She signed one of her letters "Eusebiana." It would be interesting to know how closely Clara read Schumann's music, and whether she knew the full extent of her role in his compositions.

*oon after arriving in Vienna, Schumann visited the Währinger Cemetery to lay flowers at the grave of Beethoven and, nearby, at the untended grave of Schubert. He found a pen on Beethoven's grave, which he kept, and he left flowers on both, in homage to the two composers he loved and revered above all others, after Bach. He knew that Schubert's brother Ferdinand, who lived in Vienna, had kept Schubert's unpublished manuscripts. Schumann visited him and in effect "discovered" Schubert's great C Major Symphony, his ninth. Schumann arranged at once to have it copied and sent to Mendelssohn for performance at a Gewandhaus concert. In his journal, Schumann reviewed the symphony in terms which still resonate as a description of Schubert's imaginative power: "This symphony reveals something more than mere fine melody, mere ordinary joy and sorrow . . . it leads us into a region we never before explored . . . Here we find, besides masterly musical composition, life in every vein, coloring down to the finest grade of possibility, sharp expression in detail, meaning throughout . . . while over the whole is thrown that glow of Romanticism that everywhere accompanies Franz Schubert." Schumann also found letters from Schubert to his brother and to their parents, key documents for understanding the troubled composer with whom Schumann identified so closely. In addition to the letters, he published a strange prose piece by Schubert, "My Dream," an allegory of parental rejection and despair. This was the first publication of a document that for later generations defined Schubert's very nature as a composer. The dreamer is cruelly rejected by his father and by society. Full of love for those who scorn him, he pours his feelings into his songs. "If I would sing of love, it turned to pain; if I would sing of pain, it turned to love. Thus was I divided between love and sorrow." These lines by Schubert could have been penned by Schumann in his most despairing mood.

Arabeske; Blumenstück; Humoreske; Faschingsschwank aus Wien
The discovery of Schubert's manuscripts inspired Schumann to write compositions of his own. First came the poetic *Arabeske*, begun

in Leipzig, and the charming *Blumenstück*, both works "light and suitable for ladies," Schumann told a friend, and marked "for C." in his notes. They perfectly answered Clara's repeated requests that he compose attractive pieces she could play in public, works free of puzzling titles and obscure harmonic experiments, not too short, not too long. Schumann should have been less dismissive of these relatively simple works, especially the lovely *Arabeske*, with its lyrical beauty. It has become one of his most popular works, a poignant expression of one aspect of his Romanticism, wistful, yearning, tender-hearted. It opens with a gentle, songlike theme in C major, repeated several times in interlinked "arabeske" fashion, and two episodes in minor keys, the first one similar to the first piece of *Kinderszenen*. As it ends, the notes seem to be calling Clara, who answers reassuringly in her own key of C, with her own descending scale—a sequence recalled in a final cadence, with a radiant C-major arpeggio. (If Clara was attuned to the message, she might have thought back to the transcendent third movement of the C Major Fantasie.) *Blumenstück*, too, has a quality of its own, simple but expressive. Schumann wrote to Clara that a work he thought of calling *Guirlande* (Garland) was "a set of variations *not* on a theme, closely intertwined." This could be a description of the piece that became *Blumenstück*, with its three closely related and intertwined sections. With his love of puzzles, Schumann might have thought the original title provided too definite a clue to the unusual structure of the piece.

Greater works were to come. *Humoreske*, its opening section composed in Leipzig, was completed in Vienna in March. He described it to Clara thus: "All week I sat at the piano and composed, wrote, laughed and cried all together. You will find this all nicely evoked in my op. 20, the grand *Humoreske*, which is about to be engraved. You see how fast things are going with me now. Conceived, written down, printed." To his friend Ernst Becker he described *Humoreske* as "not very merry, and perhaps my most melancholy work." A revelation of his inmost feelings, it is suffused by melancholy, reflecting his state during much of his time in Vienna. But it is also enlivened by quirky episodes in the style of Florestan or Arlequin, suggesting the darker side of "humor," intellectual games rather than merriment.

Humoreske is a fascinating work, somewhat neglected in concert performance, although it has been recorded by several great Schumann enthusiasts, including Vladimir Horowitz, Claudio Arrau, and Radu Lupu. More than his other extended works for piano—*Davidsbündlertänze, Kreisleriana*—it reads as if it were improvised dreamily at the piano, the composer thinking all the while of his beloved, his long separation from her, their union, so long delayed. It is restricted to a single key signature and its close relations, and to what seems to be a single motif, varied in ingenious ways—a challenge to the performer to improvise along with the composer.

It is tempting to understand *Humoreske* as an expansion of Schumann's idea of variations *not* on a theme, so typical of his playful approach to traditional forms. Unlike his earlier sets of variations, its contrasting sections are not separated by number or title, but constitute a single continuous work. What might seem to be a "humorous" violation of formal expectations has led to some disagreement among editors, one of them discovering fifteen separate sections. Another possibility is to see the sections as five "movements," the opening movement consisting of frames within frames—as if Schumann had more material than he could fit together in a coherent way. Or one can simply take Schumann's scheme as a series of closely intertwined variations. What is certain is that Schumann is experimenting with new ways of developing and linking the individual parts of an extended work, with disguised motivic echoes and deliciously inventive harmonic and rhythmic variation. Though it bears certain resemblances to the earlier piano cycles, *Humoreske* stands alone. In performance, it runs to just under twenty-six minutes, not far off from the thirty-two minutes of *Kreisleriana*'s eight pieces, or the thirty-five minutes of the three-movement Fantasie in C. These are three of the greatest works of this time, each one different from the others, unrepeatable in form and feeling.

No sooner had Schumann finished *Humoreske* than he began *Faschingsschwank aus Wien* (Carnival Jest from Vienna). The five-movement work sums up his time in the Austrian capital and his mixed feelings about its closed society, pleasure-loving but oppressive, its unthinking worship of Beethoven and callous disregard of Schubert. Schumann wrote a substantial opening movement and sketched the others, intending to complete the work later.

Faschingsschwank follows *Papillons* and *Carnaval* as a masquerade, with a cast of carnival characters parading, performing tricks, mocking the official world. Schumann thought of the first movement, which returns to its opening theme several times, as a "rondolet," but he also spoke of the entire five-movement work as a "grand *Romantic* sonata." *Faschingsschwank* marks the final appearance of Florestan and Eusebius in their own characteristic notes and keys and contrasting styles, although they are unnamed. As in *Carnaval*, Schubert is a vital presence, appropriate for Vienna, with echoes of his dances (especially his *Hommage aux belles Viennoises*) dominating the opening movement. Schumann's scorn of Austrian censorship appears in the cleverly announced but well-disguised entry of the "Marseillaise," just as the Schubertian dance reaches its climax. The great anthem of revolution was banned in Vienna, and Schumann knew his Viennese publisher, Pietro Mechetti, might be taking a risk in publishing the work. Marked *fortissimo* and framed by the traditional "Grandfather's Dance" also quoted in *Papillons* and *Carnaval*, the "Marseillaise" wonderfully expresses Schumann's feelings about government authority and the need for artistic and political freedom.

The second movement is a slow and tender Romanze in which Clara makes a secret appearance. The theme of her Notturno is adapted as the chief motif, a slow descending scale starting on D, repeated again and again over Eusebius's sustained E-flat in the middle voice, the diminished octave which is so expressive of love and longing. In a middle section in C major, a radiant answer to the opening lament, it seems that Clara herself is speaking, reassuring Eusebius that she loves him fervently, and that all will be well. The third movement is a carnivalesque Scherzino, in which Florestan cavorts cheerfully, landing now and again on his keynote of F. Both aspects of Schumann join forces in the impassioned Intermezzo that follows, a cry from the heart, like the F Minor Sonata, lamenting Schumann's separation from Clara and his longing to join her in marriage. The bravura Finale celebrates the triumph of freedom and love, with allusions to Beethoven at his most heroic and optimistic. Like the "March of the *Davidsbündler* Against the Philistines" that ends *Carnaval*, all the revelers are brought together in a final affirmation of hope, the spirit of *Witz* (humor, intellect, fun) and *Geist* or *Gemütlichkeit* (inner spirit, feeling, love) united in harmony. Thus the spirits of Schubert and Beethoven frame Schumann's farewell to the city that treated their dedicated musical heir as a rank outsider.

CLARA IN PARIS

While Schumann was struggling with Viennese bureaucracy, Clara had set off to Paris by way of Nuremberg, Stuttgart, and Karlsruhe, giving concerts in each city. Although Wieck had originally agreed to join her, he changed his mind, confident that she would fail without his support. She was accompanied only by a disagreeable Frenchwoman whom Wieck had hired to travel with her. It was the first time she had toured without her father, and she rose to the challenge in a way that Schumann could only admire. He was stunned by her bravery and her practical competence. She made all travel arrangements, found accommodation for herself and her unwelcome companion, and kept close track of expenses. Despite severe winter weather, spells of melancholy and frequent headaches (a recurring theme in her letters), she arranged her own concerts, appeared at court in Stuttgart, and saved enough money to pay for her time in Paris. In Stuttgart she fell for the wily overtures of one Dr. Gustav Schilling, a known speculator and seducer, who offered to help Schumann by making him a partner in a music journal he was planning to found. Schumann was furious at Schilling, and annoyed at Clara's naïveté in encouraging him. It was one of the few sour notes in the lovers' correspondence.

Clara faced each challenge with courage and determination. She half-adopted a young music student in Stuttgart, dismissing the Frenchwoman when the three of them reached Paris. There Clara found her childhood friend Emilie List, who welcomed Clara into her family home. Clara worried constantly about Schumann's mental state. She was the strong one, while Schumann was always vulnerable. His pride was offended by the machinations of Schilling (as if the scoundrel were in a position to help an established editor!) and by Clara's continued reliance on her father. She expected Wieck to join her at any point, possibly in Paris, or on a later tour to Holland, Belgium, and Germany. Schumann dreamed of their quiet private life after marriage. At the same time he urged Clara to travel from Paris to London, where he was sure she could make her name and possibly her fortune; he had friends who would assist her. After London, perhaps she might go to St. Petersburg, where she was sure to succeed, following in the steps of Thalberg and Liszt.

Events gave a new turn to their plans. In March, the publisher Robert Friese, Schumann's Leipzig partner, wrote that he was unable to continue producing the *Journal* past July. Schumann decided that he must return to Leipzig as soon as possible. Traveling to Leipzig in April, he received news of the death of his brother Eduard, Therese's husband. He hastened to Zwickau, too late for the funeral. Zwickau seemed to him like a graveyard, where so many people he loved were absent—his sister-in-law Rosalie, his brother Julius, his mother, and now Eduard. Nonetheless, there was another side to his grief. It occurred to him that he might take over the publishing business that their father had established and Eduard had been managing. The estate and the viability of the business had to be assessed. But Schumann was strongly tempted. It would mean an assured income adequate for their needs, and it would meet the financial conditions Wieck had set.

Wieck had other ideas. He wrote confidentially to Emilie List that unless Clara left Schumann, he would no longer consider her his child. He would take away her inheritance and begin a lawsuit against both Schumann and Clara, which could last from three to five years.

Schumann consulted his lawyer friends in Leipzig. It appeared that a girl could marry from the age of fifteen, but parental consent was necessary at any age. Schumann proposed to write a formal letter to Wieck requesting his consent. If Wieck refused, the Royal

Court of Appeal could override his decision. Schumann was assured that the court's decision should take no more than six weeks.

Ever devious, Wieck suddenly offered to consent to the marriage if Clara and Schumann signed a formal list of conditions. These were obviously formulated to humiliate Schumann. Wieck hoped that Clara would be tempted, while Schumann would be outraged at the attack on his character. But Clara was equally outraged by the conditions: (1) that they would not live in Saxony for five years after marrying, as long as Wieck maintained his residence in Saxony; (2) that he would retain two thousand thalers of Clara's capital for five years; (3) that Schumann must provide documentation of his income to be sent to Wieck's lawyer; (4) that he never request any meeting or conversation with Wieck unless so invited; (5) that Clara never seek to inherit money from her father.

Wieck's ultimatum confirmed Schumann's decision to appeal for legal permission to marry. It was the beginning of a court battle that dragged on for more than a year. Wieck instituted a countersuit, failed to turn up for required court appearances, and continued to devise new ways to attack his former friend and pupil and the daughter who had finally defied him.

Both Schumann and Clara tried every feasible means of making their marriage possible, answering Wieck's objections or trying in vain to meet his changing conditions, designed simply to postpone matters. It was only as a last resort that they decided to go beyond Wieck's parental authority to the courts.

Throughout this time, Clara had to deal with two difficult men, sworn enemies, each one claiming her for his own. She was passionately committed to Schumann. She promised him that she would remain steadfast "unto death." But she also continued to love her father, and hoped against hope that he would relent.

Schumann continued to have moments of despair. He was assailed by the conviction that the marriage would never take place, that Clara would find someone else, that he would die before they were "united forever." He described a strange experience to Clara. "I want to tell you about last night. I woke up and could not get back to sleep, and as I thought myself deeper and deeper into you and your soul and dream life, I spoke out all at once with inner strength, 'Clara, I'm calling you'—and then I heard, out loud as though it were beside me, 'Robert, I am with you.' A sort of terror came over me, how spirits can traffic with one another across the broad earth's miles. I shall not do it again, this calling." But this is exactly what he did in his music, calling to Clara, listening for her answer, transcribing their longing for each other into musical notes.

Clara too suffered from terrifying dreams, experiences almost supernatural in their vividness.

> I dreamed I was lying in a white dress and a white wreath lay on my coffin, and you and Henriette were kneeling at my side, smiling sadly, and I was constantly hearing the sound of heavenly bells, they sounded so heavenly and yet so horrific! I had a white veil on with silver stars that gleamed like the stars in the sky—I was in heaven, but I was so sad! Oh, Robert, I had thought a hundred times before, "If only you could see your Robert just once more"—I saw you, but I could only see you in my coffin! Away with these gloomy thoughts! No, my Robert, we will see each other again and in this life, and we shall be happy, in this world!

Confiding their dreams, their fears, their undying love to each other, they were well matched despite the nine-year difference in age and the disparity in their life experience. Still, the problems that surfaced repeatedly in these years of enforced separation, ecstatic reunions, plans agreed to and abandoned were to recur in the years of their marriage. Schumann knew that Clara would never give up her career, nor did he ever want her to give up her music. But he imagined an idyllic life in a cottage, with Clara playing for him alone. Clara had her heart set on a Russian tour, in which she could earn enough to enable Schumann to devote all his time to composing. What neither of them could anticipate was that Schumann would be plagued by spells of severe mental and physical ill health, forcing him to abandon all work for months at a time, and casting a deepening shadow over their lives.

9

FINAL COURT BATTLE

Leipzig, June 1839–August 1840

After taking legal advice, Schumann composed an official document requesting permission to marry, which he sent to Clara for her signature. Their agreement to go over Wieck's head to the Court of Appeals marked a new stage in their lives, and it was Schumann who now took charge. There could be no going back, no concessions. Clara, still in Paris, perfecting her French, was hoping to prepare for a winter season of concerts, building upon her earlier, unpaid appearances at private soirees. Schumann consulted her at each stage of the court proceedings, determined to put an end to their corrosive battle with her father. His first act was to write to Wieck in "mild and conciliatory" terms. But he told Clara that his whole body was shaking when he sent the letter.

> Honored Sir, Clara tells me that you yourself wish that we could bring this to an end; I gladly offer you my hand in peace. If you let me know your wishes, I am ready to do whatever it lies in my power to achieve. If you do not respond to my inquiry within a week, I will take it as a definite refusal. Yours very truly,
>
> R. Schumann.

As Schumann expected, Wieck let the week pass without responding. It was time to proceed to legal action. Schumann engaged Wilhelm Einert, reputed to be the best lawyer in Leipzig. Following correct protocol, Einert approached Wieck twice with offers of mediation, which Wieck refused.

Given her father's obduracy, Einert suggested that it might be useful to approach Clara's mother for her consent. In July 1839 Schumann decided to visit Mariane Bargiel in Berlin. To his joy, Mariane embraced him as a son. Adolf Bargiel, her husband, had suffered a stroke and was a virtual invalid. Mariane was supporting herself, Bargiel, and their two surviving children by private teaching. (Schumann and Clara both contributed later toward the family's expenses.) Clara had told Schumann that she was unable to feel comfortable with Bargiel, the false friend who had caused her father so much suffering. Having suffered himself from Wieck's relentless egotism, Schumann could imagine Mariane's unhappiness as Wieck's wife. He wrote to Clara: "I have been so vividly reminded of you here, by your mother; I really love her; she has your eyes, and I just cannot tear myself away from her . . . She received me so kindly and cordially, and seems to have taken a liking to me." No doubt Wieck was tortured by the resemblance between mother and daughter which so delighted Schumann. He feared that the child he had shaped in his own image, his route to fame and fortune, was following her mother in choosing love above her duty toward him.

Schumann returned to Leipzig with Mariane's written consent and her promise to help the young couple. A hearing with Archdeacon Rudolf Fischer, the official mediator appointed by the court, was set for the last week of August. All three parties, Clara, Schumann, and Wieck, were required to appear.

Clara, estranged from her father, was appalled by the prospect of returning from Paris to Leipzig. What if Wieck insisted that she live in the family home, surrounded by her enemies—her stepmother, Clementine; her brother Alwin—commissioned to spy on her? Schumann was firm: she had to appear in person at the court hearing. He sent her precise directions. She was to arrive in Frankfurt on August 19th, proceed to Naumburg on the 21st, and wait for the coach to Altenburg, where Schumann would meet her.

They met at Altenburg as planned. Schumann was waiting anxiously for the coach to arrive. "At six she was there, in my arms. The beloved, the darling, had become even more lovable, more adorable." They walked together arm in arm, gazed at the moon, all was "unforgettable." They spent several days together, traveling to Zwickau and Schneeberg to visit Schumann's family. On the day before the hearing, they went to Leipzig, where Clara, banned from her own home, stayed with Robert Friese's family.

At the mediation hearing, Wieck failed to appear, pleading urgent business elsewhere. Girding for battle, he began his own legal attack on Schumann. He submitted a "declaration" alleging Schumann's unsuitability to marry Clara, adding a few new charges to his old list of grievances. Not only was Schumann financially irresponsible, his works were incomprehensible, his speech was poor, his manners clumsy, his handwriting illegible. Trivial as the accusations were, Wieck won one postponement after another. Although the court eventually threw out all but one of his charges against Schumann, they permitted Wieck a six-week delay to prove that Schumann drank excessively. It was the start of a series of charges and counter-charges, with Schumann finally suing Wieck for defamation of character, a suit he won. Wieck was sentenced to eighteen days in jail.

Clara's mother arrived in Leipzig the day after the August hearing, and two days later Clara returned with her to Berlin. They began to know each other as mother and daughter. Clara found her mother caring for a depressed and demanding invalid. Bargiel had been cursed in all his business efforts, and now Mariane could barely make ends meet. Distressed at the family's poverty, Clara soon set to work finding a good piano, arranging concerts, distracting herself with practical matters. She longed for Schumann to join her.

In late September, Clara returned to Leipzig to meet Wieck privately, at his request. A second hearing was scheduled for October 2nd, which Wieck again boycotted, forcing a postponement to mid-December. His rage was now directed at Clara. "I know no Fräulein Wieck," he told the maid sent to ask for Clara's winter coat. He demanded that she pay four hundred thalers for her piano. Her brother Alwin told Clara that Wieck took her portrait down, hid it under the bureau, and said that he was "burying" her.

Hurtful as it was, good things came of Wieck's malice. Since Clara had to appear in person at successive court hearings, she and Schumann spent time in intimate talk, planning their future. They confirmed their love ever more passionately, reaching new depths of mutual understanding. And both Clara and Schumann came to know Clara's mother, forming warm and lasting relationships.

After the aborted October hearing, Clara returned to Berlin and arranged a short concert tour, with her mother accompanying her. The concerts at Frankfurt on the Oder, Stettin, Rostock, and other small towns enabled Clara to contribute substantially to her mother's finances. She was moved by Mariane's loving welcome to Schumann and her eagerness to help them. Brought up to regard her mother as a depraved woman who had betrayed her beloved father, Clara gradually developed the affectionate relationship she had been denied for so many years. Bargiel died in 1841, and Mariane became a staunch friend, resuming an important role in Clara's life when Schumann suffered his final illness.

HENRIETTE VOIGT, *AMIE INTIME*

In October 1839, Schumann's patron and confidante Henriette Voigt died of tuberculosis, aged thirty. His relationship with the woman he called "Eleonore," after Florestan's devoted wife, Leonore, in Beethoven's *Fidelio,* went back to 1834, shortly after the young pianist and composer Ludwig Schunke appeared in Leipzig. He and Schumann immediately struck up a close friendship, and the two young men soon became central figures in Henriette's musical salon, meeting most evenings to play Schubert's piano works for two and four hands. In the summer of 1834, when Schumann was paying court to the seventeen-year-old Ernestine von Fricken, the twenty-six-year-old Henriette, a respectable married woman with a young daughter, passed letters back and forth between the lovers and arranged times for them to meet at her home. Schumann wrote to Henriette about his idea for a series of "scenes" based on Schubert's "Sehnsucht" Waltz in A-flat. "They are love lilies, held together by the 'Sehnsucht' Waltz. The dedication deserves an

A-flat-major soul; that is, one you resemble; that is, you alone, my dear friend—Robert S." The next day he told Henriette about the remarkable coincidence he had discovered, that the musical letters of Ernestine's birthplace, ASCH, were also to be found in his own name, SCHumAnn—the germ of *Carnaval*. He was truly in love with Ernestine, he told Henriette; he also loved Henriette. It is not surprising that her friendship with Schumann soon took on deeper coloring, especially as his passion for Ernestine cooled. They had music in common—not only Schubert's dances and four-hand works, but Beethoven's sonatas and Bach's *Well-Tempered Clavier*. They shared a love of Ludwig Schunke and grief at his early death. Schumann was attractive to women; he had close relations with his sisters-in-law, and had fantasised happily about Agnes Carus. The correspondence between Schumann and Henriette—more than fifty letters—suggests that there were danger signals on both sides. The *Du* was never exchanged, but Henriette took to signing her letters "Eleonore," "Leonore," "Your Lenore," and, once, "Lenore F," hinting at a private relationship with Florestan. Schumann, in turn, addressed one letter simply "Liebe," signing it "Your Robert," otherwise it was "RS" or "R."

A comparison of Schumann's letters to Henriette with his letters to Clara suggests his wild emotional swings during this time. His tone to his mentor Henriette is confessional and loving. "Do not abandon me!—I am forever Your R." But he is writing to an *amie intime*, not to a promised bride. He assures Henriette that the holiest things one can name are friendship and love. "My dear friend—how I love and honor you in my inmost being . . . You stand before me, faithful as a picture . . . Remain mine, my dear friend." Henriette matches Schumann in feeling when Ludwig Schunke dies. "With trembling hand I write to you, my dear friend—our Ludwig is gone—he is to be buried midweek—O come, my friend . . . travel here at once . . . Heaven give us the power to bear this calmly . . . Your faithful friend Henriette V." Schumann draws a broad crescendo in Henriette's Album, signing it with the words: "This is the crescendo of our friendship." On January 5th, 1837, the date (or so he guesses) when Christel gives birth to the child he has fathered, he addresses Henriette as "Liebe . . . I think of you often. Adieu. Your RS." His diary notes in 1836–1837, when Schumann is convinced that Clara is lost to him, record private encounters with "Eleonore," "Christel," and "La Faneuse," until on the 12th of August, 1837, he notes "a change from then on in my way of life, and true longing for one woman [only]." It is possible that the "other women" he longed for were not only Christel and La Faneuse, but also Henriette, to whom he had also been making love, if not physically, then emotionally. When he and Clara were at last reunited and determined to marry, he assured her that "Madame Voigt" knew nothing about their new relations; they had vowed secrecy to avoid Wieck's rage. This was in Schumann's interest as well as Clara's. When Clara was in Paris, Schumann invited Henriette to be his pianist at the quartet mornings he held in his rooms. He does not mention this in his letters to Clara.

Six months after Schumann and Clara reconfirmed their love, Henriette's letters take on a new, passionate tone. "How much I have to tell you . . . I am playing only Florestan and Eusebius now, and I am blissfully happy to understand these two. Come soon, so that I can pour out my feelings . . . write me just a few words—oh, please. With old faith, Leonore." She hasn't seen him or heard from him for several days. "Shall I then hear nothing more from you, dear friend? Have you received my last lines? Each day I await a sign from your dear hand. If you only knew how deeply enwrapped in your tone poems I have been, you would send me a friendly word. . . . Oh, do not remain so silent—think back to the past, to so many happy hours, let me have one more through your answer . . . If you do not answer me this time, I too must be silent. Your faithful friend, Lenore F." At the same time, Schumann describes his reformed life in his diary and his letters to Clara. He is at home each night by nine, living a clean life, no drinking in the evenings; he has been composing much music. He visits the Voigts, but with no hint of anything irregular. He attends a ball at the Voigts' at which he misbehaves, refusing to dance. He wants to dance only with Clara.

Henriette was usually surrounded by people, visitors from

abroad and fellow musicians arriving each evening for music, food, and wine. An intimate private relationship would have been difficult to maintain, a sexual relationship virtually impossible. Clara's letters show obvious signs of jealousy. She did not like Madame Voigt at all. She considered her a "snake," and not only because she had supported Schumann's secret engagement to Ernestine. Clara resented Schumann's close friendship with an older woman of substance who was evidently devoted to him. Even more insulting to Clara, he showed "the Voigt" each of his works as soon as they were finished. How annoyed Clara would have been if she had seen Schumann's letter to Henriette asking her to show the Sonata in F Minor to Clara. "I'd like to know what she thinks of it and if she understands it." Henriette understood Schumann's music instinctively, as if she shared his most intimate thoughts and feelings; so she assured him repeatedly.

After Clara turned fifteen, Schumann had suggested to Henriette that she might educate the young prodigy, providing the rounded background lacking in Wieck's home, and Clara visited for two weeks. Henriette provided Clara with a new piano, and in return Clara dedicated her *Soirées musicales* to Henriette. But she continued to resent the accomplished woman whom Schumann found so congenial.

When Schumann's G Minor Sonata—Clara's favorite—was finally published in 1839, it bore a dedication to "Madame Henriette Voigt, *geb*. Kunze." Schumann explained this apologetically to Clara as the result of an old promise. To Henriette he wrote: "Now I wish only that the sonata had arrived so that the world would know to whom I dedicated it in age-old affection."

Henriette gave birth to a second daughter in May 1839. Schumann served as godfather at the baptism, the prospect of which, he told Clara, he found ridiculous. Next came the news that Henriette was desperately ill, suffering the last stages of consumption. From Paris, Clara wrote to Schumann that she was sorry for Madame Voigt, though she could not like her. Still, she promised to write to her. Schumann told Clara that she should not be so hard on "the snake," who was not a happy woman. Clara's letter to the "dear friend" she addressed as "Jettchen," and with *Du*, was loving and tender, with no sign of her real feelings.

Henriette died on October 9th, 1839. Writing jointly as Eusebius and Florestan, Schumann published "Reminiscences of a Lady Friend" in the *New Journal*, a warm tribute to Henriette's central place in Leipzig's musical life. He was saying goodbye to his early years, his first meetings with Mendelssohn and Chopin, his close friendship with the gifted Ludwig Schunke, his special relationship with Henriette and the entire "clique" who met at her home. "Eusebius" quotes from her diary: "September 13th, 1836: Chopin was here yesterday, and played for half an hour on my grand pianoforte—fantasies and new études of his own. Interesting man—yet more interesting performance—he affected me to a most uncommon degree." Two days later, writing about Mendelssohn's oratorio *St. Paul*: "This year as well as last, I practiced at every rehearsal, and now know the work by heart . . . What delight, to sing it under his direction, to perform it according to his own wishes!" Mendelssohn was being urged to move from Leipzig to Berlin; he too would soon be gone. Schumann knew that Henriette's death was the end of an era. It was the end of his youthful flirtations with married women, his overindulgence in drink, his sexual adventures, his life as a free man.

After the December court hearing, Schumann traveled to Berlin with Clara, spending Christmas with her. He returned to Leipzig before New Year's Eve to work on the *New Journal*. Another separation meant more strains and further attacks by Wieck, who was circulating copies of his infamous declaration attacking both of them. Schumann wrote to Clara on January 10th: "If I didn't have you, if you weren't such a strong German girl, I would long ago have gone under." And on the 12th: "I am writing so much to you as children drive away the spirits' midnight hour by talking . . . The evil spirit is your father."

But Schumann was at last able to compose. Apart from abortive attempts at string quartets, he had completed only two piano works after returning from Vienna: the strange *Night Pieces*, originally titled *Leichenfantasie* (Funeral Fantasy), a response to the death of his brother Eduard, who had died just as Schumann was returning to Zwickau from Vienna; and a set of *Drei Romanzen*, tender, lyrical pieces composed as a Christmas present for Clara. Her own Romance in G Minor reminded him of a similar motif in his *Humoreske*. He told her: "You complement me as a composer as I do you. Every one of your [musical] thoughts emanates from my soul, just as I have you to thank for all my music." In January he returned to the *Faschingsschwank aus Wien*, finishing all but the last movement. "It will amuse you greatly," he wrote to Clara. He depended on Clara as his other self, his "Eusebiana." Yet when she wrote to him in high spirits, having discovered that he had "stolen" a passage from Beethoven's *Hammerklavier* Sonata, he was affronted. "I thought for a long time about what I was supposed to have stolen from Beethoven and laughed out loud when I got to the bottom of it—that is, I laughed at you . . . If I steal something, I will be more subtle, as you already know from your own experience—that is, with your heart." His mind was full of the music he loved, and allusions to Beethoven, Schubert, Bach, and others often can be heard in his compositions. But these allusions, sometimes no more than hints, are altered in subtle ways, transformed, incorporated into a Schumannesque design with its own meaning. He knew how original he was, and was eager for Clara to understand this central aspect of his very being.

Song Fever: *Myrthen; Liederkreis op. 24; Liederkreis op. 39; Dichterliebe; Frauenliebe und Leben*

In February, often Schumann's best time for composing, there was an astonishing breakthrough. "I am full of music," he told Clara. "You will wonder what I've written—no piano works. You know that today is the 7th of February—Thursday in Dresden 1836—when you were with me, so lovely and happy . . . Ah, my Klara, you make me so happy with your love." He was composing songs to poems he had treasured for years. On February 12th: "I've been very busy at the piano, you always appear to me there . . . I am happiest when I can compose and forget for hours the wicked man who would poison my life." On February 16th: "I will only tell you I have written six groups of songs, ballads and quartets . . . they will please you." Included were most of the songs later published as *Myrthen* (Myrtle Leaves), the collection he was planning as a wedding present for Clara. A week later: "Since yesterday morning I have written twenty-four pages of music—something new, which I can't tell you about, except that I laughed and wept from joy . . . Ah, dearest Klara, beloved darling, I have an unbelievable longing for you." The new work was the first of the great song cycles, a sequence of nine poems by Heine, published a year later as *Liederkreis* op. 24.

The songs composed during these months are among Schumann's most original and magical works. His lifelong passions for literature and music were now effortlessly coming together. The new song cycles were a natural extension of his piano cycles, many of them linked to literary works or ideas. His *Novelletten* were short stories without words (on the analogy of Mendelssohn's *Songs Without Words*); the "scenes" of *Carnaval*, the *Fantasiestücke*, and *Kinderszenen* all had poetic titles suggesting extra-musical meaning. He prefaced his C Major Fantasie and *Davidsbündlertänze* with verse mottos, as he did each issue of his *New Journal*, using poetry and prose as a complement to music and music criticism.

His musical taste, like his literary taste, had matured since the enthusiasms of his student years. He had outgrown the popular virtuoso composers, now mainly forgotten, whose works he had first studied and performed. His true masters were Bach, Mozart, Schubert, and Beethoven, and he studied their works with meticulous care. Their compositions in every genre, secular and religious, small and large, instrumental and vocal, served as the foundation of the new Romanticism espoused in his writings and realized in his own works.

As for his literary idols, he never relinquished his love of Jean Paul, but increasingly he sought inspiration in the fantastic tales of E. T. A. Hoffmann and the works of Goethe and Shakespeare. For texts for his songs, he turned to the leading poets of Germany:

Heine, Rückert, Eichendorff, Chamisso. He also chose poems by the English and Scottish writers his father had loved, all in German translation.

Many singers and music lovers consider the song cycles Schumann composed during the months before his marriage among his greatest works, on the same level as Schubert's song cycles, *Die schöne Müllerin* and *Winterreise*. Hugo Wolf, Debussy, Ravel, Mahler, and Richard Strauss took Schumann as their model and inspiration. For these later composers, as for Schumann himself, the meaning of songs depends on the intimate relationship between words and music. The texts were of prime importance.

When Schumann wrote to Clara that he "laughed and wept for joy" as he composed the songs, he was describing their source in his own feelings. The emotional extremes that shaped so many of his piano works found yet another form of expression in texts composed by the poets he loved—his ecstatic joy in Clara's love, as well as his strange feelings of negation, his recurrent terror of death when he lost faith in her. Instead of composing at the piano, his usual method, he composed while taking walks in which the poems assumed melodic shape. The piano accompaniments were added later, at his desk or at the piano. What comes through most vividly in his letters is his delight at the flow of inspiration.

It was not his first experience of song-writing. Some of the songs he had composed a decade before served him well as slow movements for his piano sonatas. But the new songs were different in quality. At one time he thought of vocal music as a poor relation of instrumental music. Songs were a popular form of musical entertainment, presenting few challenges to singer or accompanist. In a review of Schubert's C Major Symphony, he lamented that the composer was known only for his songs, not for his major instrumental works. Later he wrote that songs were among the very few musical forms to show signs of real progress. His letters suggest that he was simply overtaken by a songwriting fever which answered his emotional needs.

In the songs that made their way into *Myrthen,* his wedding present for Clara, voice and piano accompaniment, poetic text and musical setting are in continuous intimate dialogue. Schubert was his model for the vocal lines and for many aspects of the piano writing: the use of a prelude and matching or expanded postlude, sometimes with an independent motif; the emotional shift from minor to major, major to minor, as a new stanza begins. Schumann was building on Schubert's precedent. But his own songs and song cycles took vocal music to new levels of expressiveness. Preludes and postludes enable the piano to contribute on its own, the piano postludes often resembling the final coda to piano works in which "the poet speaks." The piano may support a lyrical vocal melody with a chromatic dissonance or suspension, a deeper harmony; the vocal line often soars above staccato chords or flowing arpeggios in the piano.

It is fascinating to see how Schumann moves from the pianistic daring of the piano cycles to the challenge of song accompaniment, with its built-in limitations. As he sets each poem to music, Schumann's natural gift for melody seems inexhaustible, responding perfectly to each text. In the accompaniments, he brings out the nuances of the texts with subtle changes of harmony and rhythm, calling on the special resources of the piano as a natural partner to the voice, supporting the vocal line, occasionally anticipating it, adding its own comments and private thoughts—much as lovers support and converse with each other, occasionally disagreeing, resolving their differences, reaffirming their love.

The poets he chose for Clara's "myrtle wreath" were liberal, free-thinking, international, Romantic in every sense: Byron and the Irish poet Thomas Moore, Byron's friend and biographer; the Scottish populist poet Robert Burns; Heine and Goethe. The texts range across place and time, evoking ancient Persia, Venice, the Scottish Highlands, Jerusalem. Most of the poets were represented in the mottos Schumann reprinted in each issue of his *New Journal*. He shared his best-loved poets and their thoughts about love and life with Clara. He sometimes included copies of favorite poems in his letters, and he often asked Clara what she was reading. She explained that she had no time for reading; every minute was taken up with practicing, French lessons, visiting, performing.

Clara is always implied in these songs as the listener, the beloved for whom the braided, intertwined poems of *Myrthen* are intended. As wedding gifts, they presented Clara with Schumann's inmost self, his true face, his joy, his fears, his wild alternations of feeling, his hopes for their future. In an ecstasy of longing for Clara, he was drawn to poems that seemed to him to tell his own story. Almost all the poems he chose reflect in some way on his passionate love for Clara and Clara's love for him, the obstacles they had faced, his despair when Clara seemed lost to him.

Not all the texts are obviously autobiographical. He was giving musical voice to the poets he revered and to their own literary creations: Burns's patriotic Highlanders; Goethe's Suleika, singing of her illicit love for the poet Hatem (code names for Goethe and his intimate friend Marianne von Willmer); King Saul, in Byron's *Hebrew Melodies*, longing for the healing music of the shepherd David; Moore recording the songs of the Venetian gondoliers who took Byron to assignations with "Nanetta" and many others. Schumann no longer needed Florestan and Eusebius to speak for him. He had a full range of sympathetic figures, real and invented, whose feelings he could express in his own musical language.

The first Goethe poem in *Myrthen*, coming just after the opening "Widmung" (Dedication) by Friedrich Rückert, is "Freisinn" (Free Spirit), from the *West-Eastern Divan*, a collection of poems composed in imitation of the Persian poet Hafiz, idealizing a past world gloriously free of bourgeois prejudices. An Arab horseman rides "free and gay" in his saddle, under the stars of heaven, far from the huts and tents of his village. The image was the Romantic antithesis of Schumann's Saxony—the familiar world of commercial Leipzig, the sleepy town of Zwickau, Dresden with its royal court. It would be stretching the point to see Goethe's poem as autobiographical, either for Goethe or for Schumann. Another poem from the *West-Eastern Divan*, "Talismane," celebrates the universality of Eastern religion—"God's is the East! God's is the West!" Schumann sympathized with Goethe's enlightened deism. But the final stanza had more personal resonance for him:

Error may lead me astray;
But Thou knowest how to extricate me;
In my deeds and my works,
May you guide me the right way.

The two Rückert poems he placed as a frame for the collection consisted of words he could have written himself. "Widmung"—the dedication is clearly to Clara—reads:

You are my soul, my bliss, my joy, my pain;
You are my world, in which I live,
My heaven, which I aspire to . . .
My guardian angel, my better self!

Schumann knew the second stanza of the poem, "Du bist die Ruh" (You are peace itself), in Schubert's setting of a longer Rückert poem with the same opening line. Thus he could pay tribute to Schubert and to Clara in the first poem of the collection, when he echoes Schubert's setting without actually quoting it. The final Rückert poem, with Schumann's title, "Zum Schluss" (In Conclusion), is touched by melancholy but equally appropriate:

Here in this earthbound air,
Weighed down by sorrow,
I have woven an imperfect wreath
For you, my sister, my bride!

Myrthen is held together by pairs of related texts, often in the same key—two cheerful drinking songs by Goethe (possibly a snub to Wieck and his accusation of drunkenness), two gondoliers' songs by Moore, two "Songs of a Bride-to-Be" by Rückert, two poems by Byron (one of which, ascribed to Byron, was actually by Catherine Fanshawe), a pair of Highland songs by Burns. Another pair by Burns, "Jemand" (Someone) and "Niemand" (No One), are obviously linked but are separated, providing more structure for the sequence. Burns contributes the largest number of poems, which in German translations convey only an approximate sense of the original love poems: "My Heart's in the Highlands," "Hee Balou," "The Captain's Lady." The poems represent the democratic, radical Burns, speaking for the oppressed Highlanders, celebrating the loyalty of their wives and lovers. As a committed defender of the underdog, a free spirit, a popular love poet, Burns could have been an honorary member of the *Davidsbund*. Schumann's settings include a folk-song element, a tribute to "the people's poet."

Five texts are by Goethe, all from the *West-Eastern Divan*: "Freisinn" and "Talismane," two drinking songs, and "Lied der Suleika." Schumann had portrayed "Suleika and the Saracen" in the second of the *Novelletten;* Schubert, too, set two "Suleika" songs. For Schumann, as for Schubert before him, Goethe's Suleika was a noble heroine, like Count Egmont's Klärchen and Florestan's Leonore, defying convention for the sake of love. Clara, too, she told Schumann, was ready to fly to him if there was no other way for them to live together.

The most erotic songs in *Myrthen* are two poems by Heine, which virtually leap from the score in their evocative power. "Die Lotosblume" (The Lotus Flower) describes the innocent flower unveiling her face to her lover, the moon, and "trembling for love and the pain of love." "Du bist wie eine Blume" (You Are Like a Flower) praises the beloved in a state of innocence, her future life anticipated as the lover lays his hands on her head in prayer, blessing her, claiming her for his own. "Der Nussbaum" (The Walnut Tree), by the little-known poet Julius Mosen, also uses natural imagery erotically. The tree's fragrant blossoms whisper softly as they are kissed by the wind. Seduced by the gentle sound, the sleeping girl dreams of "a bridegroom and the coming year"—a parallel to Schumann's hopes, promising sexual consummation. The opening "Dedication," too, is touched by erotic feeling. Schumann must have loved the way Schubert's setting of "Du bist die Ruh" enhances the poetic text, lingering on the rhyme words. His own setting returns to the opening stanza of the Rückert poem with a soaring melody, giving voice to two themes in one, the perfection of his beloved and his longing for her.

Although the songs of *Myrthen* make a lovely collection, and are called a *Liederkreis*, or song cycle, on the title page, they were unlikely to be performed as a whole, even at a private musicale. Ideally two voices, male and female, are required; at least eight songs are in a woman's voice, and Schumann supplied some alternative melodic lines. (The published scores of *Myrthen* and the other song cycles were all for soprano or mezzo voice; *Liederkreis* op. 24 was dedicated to Pauline Viardot Garcia, *Dichterliebe* to Wilhelmine Schröder-Devrient, two of the most prominent women singers of the time.) The greatest songs of *Myrthen* are usually sung on their own even now—the Heine settings, the opening "Widmung," "Der Nussbaum."

Schumann also set to music several dramatic ballads by Heine, including "Belsatzar," "Der arme Peter" (Poor Peter), and "Die beiden Grenadiere" (The Two Grenadiers). His model was Schubert, whose "Erlkönig," "Der Junge Nonne," and other ballads were popular both as songs and in Liszt's piano transcriptions. Carl Loewe's ballads also provided a precedent. Schumann's ballads have a strong political dimension, especially "The Two Grenadiers"—a protest against the futility of war and the worship of Napoleon by those who suffered most from his imperial ambitions.

The next song cycles composed at this time are ideally performed as a whole: the Heine *Liederkreis*, op. 24, and *Dichterliebe* (A Poet's Love); the Eichendorff *Liederkreis*, op. 39; and Chamisso's *Frauenliebe und Leben* (A Woman's Love and Life). Although individual songs seem like spontaneous outpourings of feeling, as cycles they are closely linked by key and by overlapping themes, each with an emotional curve that gives the cycle greater scope and intensity than the individual poetic texts taken on their own.

The first of the song cycles, composed in two days in late February and published as *Liederkreis* op. 24, sets a sequence of untitled songs from Heine's popular collection *Buch der Lieder*, composed when the poet was in his twenties. Schumann follows the order of the nine poems grouped together in the first section of Heine's book, called (with a hint of irony) *The Sorrows of Youth*, after Goethe's novel *The Sorrows of Young Werther*. The poems are full of sound and movement: birdsong; the lover's pounding heart; the banging and hammering of the carpenter fashioning a coffin; the lover driven this way and that, dragging along, staff in hand, as his boat sails on merrily. Schumann's settings realize these images with the sensitivity of a composer alert to every nuance of his text.

The first and second songs, "Each morning I wake and ask: / Will my sweetheart come today?" and "I'm driven this way, driven that!" respond to the rhythms of the untitled texts, with light syncopated staccato chords anticipating and echoing the melody; the second song building upon the first in increasing agitation. "I wandered under the trees" opens with a haunting melody for piano alone, which reappears only in the piano postlude. Prelude and postlude frame one of Heine's most original and mysterious images, an imagined exchange between the lover and the birds whispering above him in the trees. Most ingenious is Schumann's rendering of the riddling song of the birds, which he sets as a series of high chords in the surprising key of G, returning to earth (back to B major), and the lover's angry rejection of such mysteries. "My dearest, lay your hands on my heart" reverts to the opening mood, echoing the earlier settings with syncopated staccato chords, leading to the morbid image of a carpenter hammering a coffin in the lover's heart. The climactic "Lovely cradle of my sorrows" takes wing again in new excitement, evoking the anguish and terror of love. The last two poems in the cycle are linked: a four-line quatrain is set as a chorale, solemn chords under a simple melodic line, ending with the unresolved question torturing the lover: how can he bear the ordeal? The final song, "With myrtles and roses, sweet and fair," provides the answer, as it returns to the key of the first song. Opening with a deceptively cheerful piano prelude, the song is a farewell to love and life. The poet's only hope is that his songs, put together in a coffinlike binding of myrtles and roses, will reach his beloved after his death. Hope and despair, linked inextricably in Heine's texts and Schumann's settings, make a perfect "circle" of romantic love, ending where it began.

Schumann interrupted his songwriting in mid-March when Liszt made a long-planned visit to Dresden and Leipzig. It was Schumann's second meeting with the composer who had written to him so warmly about his piano compositions. After Liszt's Dresden concert, Schumann traveled back with him to Leipzig, spending the next two weeks with the Hungarian pianist. Liszt was the embodiment of the free spirit Schumann admired in Goethe's poetry. A year younger than Schumann, he was already as famous for his personal glamour as for his dazzling performances. He was a true multilingual European. Born in Hungary, he had pursued his music education in Vienna as a pupil of Czerny, and he lived for years in Paris. He and his mistress, Countess Marie d'Agoult, who wrote under the pen name of Daniel Stern, had been instrumental in promoting the ill-starred love affair between Liszt's friend Chopin and Marie's friend (and rumored lover) Aurore Dudevant, better known as George Sand. The musical world of Leipzig, which was held to strict artistic and moral standards by Mendelssohn, must have seemed hopelessly staid to the flamboyant pianist. Yet it was Liszt who had recognized Schumann's originality, writing to him (in French) on receiving copies of *Carnaval* and the *Fantasiestücke*: "Without knowing each other, we hold each other in esteem and love each other . . . all I know of you and of your talent inspires me with a profound and lively sympathy." He wrote that *Kinderszenen* had given him one of the greatest pleasures of his life; he played it for his three-year-old daughter two or three times a week. He had already performed *Carnaval* and *Kinderszenen* for the public who idolized him. But he feared that *Kreisleriana* and the Fantasie were "too difficult for the public to digest"—which proved true at the time, and for much of the later nineteenth century.

Clara and her mother came to Leipzig from Berlin to hear Liszt's final concert, a benefit for the Leipzig Institute for Aged and Ill Musicians. Liszt included most of *Carnaval*, along with Mendelssohn's D Minor Piano Concerto (read at sight a few days earlier) and works and transcriptions of his own. In his review, Schumann described Liszt's extraordinary generosity, the aura of excitement he created with each appearance, the glamour of the man himself, with his leonine looks, the "energy and boldness" of his playing. Schumann was less enthusiastic about Liszt's choice of music. He could unreservedly praise only the Weber Konzertstück and a Chopin étude. In an earlier article he contrasted Liszt's Romantic compositions with those of Chopin, who, he wrote, "always has form; and under the marvelous creations of his music . . . always spins out a rose-colored thread of melody." Schumann preferred the originals to Liszt's piano transcriptions of Schubert songs and Beethoven symphonies.

Clara remained in Leipzig for over two weeks, and Schumann accompanied her back to Berlin. They knew it was just a matter of time before they could marry. On his return to Leipzig, two weeks later, Schumann threw himself again into songwriting, as if the pause had inspired him to even greater invention. He was composing vocal works so original in scope and variety that they marked a new phase in the art.

Schumann chose the texts for the Eichendorff *Liederkreis* from the 1837 collection of Eichendorff's poems, extracted from his earlier prose works. Schumann simply selected poems that appealed to him, and he organized them loosely, relying on opening and closing verses to provide a structure. Unlike the poems of the Heine *Liederkreis*, there is no implied plot. Instead the poems touch on all the Romantic themes: myths and legends (the old knight of the castle, the enchanting witch Lorelei), images of moon and stars, nightingales, flowers in bloom, birds in flight, all linked by the perennial subjects of love and death. Several poems lend themselves to an autobiographical reading. The melancholy opening poem, "In der Fremde" (In a Strange Land), corresponds to Schumann's despair on returning to Zwickau after his brother Eduard's death: "Father and mother have long been dead, / Now no one knows me there." He could have written the second poem, "Intermezzo," about the portrait Clara had given him: "I bear your beautiful likeness / Deep within my heart, / Each hour it gazes at me / So freshly and joyfully." (He was to repeat the theme, with the words unspoken but implied, five years later in his F Major Piano Trio.) "Die Stille" (Silence) includes words that Clara had spoken as a child: "How happy I am, how happy!" Poems predicting future happiness, the wonderful "Mondnacht" (Moonlit Night), hymning the marriage of heaven and earth, and the final song of love reciprocated, "Frühlingsnacht" (Spring Night), directly express Schumann's joy in his knowledge that Clara was "faithful unto death." "Mondnacht" is a musical representation of erotic consummation. A sustained vocal line represents the sky kissing the sleeping earth (descending slowly from the high treble to the bass by fourths and fifths), while the repeated piano accompaniment suggests the human heartbeat. In the final stanza the soul "spreads wide its wings" to fly over the silent countryside, as if flying home—not to the heaven of the opening stanza, but to the enfolding warmth of the beloved. So the rising ecstasy of Schumann's music suggests.

The remaining texts wander in different directions, associating joy with sorrow, with the fears aroused by dusk and nighttime, the Romantic landscape of forests and mountains. What unites the poems is the glorious music to which they are set, from the melancholy brooding of the first song, anticipating the poet's lonely death, to the dramatic excitement of "Frühlingsnacht" as the poet claims his beloved: "She is thine! she is thine!" Schumann provides the sense of a "circle" by setting the opening poem in F-sharp minor and "Frühlingsnacht" the final poem, in F-sharp major, which closes the cycle on the appropriate upbeat note. There are overlapping motifs, an enchanting variety of tone, tempo, mood, and a surging climax at the end, embodied in the contrast between the piano's pounding triplets and the voice rising above them in bliss.

No sooner had Schumann finished the Eichendorff *Liederkreis* than he turned again to Heine and the section of his *Book of Songs* called *Lyric Intermezzo*. Schumann selected twenty of the sixty-five lyrics and arranged them into two books of contrasting pairs. He later reduced the number to sixteen, arranged in two books of eight, and he called the whole *Dichterliebe* (A Poet's Love). The title came from a Rückert poem, linking the themes of poetry and love. Schumann thought of poetry and song as two faces of the same art, as they were for Heine and for the troubadours to whom Heine pays tribute. The poems collected as *Lyric Intermezzo* are prefaced by a tale of a melancholy knight seduced by a fickle wood nymph. Old tales and legends—the holy Rhine and the image of Our Lady in Cologne Cathedral, fairy tales of a land of infinite delight, age-old stories and songs of love betrayed—reinforce the poet's songs of his own tormented love. Sexual longings find release in kisses real or remembered and in erotic flower imagery: the chalice of the lily, in which the singer wants to plunge his soul.

The spirit of Schubert hovers over *Dichterliebe*, in his own settings of Heine's poems, and the allegorical "Dream" which Schumann discovered and published, with its central thought: when the dreamer, a poet himself, sings of love, it turns to pain; when he sings of pain, it turns to love. In Heine's lyrics, the lover dreams of happiness but awakens to the reality of lost love.

Schumann's settings realize the double nature of romantic love in his own expressive musical idiom—incorporating dark forebodings even as he gives voice to the ecstasy of the lover, tempering the lover's tears with recollections of past joy. The joy of the opening poem, "In the wondrous month of May," in which the lover confesses his longing and desire to the beloved, opens with a strange dissonant piano prelude, its haunting plaint unresolved until a few bars after the singer enters. The prelude is repeated between the two stanzas and again in the postlude, still unresolved. The motif recurs at intervals throughout the cycle, in varying form, until it is recalled in the piano coda that ends the cycle, expanded to contain all the elements of the enclosed songs, their melancholy and their joy.

In addition to setting each poem in a way that perfectly realizes its mood and imagery, Schumann organizes the cycle with attention to its overall form. He follows the order of Heine's *Lyric Intermezzo* for the first seven songs, linking them by related keys and the subtle overlapping of a keynote in the final bar of one song and the opening bar of the next. The cycle as a whole moves around the circle of fifths in a way that corresponds to the emotional curve of the poet's love—moving up from three sharps (the brightness of A major) to C major, then down the flat side as the poems grow increasingly dark. Songs are linked in pairs or across the cycle by key, by the imagery of flowers, birdsong, dreams, and by related musical motifs.

"On a bright summer morning" echoes the plaintive piano motif of the opening song. In the final song, "The old, ugly songs"—also the last in Heine's collection—the poet calls for a coffin to be built and borne to the sea, so that his love and also his pain can be buried there. The music echoes the dramatic setting of "In the Rhine, the holy river."

Although Schumann believed that music was essentially poetic, he also believed that form, in which he considered harmony to be the key element, was equally necessary to a work of art. The untitled songs in *Dichterliebe* carry poetry to its most expressive heights. The form of the cycle, its unifying harmonic structure, contributes to its enduring life as one of the greatest of all song cycles.

Schumann obviously felt drawn to Heine's lyrics portraying "the sorrows of youth." But *Dichterliebe* is not primarily autobiographical. It stands independently as a new creation, melancholy, tender, a portrait of the generic Poet in Love, as represented by the young Heine, poet and lover, with a glance at his alter ego, the troubadour singing of a love that can be realized only in his dreams.

Dichterliebe was not published until 1844, when four of the original twenty songs were omitted. It was performed in full only in 1861, five years after Schumann's death, when Brahms accompanied the young baritone Julius Stockhausen in a pioneering lieder recital, setting a precedent that has now become common practice.

The last of the major song cycles composed during this time was *Frauenliebe und Leben* (A Woman's Love and Life), a cycle of poems by Adelbert von Chamisso. The cycle is presented entirely from the woman's point of view, and at first sight has no obvious autobiographical connection to Schumann. He was attracted to Chamisso for his political sympathies, his poems of the working classes, his allegiance to the ideals of the French Revolution. (His French family had fled to Prussia when Chamisso was a child.) Chamisso translated poems of the populist French poet Pierre Béranger, two of which Schumann set, along with Chamisso's own ballad "The Lion's Bride" and a group of poems by the Danish writer Hans Christian Andersen, which Chamisso adapted.

Chamisso's poems tell the story of a woman transfigured and

destroyed by love. The protagonist, a young girl of humble birth, is an adoring worshipper of her lover. In a solemn address to her engagement ring, she pledges her love forever: "I shall serve him, live for him, belong to him entirely, give myself to him alone, and be transfigured in his glance." In another song she cries: "Are you here, my beloved? Do you shine on me, O my sun? Let me bow to my master in all humility." Her whole being is defined in terms of the godlike man she loves, first as an unattainable ideal, next as fiancé, husband, the father of her child. In the final song, when her beloved has died, she laments that her life is now meaningless, her world destroyed, her sorrow unending. A setting of the same cycle by Carl Loewe includes a final poem omitted by Schumann, which is spoken by the protagonist as a grandmother, looking back on the great love of her life, and reconciled to living through her memories. Schumann's more dramatic version turns the cycle into a tragedy not only of lost love but of life destroyed.

Frauenliebe und Leben is among the greatest song cycles written for female voice, and most singers readily enter into the inner life of the protagonist. The young woman's "love and life" are not typical; they are a consequence of her childish innocence and inexperience and, above all, her humble origins. This is a drama of period and class, in which Schumann's early sexual experience with a woman of low birth may have played a role. His relationship with the servant known as Christel might have enabled him to sympathize with the protagonist of Chamisso's poems at each stage of her drama, and to capture her conflicting emotions: her initial wonder; her ecstatic happiness, tinged with disbelief; her joy in marriage and motherhood; her final despair. His sympathy for Ernestine von Fricken might also have affected his feelings. He had suffered from guilt at breaking their engagement. Instead of cooperating with Wieck when he asked her to testify against Schumann, Ernestine indignantly refused. Schumann and Clara were both relieved when she married, and dismayed when her husband died, leaving her childless and impoverished. Thoughts of Christel and guilt about Ernestine might well have entered into Schumann's music. Or perhaps, having portrayed in *Dichterliebe* the anguish and ecstasy of the poet-in-love,

Schumann wanted to give voice to the woman-in-love, as realized so vividly in Chamisso's poems.

Unlike the other song cycles Schumann had just composed, this set of eight short poems has a true plot, a dramatic reversal, and a sequence of events evoking strong sympathy. Schumann realizes these elements with assurance, building upon all his recent experience of writing for voice and piano. As in the Heine song cycles, the emotional curve moves from initial joy to dark grief. Each song marks a new stage of life, from love, engagement, marriage, and the birth of a child to the final catastrophe of the husband's unexplained death. Schumann gives the cycle a beautifully sustained form, with close harmonic links between the end of each song and the beginning of the next. Each song is individually realized, with a special intensity of feeling. Subtle hints of coming disaster are included in the mood of joyful anticipation that dominates most of the songs. The cycle moves inexorably to its climactic ending, returning to the first song with a soft piano coda, a recapitulation that closes the cycle and gives its initial joy new meaning.

Schumann continued to write songs during July, including four poems by Hans Christian Andersen, translated by Chamisso, and a set of poems by Robert Reinick. But he was mainly absorbed in preparations for his marriage to Clara. She rejoined Schumann in Leipzig for his birthday in June. In July, as court proceedings were approaching an end, they looked for lodgings in Leipzig, settling at last on a first-floor apartment in the new district of Friedrichstadt.

Wieck had by this time removed his business and family to Dresden, and he failed to turn up at the final court hearing. In August Schumann and Clara finally received the court's official permission to marry. Clara left for a short concert tour, and Schumann surprised her at her final concert in Weimar on September 3rd. He wrote in his diary on September 4th: "From then on with her forever."

"WITH HER FOREVER"

Leipzig, September 1840–1842

MARRIED LIFE

The marriage took place on the 12th of September, 1840, in Schöne-feld, northeast of Leipzig—a village that had been destroyed in 1813, during the Battle of Leipzig, but was later rebuilt. It was a simple ceremony, with Clara's mother, Mariane Bargiel, and Schumann's friend Ernst Becker as witnesses. The newly married couple moved at once to their lodgings at Inselstrasse 5 (now Inselstrasse 18) on the eastern outskirts of Leipzig, a district soon to be occupied by printers and publishers. Leipzig was already a European center of music publishing; Breitkopf & Härtel and C. F. Peters were founded in Leipzig and had their headquarters there until Leipzig became part of East Germany after 1945.

Robert and Clara Schumann now lived together in a pleasant apartment on the first floor of a handsome, three-story neoclassical building. The central room was spacious enough for music-making with friends, one of the great pleasures of their married lives. During the next four years they would be visited in these rooms by Berlioz, Liszt, Mendelssohn (a frequent visitor), and his sister Fanny Hensel, the singer Pauline Viardot-Garcia, Richard Wagner, and many other leading European musicians.

The evening before their wedding, Schumann presented Clara with a beautifully engraved printing of the bridal wreath of songs he called *Myrthen*. The "myrtle wreath" was an intimate private gift to Clara that would endure for all time.

Clara turned twenty-one on September 13th. Schumann presented her with another nicely bound book, which was to serve as their joint diary, signed by each of them with a promise that "all the joys and sorrows of a marital life should be written down here as a true history." They were to take turns writing each week, exchanging the diary on Sunday mornings, after coffee. Schumann knew that Mendelssohn and his wife had kept a joint diary on their honeymoon, but they let it lapse after their marriage began in earnest. Schumann assured Clara that they would continue the joint diary indefinitely. But in its nineteenth week (17–24 January 1841), Clara took over the diary for five consecutive weeks, and after they returned from their Russian tour, in May 1844, they kept separate diaries, as they had done before their marriage.

The "true history," which was meant for husband and wife alone, was published in the second volume of Schumann's diaries in 1987. It makes curious reading, both for what is said and for what is left unsaid. Clara begins each entry by reaffirming her love for her husband, unconsciously echoing the young woman of *Frauenliebe und -leben*: "I can truly say I live *only* through you." She wants to be the perfect *Hausfrau*, cooking (or at least supervising the cook the young couple engaged), entertaining Schumann's large circle of friends and acquaintances, her close friends Elise and Emilie List, and a constant stream of well-wishers. At the same time, she remained her professional self, and she was miserable when she was unable to practice. Schumann could hear her grand piano when he was working in his study, which meant that she was limited to an hour's practice each afternoon. Elise List was nervous about singing in a Gewandhaus concert, and Clara explained how best to deal with stage fright. She turned down repeated requests to perform at the Gewandhaus, until Mendelssohn returned from a trip to England and invited her to play the Bach Concerto for Three Keyboards with him and his friend Ignaz Moscheles. The prospect of performing Bach with Mendelssohn was irresistible, and Clara agreed. Married life did not find Clara relaxing her standards; she thought Moscheles's playing was sadly diminished and concluded that he was too old to perform in public.

Suddenly she was extremely unwell. She could not play at all, could not even leave the house. The illness passed, but she was still exhausted. As they were about to celebrate Christmas, she knew that she was expecting a child.

Schumann, too, was unwell, with the usual set of complaints, but since he was also very happy, the complaints were minimal. A few days after Clara's birthday, he proposed that they study Bach's *Well-Tempered Clavier* together, one prelude and fugue each day. His Christmas present to Clara was Beethoven's complete piano sonatas. Clara had often performed the *Appasionata* and a few Bach fugues (the C-sharp Minor Fugue from book 2 of *The Well-Tempered Clavier* was her favorite). Schumann wanted to share his comprehensive knowledge of Bach and Beethoven with his beloved wife, subtly hinting that she might think of expanding her repertoire.

It was at this time that Schumann's best friends and alter egos, Florestan and Eusebius, receded from his life. He no longer enlisted them as fellow composers, signing their names to his more exuberant and personal compositions—the Sonata op. 11, dedicated to Clara "by Florestan and Eusebius," and *Davidsbündlertänze*, signed with the initials "F" and "E." No longer do they sign his reviews in the *New Journal*, where the editor "Rob. Schumann" takes full responsibility for his considered judgment of composers past and present.

Suddenly Schumann was enormously productive. His newfound happiness triggered a series of large-scale orchestral works. A *Spring* Symphony in B-flat was sketched in four days and orchestrated in a matter of weeks. He was inspired to write an overture on no particular theme, which soon acquired a scherzo and a finale, not quite making up a symphony. At the same time he began the one-movement Phantasie for Piano and Orchestra, which later acquired two additional movements to become the Piano Concerto in A Minor.

In late November, Schumann wrote in the shared diary that his setting of a small group of poems by Justinus Kerner was ready, adding for Clara's benefit that he knew he was giving her pleasure as well as pain, "since she must purchase my love so often with silence and invisibility." He kept adding to the cycle, eventually setting twelve poems by Kerner for a group he called *Liederreihe* (Row of lieder) rather than *Liederkreis*, since they were not linked in a circular pattern, but simply followed one another in no particular order. Schumann's first songs, composed ten years before, had been settings of poems by Kerner, a doctor and botanist with a strong mystical streak. Schumann set the new collection of songs, which treat the bliss and the sorrow of love, with the consummate skill which was now second nature to him. Although they are seldom performed as a group, three of the Kerner songs are among singers' favorites: "Erstes Grün" (First Green), "Stille Liebe" (Silent Love), and "Stille Tränen" (Silent Tears). Like the songs composed before Schumann's marriage, all three are marked by the poetic interplay of a tender vocal line and an independent piano accompaniment, words and music joined in harmony.

In November Schumann noted in the marriage diary that he had set to music the "beautiful" "Rheinlied" by Nikolaus Becker, "which all Germany is talking about." The popular song opened with these words: "Never shall they have it, / The free German Rhine"—an attack on the defeated French, who had recently demanded that France regain ownership of the left bank of the Rhine, its "natural" border. Schumann's settings, published as "Patriotic Song," first for voice and piano, later for chorus, were a gratifying source of income, although he did not win the prize offered for the best setting. Liszt and many others took up the song enthusiastically. Mendelssohn found its nationalism odious and refused to set the poem, writing to his friend Karl Klingemann: "The whole town here is ringing with a song, supposed to have a political tendency against the French . . . everyone is speaking of the 'Rheinlied,' or the 'Colognaise,' as they call it [a play on the "Marseillaise"] . . . it seems to me so sterile and futile . . . Yesterday they said I had also set the song, while I never even dreamed of setting such a thing into music."

Mendelssohn's scorn for the patriotic song and Schumann's unreflecting enthusiasm hint at the complicated relationship between the two friends. Schumann admired Mendelssohn above all other musicians, but there were recurrent tensions. An entry in the marriage diary reveals his ambivalence, tinged with the anti-Semitism that was endemic at the time, an insidious mixture of envy and resentment. "Clara told me that I seemed to have changed toward Mendelssohn; surely not toward him as an artist, as you know—for years I have contributed so much to promoting him, more than almost anyone else. In the meantime—let us not neglect ourselves too much. Jews remain Jews; first they take a seat ten times for themselves, then come the Christians. The stones we have helped gather for their Temple of Glory they occasionally throw at us . . . We must also work for ourselves." Clara responded in kind. Perhaps they should not be as friendly to Mendelssohn as before.

The question of anti-Semitism was to plague later studies of both Schumann and Mendelssohn. At the height of the Nazi period, the musicologist Wolfgang Boetticher published a massive biography of Schumann, presenting the composer as a dedicated anti-Semite. Schumann was to be a musical hero for Nazi Germany, in contrast to Mendelssohn, born to a Jewish family, although he had been baptized as a child, was a practicing Lutheran, and had married the daughter of a Huguenot pastor. Mendelssohn's works were banned, and his statue was removed from its place of honor in front of St. Thomas's Church and destroyed. In the index to Boetticher's 1942 biography, in accord with Nazi practice, the names of all persons with Jewish ancestry were starred. In addition to Mendelssohn and his family members, most of whom had converted to one or another form of Christianity, these included a large number of artists, composers, and publishers, many of them close associates of Schumann: the violinist Ferdinand David; the pianist and composer Ignaz Moscheles; the young Joseph Joachim, who joked with his friend Brahms that Brahms, too, probably had Jewish ancestry, since his family name could easily be a shortened version of "Abrahamson." The name of Heinrich Heine, whose poems inspired so many of Schumann's songs, was starred. He had converted to the Protestant faith as a medical student, since the profession was barred to Jews, and he later wrote scathingly—and prophetically—about the powerful religious and nationalistic forces in German life.

After those first grudging remarks in the marriage diary, Schumann expresses nothing but admiration for Mendelssohn. He was, after all, a supreme artist. Following a soiree: "He played—as only Mendelssohn can play!" Mendelssohn visited one afternoon and played a Bach concerto for two keyboards with Clara, followed by a Mozart sonata: "Love and veneration are the feelings he always inspires." Whatever ambivalence Schumann felt toward his friend was set to rest by two major events: the orchestration of the *Spring* Symphony in March 1841 and the birth of the Schumanns' first child, Marie, six months later.

SYMPHONIC FEVER

The first movement of the *Spring* Symphony was begun on January 23rd, 1841, the Adagio and Scherzo sketched the next day. In his household book, mainly devoted to financial accounts, Schumann noted "symphonic fever" and "sleepless nights" as the last movement germinated; and on January 26th: "Hoorah! [*Juche!*] Symphony finished!" He orchestrated the symphony during February, and in early March showed it to Mendelssohn. "Joy at Mendelssohn's judgment," he records in his household book, and in the marriage diary: "I was anxious to hear his opinion of [the symphony]. I was overjoyed by what he said. He always perceives and hits on the right thing."

Schumann had set aside his first attempt at a symphony, composed a decade earlier, as a work of his untutored youth. In the *Spring* Symphony he was challenging comparison with Beethoven, Schubert, and his own eminent contemporaries. He was delighted when Mendelssohn paid him a visit a week after the first reading and spent hours with him going over the score. Mendelssohn also brought Clara a wedding gift of Goethe's epic poem *Hermann and Dorothea,* specially bound, which seems to have canceled her own ambivalent feelings toward their friend and colleague.

Mendelssohn's detailed reading of the *Spring* Symphony marked a new stage in his relations with Schumann. In an earlier letter to his mother, Mendelssohn had described Schumann as the founder of a music journal and a composer of "several piano pieces," adding, "I am very fond of him and he has been consistently good and friendly to me from my first arrival here." Mendelssohn now saw Schumann for the first time as an equal. He had no suspicion of the negative feelings that Schumann and Clara had expressed in their private diary. It was natural for Schumann to seek his advice, in view of his expertise as the most highly regarded composer of his time. But Mendelssohn was genuinely pleased at Schumann's mastery of this most ambitious of musical forms. It was a great achievement, as Mendelssohn knew from his own struggles with symphonic composition. Schumann had in a matter of weeks produced a beautiful, coherent "classical" work in his own Romantic style.

The *Spring* Symphony opens with an evocative horn call, doubled by trumpets, summoning the spring, and repeated in unison by the full orchestra, woodwinds, brass, and strings—as if all creation is joining in the call for a renewal of life and hope. The orchestra answers the horn summons in a rapid scale rising from low bass to high treble, descending by steps to the home key, and sustained with continued anticipation until the Allegro—echoing the opening horn call—affirms that spring has indeed arrived. The second movement, a tender Larghetto, echoes the last four notes of the horn call, transposed and in an altered rhythm, but recognizable. A few bars from the end of the Larghetto, a short melodic motif by two trombones, also derived from the opening theme, leads seamlessly into the opening notes of the third movement, a Beethovenian Scherzo. Marked *molto vivace*, the Scherzo has strong accents, off-rhythms, and several repeats, along with two contrasting trios. A joyful finale returns to the key of the first movement, with delightful reminders of its motifs.

Probably the dominant role of its opening horn theme was what made it possible for Schumann to draft all four movements of the symphony in four days. There are flashes of free improvisation, solo cadenzas in the first and final movements for flute (with a suggestion of bird calls), and secondary themes with a "Schumannesque" lyrical shape which plays against the rhythmic insistence of the horn motif. But the symphony observes classical principles without any obvious strain. It is clear that Schumann has made a close study of

Beethoven's symphonies—for instance, the way the famous opening motif of the Fifth Symphony (fate knocking at the door) generates the theme of the Allegro and much that follows, and a similar pattern linking the Introduction and Allegro of Beethoven's A Major Symphony, no. 7, which Schumann had just heard performed. The closest parallel to the *Spring* Symphony is Beethoven's Symphony no. 4, also in B-flat—the work with which Mendelssohn had opened his first Gewandhaus concert. As part of their joint studies of Bach and Beethoven, Robert and Clara had recently made a piano arrangement of the Fourth Symphony. Schumann absorbed the symphony in its entirety and used it as inspiration for his own symphony, reversing Beethoven's motifs and in his introduction echoing a horn call that appears in Beethoven's introductory Adagio. But the emotional trajectory of Schumann's symphony is distinctively Romantic—the excitement of the ascending horn motif, the sense of rhythmical excess, the melodic lyricism of the Larghetto all contributing to the expression of romantic energy.

Mendelssohn immediately offered to conduct the symphony at a Gewandhaus concert organized by the Schumanns, with Clara also playing—a tribute to the combined musical gifts of the artistic couple. It is easy to see why Mendelssohn was so warmly appreciative of the symphony and its poetic spirit. He must have relished not only its joyful welcome of spring, but each detail of the symphony's structure, the satisfying way in which the opening horn call generates the material that follows and plays in canon against each new subject. Clara wrote in the marriage diary that the symphony was inspired by a poem by Adolf Böttger, a Leipzig poet who translated the complete works of Byron, and who had recently visited the Schumanns. The last line of Böttger's stanza, taken from a series of "Spring" poems, fits the rhythm of the opening horn call: "Im Thale blüht der Frühling auf" (literally, "In the valley blossoms forth the spring"). Even before writing the draft of the first movement, Schumann had noted in early January: "However old one is, each year the longing for spring returns again." He disclaimed a program for the symphony, keeping the title *Spring* Symphony but discarding early names for each movement ("The Arrival of Spring," "Evening," "Merry Play," "Spring at the Full"). The symphony is lit by sunshine, the tone similar to Mendelssohn's early orchestral works, which Schumann admired so much. As Mendelssohn had done so memorably in the *Hebrides* Overture, Schumann evokes the sounds and sights of the natural world in writing that is full of melodic inspiration. Schumann's signature is unmistakable in each surging rhythmic sequence, each sudden pause to take breath, to collect the musical forces and begin again. The principal feeling is one of longing and eager anticipation—longing for the renewal of spring, anticipation of life and love fulfilled, as the natural cycle takes its welcome course.

Schumann incorporated Mendelssohn's suggestions in his final score, pleased that they often conformed to his first ideas. Rehearsals began at the end of March, and the premiere was given at the Gewandhaus on the 31st of March, with Mendelssohn conducting. Clara opened the concert with two movements of Chopin's Piano Concerto in F Minor, the Duo Mendelssohn had composed to perform with her, and solo pieces by Scarlatti, Mendelssohn, Schumann, and Chopin. The audience was enthusiastic, and a review in the conservative Leipzig music journal *Allgemeine musicalische Zeitung* praised the technical skill of the symphony and the naturalness of the style—qualities that ensure its popularity to this day. It marked the beginning of Schumann's recognition as a major composer.

Mendelssohn was under intense family pressure to move to Berlin, where the Prussian king had been urging him to accept a vaguely defined position as the head of a musical academy, or (Mendelssohn's preference) as Kapellmeister. Mendelssohn was strongly attached to Leipzig's musical life, and he intended to continue his relationship with the Gewandhaus Orchestra. The two cities were now linked by rail, six and a half hours' travel apart. Mendelssohn was already planning to found a Leipzig Conservatory, at which both Clara and Schumann were invited to teach. When Mendelssohn moved to Berlin in July, he ended his parting letter to Schumann with these words: "Do not forget us, and that we remember you [both] in love and friendship always."

Clara gave birth to her first child, Marie, on September 1st, and

Schumann wrote to Mendelssohn, without salutation, in excited phrases—joyful, bewildered, happy, confused—and profoundly grateful, he wrote, "for your last loving lines, which must not be the very last—you shall soon hear more from me, also about music." Mendelssohn wrote back at once, begging Schumann to be "truly and pedantically anxious" in the first weeks, adding: "Laugh at this if you will, but do as I say." His son's birth three years before had been a source of great worry.

Here was another bond between these two sensitive, prickly composers of genius. They both adored children, and were happiest in their own homes, with their young families, cushioned against the intrusive demands of the outside world. After consulting Clara, Schumann wrote again, asking Mendelssohn if he would consent to be a godparent to the infant. Mendelssohn wrote that he was over-joyed to be asked, was tempted to take the new railway to Leipzig to be present at the christening but, alas, couldn't do so. "May you be happy, healthy, and lucky on the day and in all that is wished for you from the whole heart of your *Gevatter* [godfather]" was his wish for the infant and her parents. He later addressed Clara as "Frau Gevatterin"—as if they were now truly "bound together" (Schumann's words) as family.

Soon after the successful premiere of the *Spring* Symphony, Schumann quickly sketched a symphonic work which he thought of first as a *sinfoniette,* and finally published as Overture, Scherzo and Finale. The opening movement has a structure and feeling simi-lar to that of Mendelssohn's *Hebrides* Overture, though in a playful variation on conventional symphonic form, it is an overture to noth-ing in particular. A lyrical Andante con moto leads to an exuberant Allegro. A week later, Schumann added a Scherzo and Finale, with themes related to the overture.

Like all Schumann's music, the delightful score of the Overture, Scherzo and Finale must be performed with sensitive attention both to details and to the relationship of each motif to its later variations. The whole is poetic throughout, joyful and exuberant. Schumann soon followed this unusual "little symphony" with an equally origi-nal one-movement Phantasie for Piano and Orchestra. No doubt if

Schumann had found a publisher, the three-movement "little symphony" and the one-movement Phantasie would have entered the repertoire as they were first composed. Instead, the Phantasie had to wait four years to be transformed into the Piano Concerto in A Minor, op. 54. The Overture, Scherzo and Finale was revised twice, first in 1845, with publication a year later, and again in 1853, reaching at that late date its final publication and subsequent popularity.

It was only natural that Schumann would plunge into writing a second symphony once the Overture, Scherzo and Finale and the Phantasie for Piano and Orchestra were finished. He sketched the first movement of a new Symphony in D minor at the end of May, two months after the triumphant premiere of the *Spring* Symphony. There were several interruptions—in July, a week's holiday in Dresden and the Saxon Alps, in September the birth of Marie. The D Minor Symphony was not completed until October. Schumann was eager to arrange a performance and publication. Darker in spirit than the *Spring* Symphony, each movement leads naturally to the next, as if written in one continuous arc. An Andante con moto introduction opens with a single orchestral call to attention, followed by evenly spaced sixths "walking" stepwise toward a climactic resolution, sustaining the dominant A-major suspense until the Allegro opens in the home key of D minor—a beautifully thought-out introduction to the Allegro's themes.

This manner of organizing his musical material had become natural to Schumann, who was no longer indebted to his studies of the masters, but was his own man. The second-movement Romanza, also marked Andante, opens with one of his most haunting themes, played by solo oboe in unison with solo cello, adding depth to the oboe's poignancy. Perhaps the theme was a tribute to the lovely oboe melody in the slow movement of Schubert's C Major Symphony, the great work Schumann had discovered in Vienna. The oboe theme is followed, surprisingly, by the evenly spaced sixths of the introduction to the Allegro, a subliminal hint that the oboe theme is actually derived from the initial motif. Countersubjects introduced in the first movement reappear "like a red thread" (a favorite image of Schumann's) in the following movements. A lovely solo violin passage in the Romanza reappears as the chief subject of a trio in the Scherzo; the end of the D-minor Scherzo leads into a joyful Finale in D major, its new but oddly familiar theme a development of another motif from the first movement, ingeniously treated in canon, until yet another familiar theme enters. It is all wonderfully linked together, full of poetry, haunting in its melodies, sure in its handling of each section of the orchestra, each soloist. It was another masterpiece, as Schumann must have known.

Unfortunately, Mendelssohn was unable to leave Berlin, and he was sorely missed both as a conductor and as a master of programming. The first rehearsal was conducted by Ferdinand David, concertmaster of the Gewandhaus Orchestra. The concert on December 6th, billed under Clara's name, was dominated by the appearance of Liszt, who volunteered to perform the dazzling *Hexameron* with Clara (Variations on a Theme from Bellini's *I Puritani*, originally for six pianos, by six pianists—hence the title *Hexameron*—rearranged by Liszt for two pianos). The program was extremely long. The first half began with Schumann's Overture, Scherzo and Finale, followed by Clara performing Mendelssohn's Capriccio for Piano and Orchestra, a Bach fugue, and a Chopin étude. Liszt then joined Clara for a Fantasy by Thalberg and a Diversion by the English composer William Sterndale Bennett, both for four-hands piano, followed by Liszt's setting of the patriotic "Rheinlied" for male chorus.

Schumann's Second Symphony, as it was billed, began after the intermission, when audience and musicians were exhausted. Liszt's appearance with Clara in the *Hexameron,* as a grand finale to the entire program, cast Schumann's new work into the shade. The response to the symphony was tepid. Reviewers were suspicious of its unified structure, and they gave its "good ideas" faint praise. They failed completely to appreciate the work's originality and power, from its opening bars signaling a master who was paying tribute to Beethoven and Schubert but confidently taking his own direction.

Schumann was strongly influenced by the critical response to his works, sensitive to any rebuff. He knew that his new symphony was as fine in its own way as his first, and he sent it to more than one publisher. Discouraged by their rejection letters, he set the score aside and only returned to it ten years later, when he was music director in Düsseldorf. He revised it to his satisfaction in December 1851, writing later to the Dutch composer Johannes Verhulst: "I totally reorchestrated the symphony and, of course, made it better and more effective than it was before." It was performed again, under his own direction, in May 1853, and published as his Symphony no. 4. The revised edition has been performed ever since.

But the story does not end here. In 1886, thirty years after Schumann's death, Clara Schumann gave Brahms the autograph of the original version. For several years they had worked together on editing Schumann's Collected Works, for what became the standard edition for performances. Reading over Schumann's original score, Brahms decided that he preferred it to the revised version: its "charm, ease, and clarity" had been lost in revision. He arranged to have it performed in 1889 and published in 1891. When Clara discovered that the autograph was to be published, she was furious. She told Brahms that Schumann's revised version represented his final thoughts, and to publish the earlier version was an insult to his memory. The two close friends were estranged for more than a year, until a somewhat frosty exchange of Christmas cards led to reconciliation. Clara Schumann won that battle, and it was only in 2003 that a scholarly edition of the earlier version was published.

A comparison of the two versions reveals that Schumann made few substantive changes, most of them in the first movement, and consisting mainly of thickened textures and doubled instruments, with an anticipation of the Allegro theme inserted toward the end of the introduction. The Romanza and Scherzo were left pretty much as they were, and the changes to the final movement were inconsequential.

The most important revision was a change in the tempo markings of the first and second movements, which altered the feeling of the entire symphony. Instead of marking the introduction Andante con moto (a walking pace, moving along) as in the original, Schumann changed it to *Ziemlich langsam* (Quite slow). This required a similar change in the tempo of the Romanza from Andante to *Ziemlich langsam,* so that the theme of the introduction, the evenly moving sixths, when they recur after the oboe melody, would be at the same tempo. The revised symphony thus becomes *maestoso*, heavy, somber, portentous. The slower tempo necessitated the doubling that follows, winds and brass filling out the cello octaves, as well as the early introduction of the Allegro theme in the dominant, in anticipation of its definitive appearance in the home key in the Allegro. Slowing down the Romanza makes it much harder to communicate the poignancy of the lyrical oboe-and-cello theme, as any oboe player will testify.

There are two possible reasons for Schumann's late revisions. It was only two years before his final breakdown, and he had complained at this time and earlier about disturbances in his hearing. Once he found Clara playing his Piano Quintet too quickly; he interrupted her performance and reduced her to tears. His conducting had become so erratic that members of the orchestra were asking for his resignation. His faulty sense of time might have caused him to slow down the first two movements. It is also possible that he wanted the heavy, portentous sound—a tragic D minor contrasting with the joyful mood of the E-flat *Rhenish* Symphony, composed only a year earlier, and acclaimed by audiences and critics. His musical sense was quite altered at this time, as his compositions from 1852 to February 1854 demonstrate. His works were increasingly dark, as if anticipating his final breakdown.

Whatever the reasons for Schumann's revisions, Brahms understandably preferred the lighter orchestration of the original, its elegance and clarity. The Symphony in D Minor, now no. 4, was welcomed as a masterpiece when it was performed in 1853. Had circumstances been different twelve years earlier, when Schumann's orchestral ideas were fresh, the original version would have been greeted as a worthy companion to the *Spring* Symphony—darker in coloring, but equally original, equally compelling. The D Minor Symphony is a revelation of Schumann's powers at their height.

CLARA AS COMPOSER, ARTIST, WIFE

One of Schumann's fondest ideas at this time was to publish a collection of songs that would include settings by Clara alongside his own work. Clara was finding composition difficult, if not impossible; she felt that she had no impetus to compose. But finally she put together three songs which Schumann published with his own settings as *Twelve Poems from Rückert's "Liebesfrühling,"* op. 37.

The joint publication raises a question which has surfaced many times since. Was Clara's genius stifled by her husband? Would she have become a major composer if she had not been married to Robert Schumann? It is clear that Schumann had the highest opinion of Clara's abilities, not only as a pianist but as a composer. In an early diary entry he placed "Zilia" alongside Mozart, Shakespeare, and Goethe as examples of artistic perfection. His term was *Leichtigkeit* (lightness), suggesting ease and grace, as opposed to the seriousness of Bach and the passion of Beethoven. He drew on Clara's compositions for material for his own works, and urged her repeatedly to compose. But she had a realistic sense of her abilities. As a pianist she was supreme. As a composer she had her own style but no ambition to compete with her husband.

The truth is that her life was increasingly dedicated to promoting Schumann's works. Her dedication reflected not only her love of the man but her increasing appreciation of his genius. She suffered from each rebuff that he experienced, each crisis of confidence, and, most worrying, his episodes of illness and nervous collapse. She was determined that the public should recognize him as a worthy successor to Beethoven, a contemporary master equal to Chopin and Mendelssohn. As his wedding gift of *Myrthen* affirmed in rapturous tones, she was his "good angel, [his] better self."

It was for this reason, not to promote her own career, that she was determined to undertake concert tours. She was convinced that the income she could earn from concerts would enable Schumann to devote himself to composition. This is why she undertook the first tour of their marriage, in November 1841, to the nearby town of Weimar. Later, more ambitious tours were undertaken for similar reasons. Not that Clara was averse to establishing her name in a great European city. She loved performing, and she relished the attendant fame, the invitations to great houses, the musical friendships she formed. But her priorities were always clear. She and Schumann even considered an American tour, in which they could earn enough money to subsidize their future life, though it would mean leaving their young child for several months. The American tour never happened, nor did a tour of England, which they also considered. Their lives were inextricably bound together, and each new possibility was carefully discussed. But increasingly it was Clara who made the fateful decisions.

11

IN CONFLICT, IN HARMONY

Leipzig, 1842–1844

It is absolutely necessary that we find the means to use and develop both of our talents side by side.

—ROBERT SCHUMANN

On the 18th of February, 1842, Schumann and Clara left Leipzig for a concert tour of Bremen and Hamburg. Schumann's *Spring Symphony* was to be performed in both major musical centres. The first concert was in Bremen, where Schumann was pleased: he thought the performance of his symphony went reasonably well after only one rehearsal. Clara performed Weber's popular Konzertstück, cleverly preparing the ground for Robert's symphony in the same program. From Bremen they traveled to Oldenburg, where Clara's concert included virtuoso works by Henselt and Thalberg, a Chopin nocturne, and a piece by Scarlatti, but nothing by Schumann. The brilliant young virtuoso was invited to appear at the ducal palace, an invitation that did not include Schumann. He confided to their marriage diary that it was only his weakness that allowed Clara to accept the invitation. He could not endure an argument. When Clara returned from the palace, she was delighted at the warm reception she had enjoyed. The thought of his "unworthy position" prevented Schumann from sharing her pleasure. It was a demeaning insult, not the first or last of its kind. Supremely confident of Schumann's great gifts, Clara underestimated his insecurity and his need for recognition. She was innocently pleased that she was able to include her husband's works in concerts billed under her name: "Madame Clara Schumann, née Wieck."

They returned to Bremen for more music, more concerts, then proceeded to Harburg, where they boarded a steamboat to the free Hanseatic city of Hamburg, one of the great ports of the world and a well-established musical center. At the Philharmonic concert featuring Schumann's *Spring* Symphony, Clara again played Weber's Konzertstück and works by Mendelssohn, Bach, and Liszt. The audience was delighted by the gifted young pianist. It is not clear that they fully appreciated Schumann's new work. After anguished discussion, Schumann decided to return to Leipzig alone, while Clara would continue to Copenhagen with a hired companion. They separated in Hamburg on the 10th of March.

Schumann longed to see the six-month-old Marie, and he had to resume work on the *New Journal*. He tried to drive his melancholia away by writing about the past weeks in the marriage diary. His first message was for the absent Clara:

> It was really one of the most stupid things for me to let you leave me. I feel it ever more . . . The separation has again made me feel our strangely difficult situation even more strongly. Should I neglect my talent in order to serve as your companion on trips? As for you, should you leave your talent unused because I am chained to the journal and the piano? . . . Thus I torment myself thinking . . . Yes, it is absolutely necessary that we find the means to use and develop both of our talents side by side.

In Clara's account of her decision to tour alone in Copenhagen, written after her return to Leipzig, she claimed that she found their separation as unbearable as Robert did. "[It was] the most terrible day in our marriage so far—. We separated and it seemed to me as if I would never see him again." She traveled to Kiel for a concert, but felt ill and had to cancel. Storms meant that she had to wait two weeks before taking a ship from Kiel to Copenhagen. Finally she boarded the *Christian VIII,* arriving the next day in Copenhagen, where she was met by friends. There was much visiting, new friendships, successful concerts. For Clara, it was a triumph. Her gross earnings after seven weeks of touring were 1,155 thalers—though only 100 louis d'or remained after deducting expenses. But she had realized her chief purpose, as she saw it: to earn enough money to free Schumann to realize his genius as a composer. Her ambition set a pattern that was to cause much distress in later years.

Schumann's account in the marriage diary of his life during Clara's absence was meant for her eyes. The household books he kept before and after his marriage were primarily a financial record, with small amounts listed each day for cigars and an evening beer at Poppe's, his favorite tavern. The household books also recorded works in progress and completed, concerts attended, notes on his health and state of mind (often "melancholy," rarely "cheerful"). He set down as well private thoughts omitted from the marriage diary—for instance, a note of the first time he slept with Clara (his euphemism) after Marie's birth, one month later. After his return to Leipzig, he noted his irritation with the "damned" *New Journal.* He was chafing at his continued responsibilities as editor, managing contributions from abroad, contributing his own articles, keeping track of expenses.

Schumann's detailed financial accounts shed light on the domestic arrangements that enabled Clara to pursue her professional life: the wet nurse hired for the infant and paid four thalers a month until Marie was weaned at nine months; a maid named Hanne and other *Dienstmädchen* (servant girls); a series of cooks and other household help, wages, tips, and Christmas presents all carefully noted.

Clara returned to Leipzig on the 26th of April, having been away from home for two full months. Schumann's melancholy during her Copenhagen tour had been relieved by his close study of the string quartets of Mozart, Haydn, and Beethoven. He was preparing to work seriously on string quartets of his own. He started work on the first one in June, probably thinking of a series of three, on the model of Mendelssohn's three String Quartets, op. 44, which had been published in 1839.

String Quartets; Piano Quintet;
Piano Quartet; *Fantasiestücke* for Piano Trio

Schumann was soon composing one quartet after another, each movement in turn sketched and written out in full. He completed a series of three by the end of July, all on the same crest of inspiration. In August he and Clara spent two weeks in Dresden and the Bohemian spa towns of Teplitz, Karlsbad, and Marienbad. This was a true holiday, apparently with no occasion for jealousy or resentment. Schumann wrote in the marriage diary that this was the loveliest time he had spent with Clara in their entire married life.

The three string quartets were rehearsed on the 8th of September and performed at home on the 13th, Clara's birthday. Ferdinand David's quartet performed them later in September for Mendelssohn, who was genuinely pleased with them. There was high praise again from the master whose judgment Schumann respected above all others. He told Mendelssohn he would like to dedicate the quartets to him, which he did on their publication in 1843. They also discussed Mendelssohn's hope of founding a music conservatory in Leipzig, in which Schumann would teach composition.

In his string quartets, Schumann was trying his hand at the classical genre established by Haydn, brought to perfection by Mozart, and developed beyond anyone's possible dreams by Beethoven. Schubert, too, had composed superb string quartets, though most of them had not yet been published; Schumann probably knew only *Death and the Maiden,* which had been published in 1831. But Mendelssohn's quartets, including the two early ones, op. 12 and op. 13, were a model and inspiration. While openly paying homage to Beethoven's late quartets, they were plainly Mendelssohnian in their charm, grace, and melodic fluency. Schumann's summary of musical activity for 1839 in the *New Journal* lists quartet evenings with Ferdinand David and his fellow musicians playing quartets by Haydn, Mozart, Beethoven, Cherubini, and Mendelssohn. Schumann's string quartets, like all his works, are strongly marked with his own musical signature. But there are recognizable hints of Beethoven in all three, and a Mendelssohnian lightness in the Scherzo movements.

Schumann regarded the string quartet as above all a conversation among equals, each with its own voice. The first quartet he composed was in A minor, the key closely associated with Clara. As in the symphonies composed earlier in the year, Schumann organized the quartet closely, deconstructing and varying a small number of related motifs. In the Introduzione, marked Andante espressivo, the first violin opens the discourse with a simple, tender theme, picked up by each voice in turn, a reflection of Schumann's love of counterpoint, perfectly suited to a four-way conversation. The Scherzo which follows the first movement is charming, Mendelssohnian in feeling. In the slow movement, Schumann is at his most poetic, weaving a beautiful and deeply felt melody initiated by the cello, a love song to Clara. Each instrument contributes its own lyrical embellishments, returning naturally to the poignant theme. The final movement draws the entire quartet together, with reminiscences of earlier themes, and a feeling of reconciliation, harmony achieved after sorrow endured and assuaged.

Schumann's recurrent melancholy pervades the quartet—indeed, all three quartets, though the melancholy gives way on occasion to the pleasure of composition. The Second Quartet, in F, is immediately attractive, even more appealing on first hearing than the A Minor Quartet. The first movement is lyrical, tender, in Schumann's most expressive style. Inspiration flags, for some listeners, in an Andante set of variations in A-flat, the variations adding little to a theme that has slight interest in itself. The inventive Scherzo in C minor picks up at once, of a piece with the first movement but moving in its own Presto world, rhythmically exciting, leading naturally into an equally satisfying Finale in F.

The Third Quartet, in A major, is the most personal, and for many listeners the most moving. Schumann had told Clara that he wanted to paint her name in capital letters in all his music. This has often been taken to hint at ciphers "spelling" Clara in notes (as *Carnaval* spells "Asch" in notes), though neither the *l* nor the *r* of "Clara" fits musical cipher form, and Schumann at this point was consistently spelling his beloved's name "Klara." But there is little doubt that the opening theme of the third string quartet sings, calls, speaks the name "Clara" as a falling fifth, with the stress on the first syllable. The distinctive motif is repeated all through the movement, deepening its meaning with each appearance. Once noticed, it is impossible not to hear Clara's name in the falling interval. It is unmistakable, too, in the slow movement of the A Minor Quartet. Mendelssohn, who was so appreciative of Schumann's string quartets, echoed the name and the interval in the opening *Song Without Words* of the volume he later dedicated to Clara, a falling fourth rather than a fifth, singing the name "Clara" clearly to those in the know.

The second-movement variations of the A Major Quartet have the inspirational quality missing in the variations of the F Major Quartet. Each variation is individually marked in rhythm and tone, new and yet connected. The third-movement Adagio in D, marked *sempre espressivo*, also picks up earlier motifs, weaving them into a haunting tapestry (Schumann's image of a "red thread" is appropriate), lingering over the theme as if reluctant to let it go. The Finale, Allegro molto vivace, returning to A major, provides relief, suggesting folk music in its rhythms and harmonies.

The string quartets have not been taken into standard repertoire in the same way that Schumann's symphonies have. Yet they have been recorded by most major groups, analyzed, praised for their poetic qualities and criticized for occasional repetition. It was not a genre that Schumann was to pursue. But by late September he began to sketch a Piano Quintet in E-flat, which became one of his supreme works—still at the heart of the chamber-music repertoire. The closest precedent was Schubert's enchanting *Trout* Quintet for piano, violin, viola, cello, and double bass, published in 1829, two years after Schubert's death. Schubert's Piano Trio in E-flat, op. 100, often mentioned in Schumann's early diaries, was also a direct inspiration. Written over fifteen years later, Schumann's Piano Quintet is unashamedly Romantic, a term applied to Schubert's works only with hindsight.

The Piano Quintet is a celebration of everything Schumann had learned in years of writing for the piano, now incorporated into a continuing dialogue with solo string players, each instrument responding to the others separately and together. Like the earlier Phantasie for Piano and Orchestra, the Piano Quintet was composed with Clara in mind, calling upon each quality of her playing and her musicianship—her effortless virtuosity, her ease in stretching to tenths, her faultless octave scales, her ability to move from *pianissimo* to the most bravura *fortissimo* climaxes. With each repetition and variation the pianist seems to be saying to her fellow musicians: "Wasn't that delightful? Shall we try it again, perhaps a tone lower, and with a few harmonic changes toward the end? Never fear, I'll get you back home again!" And so she does, confident that she can take the string players along with her when she moves from three flats to four, from four flats to four sharps, from C minor to G major, following her own impulse, and returning effortlessly to the home key each time.

Exhilarating from the start, the Piano Quintet is endlessly inventive, with strong overlapping motifs, wonderful figuration for the piano, from the opening Allegro brillante right through to the end. The exuberant Scherzo builds tremendous excitement with the repeated theme of an ascending and descending staccato scale, relieved by two contrasting trios in related keys. The Finale moves effortlessly through an ingenious series of modulations until, having exhausted ordinary possibilities, it rises on a series of *sforzando* dominant chords, pauses dramatically—and transforms the opening themes of the first movement and the final movement into a double fugue of Schumann's own devising, the piano leading, the strings entering in counterpoint. The entire work, closely organized as it is, has a feeling of improvisation, with each musician contributing new ideas as the music unfolds, inviting new variations, new developments. It is a truly collaborative venture, with the piano now proposing a new theme, now providing the accompaniment. Liszt condescendingly said it was too *Leipzigerisch*, presumably too plea-

surable for musicians and audiences, too conventional. It is rightly
and enduringly popular.

A Piano Quartet, also in E-flat, followed at once, like an extension of the Piano Quintet, with a similar delight in the relationship
of piano to strings, and with Clara in mind as the pianist. Its fine
qualities have been somewhat obscured by the delights of the Piano
Quintet. But it is equally original, equally revelatory in its beauty
and subtlety of form. All four movements are closely interwoven. A
slow, mysterious introduction outlines the basic harmony, followed
by a bravura Allegro (marked *sempre con molto sentimento*) full of
excitement as well as "sentiment," pausing for a brief recall of the
introduction, which is going to be recalled again, in changed form,
at the end of the Andante. But first there is a remarkable Scherzo
in G minor (two flats instead of three), in a quick *pianissimo* staccato figure, up and down the scale—another voice, like a discreet
commentary on the passion of the opening movement. The Andante
cantabile is a slow movement of surpassing lyricism, tragic in its
intensity. The movement is initiated by the cello as a sustained, lingering theme, answered by the violin and more briefly by the viola,
all accompanied quietly by the piano. It is another heart-stopping
"song without words," which came as naturally to Schumann as
quicksilver scherzos came to Mendelssohn and bravura virtuosity
to Liszt. Notable is the expressive power of the close dissonance in
which Schumann revels, minor seconds, diminished octaves, minor
ninths, close to each other in the piano accompaniment, an octave
above or below as cello, violin, and viola in turn take up the theme.
In an early issue of the *New Journal*, Schumann had singled out
the diminished octave for its expressive power, criticizing what he
called "the antichromaticists": "They should remember that the seventh once displeased as much as the diminished octave does now;
it is through harmonic development that music has attained such
a high rank among the arts, and has acquired the power of expressing the finest shades of passion, the deepest feelings of the soul."
Schumann also loves the expressive power of modulation from one
key to another, and changes of rhythm. A sudden shift midway in the

Andante moves magically from two flats (B-flat major) in three to a bar to a choralelike theme in six flats (G-flat major) in four to a bar, and back again, each time deepening the melancholy. A tender coda-like transition offers brief relief and leads with a reminiscence of earlier themes into the affirmation of the fugal Finale and the return to E-flat major. Listeners might detect a hint of the fugal finale of Beethoven's *Hammerklavier* Sonata, which Schumann no doubt would have denied. What is openly, explicitly defiant is the instruction to the cellist to tune the lowest string down from C to B-flat, to give the tonic deeper support, at the end of the third-movement Andante, retuning to C as the Finale opens, with hardly any pause between the two. Although he had briefly studied the instrument, Schumann was happy to demand the impossible from his cellist, here and several years later in the marvelous Cello Concerto. Both the Piano Quintet and the Piano Quartet are colored by Schumann's joy in exploring all possible permutations of his material, with an apparently endless fund of melody.

Soon after writing the Piano Quartet, Schumann composed a work that he entitled *Phantasiestücke für Pianoforte, Violine und Violoncello* when he published it in 1850, after many revisions. In effect it was his first piano trio. It opens with a plangent Romanze introducing a "lively" movement Schumann called Humoreske, perhaps because of its unusual "humorous" structure. Like the earlier Humoreske, op. 20, for piano, the movement consists of a theme and variations cleverly linked but contrasting in key, rhythm, and mood—as if new characters enter with each variation, return, and converse together, with the first and last section providing a frame. The piano dominates in the Romanze and Humoreske, but cello and violin come into their own in a lyrical Duett, as beautiful as anything Schumann wrote at the time or later. The melody is similar to the love duet between cello and violin in the Andante of the Piano Quartet. Perhaps Schumann simply could not let go of the idea and had to try yet another version, with the strings conversing an octave higher than in the Piano Quartet. An arpeggiated piano accompaniment gives a tender coloring to the high strings. The Finale is another set of variations, based on a simple four-square march with conventional harmonies. Schumann seems to be cleverly imitating a current style, showing that he can do it as well or better, should he be so inclined. The variations retain a basic formula but add decorations which give the whole a less martial feeling, adding charm and an element of parody. The *Phantasiestücke* works surprisingly well in performance—an example of Schumann's somewhat quirky humor and a reflection of his high spirits at this time.

There is only one mention in the household book of an unusual chamber piece in which Schumann returned to the variation form explored repeatedly in his piano works. This was a work for two pianos, two celli, and horn—a unique combination. Like the *Phantasiestücke* for piano trio, it has the air of being written quickly. The variations are largely conventional in form, with only one departure from the prevailing key of B-flat, for an E-flat variation in which the E-flat horn dominates. But it is a thoroughly engaging piece, which remained unpublished in its original form until 1893, when Brahms included it in a supplement to Clara Schumann's edition of the Collected Works. It remains a rarity in concert performance, with only a few recordings. Mendelssohn suggested reworking the piece for two pianos only, and performed it in that arrangement with Clara; this is the version published in the Collected Works as op. 46.

The other chief events of 1843, often known as the "chamber music year," were the birth of a second daughter, Elise, in April, and the launch of Mendelssohn's visionary project, the Leipzig Conservatory, also in April. For a short time, Schumann taught composition, score reading, and piano, acquiring six pupils, but he was not comfortable as a teacher and was evidently unable to communicate his own expertise with any confidence.

Wieck was now living in Dresden, no longer plotting against Schumann, no longer his mortal enemy. Clara visited her father in Dresden in February, and returned to Leipzig pleased with the younger children and even with her cold stepmother. The following December, Wieck wrote a note to Schumann, completely in character:

Dear Schumann,

Tempora mutantur et nos mutamur in eis. [Times change and we change with them.] We can no longer remain estranged from each other, in the face of Clara and the world. You too are now the father of a family—what need for further explanation?

We were always as one with regard to art. I was your teacher; my consent was decisive in your present career. I need not assure you of my sympathy for your talent and your fine and sincere efforts.

I await you in Dresden with pleasure.

Your father
Fr. Wieck
15 Decbr. 1843

Schumann knew how important it was to Clara to repair relations with her father. They joined the Wiecks in Dresden for Christmas Eve. It was true that Wieck's support had enabled Schumann to abandon law for a career in music. But it was impossible for Schumann to forget the anguish he had suffered from Wieck's vicious attacks on his reputation, undermining him at every opportunity. The poison still festered within.

Paradise and the Peri

Like most of his musician friends, Schumann dreamed of writing an opera. He shared ideas of suitable subjects with Mendelssohn, and later with Richard Wagner, whose first successful opera, *Rienzi*, was premiered in Dresden in 1842. When Clara visited her father in February 1843 on a peace mission, she attended a performance of two acts of *Rienzi*, and reported to Schumann that her chief reaction was one of displeasure. Mendelssohn and Schumann shared a grudging respect for Wagner, but agreed that he knew nothing about the rules of composition.

Schumann considered Byron's verse tale *The Corsair* a promising operatic subject, with its Romantic plot, in which a wild Greek pirate chief is saved from certain death by the selfless love of a Turkish slave. He also thought of Hoffmann's short story "Doge and Dogaressa," for which he began a libretto outline, and a Shakespeare play, possibly *Hamlet* or *Macbeth*. The subject he finally chose was "Paradise and the Peri," the second of four tales in *Lalla Rookh: An Oriental Romance* by Thomas Moore, the popular Irish poet best known for several volumes of *Irish Melodies*. Schumann had read the work in the summer of 1841, noting in the marriage diary that it had made him very happy: "Perhaps one could make something fine from it for music," he thought. "Paradise and the Peri" combined fantasy with a serious moral purpose, complementary qualities that Schumann believed to be at the very center of art. He began work on the project in 1842, consulting his friend Emil Flechsig about the text, and eventually creating his own libretto, based closely on the German translation.

Moore's *Lalla Rookh* became instantly popular on its publication in 1817, and was soon translated into several European languages, inspiring musical versions as songs, a masque, and a ballet. The poem is recited as a continuing entertainment for the Indian princess Lalla Rookh when she leaves Delhi for Kashmir, where she is to be married to the heir to the throne of "Bucharia." Four separate tales are narrated by a handsome young poet who has gained admittance to the entourage. Lalla Rookh falls in love with him, only to discover when she arrives at the imperial palace that the poet is actually the prince in disguise.

Although *Lalla Rookh* seems to be a typical example of the Oriental craze of the time, on the model of the popular *Arabian Nights*, it has a serious dimension. Moore admired his friend Lord Byron for his daring, his recklessness, and his contempt for the British establishment. He also shared Byron's political sentiments. Byron's maiden speech on entering Parliament in 1812 was in defense of the frame breakers of Nottingham, who were rioting against the mechanized looms that were displacing human labor. Byron knew Moore as a spokesman for the Irish people, oppressed by British rule and exploitation. His own Turkish tale, *The Corsair*, celebrated personal and political freedom and the loving sacrifices made by heroic women. He encouraged Moore's Eastern project, suggesting helpful background reading, and he dedicated *The Corsair* to Moore with these words:

> It is said . . . that you are engaged in the composition of a poem whose scene will be laid in the East—none can do those scenes so much justice—The wrongs of your own Country—the magnificent and fiery spirit of her sons—the beauty and feeling of her daughters may there be found . . . Your imagination will create a warmer Sun & less clouded sky—but wildness tenderness and originality are part of your national [heritage].

"Wildness tenderness and originality" were qualities that appealed above all to Schumann, who had always loved the poems of Byron and Moore. Both poets wrote about themes Schumann found irresistible: political heroism and sacrifice, guilt and repentance, "love unto death." Byron's death in Missolonghi, where he was supporting the Greek revolution against the Turks, was for liberal Europeans the enduring symbol of heroic resistance to tyranny. The political theme had central importance in Schumann's setting of "Paradise and the Peri."

Inspired by the verse tale's poetry and philosophy, its fairy-tale elements and human drama, Schumann turned "Paradise and the Peri" into a musical work of grand proportions—part oratorio, part allegory and moral fable. It was the most ambitious work he had undertaken, combining his recent experience of songwriting and orchestral composition with the challenge of setting an extended episodic plot to music. The verse text provided a narrator, a range of angelic and human characters, and several tableaux, to which Schumann added his own invented dialogue and choruses, expanding and dramatizing key moments in the tale.

He drew upon several precedents. Beethoven's incidental music to *Egmont* had moved Schumann to tears, sending him back to Goethe's drama of a heroic victim of tyranny and his devoted lover, themes also present in Moore's tale. Schumann had recently heard

Mendelssohn's cantata for soloists, chorus, and orchestra, based on another work of Goethe's, *The First Walpurgis Night*, defending an early tribe of Druid worshippers against persecution by their orthodox Christian rulers. *Israel in Egypt* and *Jephtha*, Handel's most frequently performed oratorios, also served as inspiration; they dramatized those favorite Romantic themes, an enslaved nation's resistance to tyranny and a woman's heroic sacrifice. *Paradise and the Peri* drew on these precedents but was Schumann's unique creation.

The central figure of Moore's tale is the Peri, a fairy creature of Persian and Islamic myth. She is "the child of an erring race," fallen angels who have mated with mortal women. Half mortal, half divine, she longs to return to the heaven from which she and all her race have been exiled. She weeps before the gate to the Islamic heaven, lamenting her fate, and the angel who keeps the gate takes pity on her. He tells her it is written in the Book of Fate that the erring spirit can gain admittance if she brings the dearest of gifts to heaven.

Where can she find such a gift? The angel advises her: "Go seek it and redeem thy sin / 'Tis sweet to let the Pardoned in."

Sin, redemption, forgiveness—the theme of the tale is announced at the start. But this is not a Christian morality tale. Eastern mythology and religion, reinterpreted by Romantic artists like Byron and Moore, offered an enlightened alternative to the exclusive truths of Christian doctrine, with its harsh choice of eternal punishment for sinners and eternal rewards for the chosen. In the romanticized East, there is one God, and Allah is his name—Allah the Compassionate, Allah the Merciful. Compassion is the saving virtue of *Paradise and the Peri*, the tear of pity its symbol.

The Peri must search for a suitable gift in the world of fallen humanity—half of her inheritance. And the world of humanity is at the heart of Moore's poem. The Peri's quest frames three episodes of life on earth, set in ancient Eastern lands, afflicted by disasters that have parallels in every century: the carnage of war and the catastrophe of plague. The devastating Napoleonic wars were very much in Moore's mind when he was writing the poem, and cholera outbreaks began in Asia in 1814, spreading across Europe in the 1830s.

The Peri, like Shakespeare's Ariel, can circle the world in a moment. She arrives first in India, a land of beauty ravaged by the tyrant Gazna, a rapist and a slaughterer of priests—a figure based on the eleventh-century sultan Mahmud of Ghazni, whose armies raided and looted northwestern India. One young warrior is left to oppose the tyrant. Gazna offers to spare his life if he will join the enemy. The young hero refuses, passionately loyal to his country and his fallen comrades. He sends his one remaining arrow at the tyrant's heart, but misses Gazna, who slays the youth. The Peri catches "the last glorious drop" of the hero's blood, hoping to present it as her gift to heaven: "'Tis the last libation Liberty draws / From the heart that bleeds and breaks in her cause!"

Moore writes in his notes to the poem: "Objections may be made to my use of the word Liberty . . . as totally inapplicable to any state of things that has ever existed in the East . . . yet it is no disparagement to the word to apply it to that national independence, that freedom from the interference and dictation of foreigners, without which, indeed, no liberty of any kind can exist."

In the spirit of the text, Schumann ends part 1 with a grand choral hymn to freedom, echoing the Prisoners' Chorus in Beethoven's *Fidelio,* as the political prisoners joyfully enter the world of light and freedom.

Opening part 2, the angel at heaven's gate appreciates the Peri's gift, but sadly confirms that it is not sufficient. The Peri must return to earth, to seek a gift even more precious than the drop of blood from a hero who has died fighting for liberty.

The Peri flies south to Africa, landing at the source of the Nile, and roving over the groves and vales of Egypt, where she discovers the second human catastrophe: "Who could have thought that there, even there, / Amid those scenes so still and fair, / The Demon of the Plague hath cast / From his hot wing a deadlier blast." The Peri is moved to pity. "Poor race of men! . . . Dearly ye pay for your primal Fall." Christian symbolism, but in an Oriental guise. The true virtue is pity, love, forgiveness—not judgment.

A youth dying of the plague has fled his home to die alone, taking comfort in the thought that his beloved is safe from contagion.

But she comes flying to join him. "Am I not thine—thy own lov'd bride— / The one, the chosen one, whose place / In life or death is by thy side?" The Peri's second gift will be the sigh of the expiring bride—and Schumann ends the episode with a beautiful choral lullaby for the sleeping lovers, dead in each other's arms.

Part 3 opens to find the Peri's gift rejected once again, plunging her into despair. She must return to the fallen world to resume her search. The final episode is a parable set in the Holy Land. An innocent child is playing by the wild roses in the Valley of Balbec, in Syria, when a weary man appears, a criminal dying of thirst. At the call of a thousand minarets, the child drops to his knees in prayer. Moved by the sight, the sinful man repents the vicious crimes of his youth, drops to his knees next to the child, and prays for forgiveness. The tear of a repentant criminal proves to be the supreme gift, opening the gate of heaven, at last, to the Peri.

The first challenge for Schumann was to portray in music the emotions of a creature half human, half divine. He opens the overture with a poignant motif that symbolizes the Peri's quest, a leitmotif, anticipating Wagner's radical expansion of the technique. Schumann gives the Peri a distinctive voice, a high, pure, lyrical vocal line, intensely expressive at each stage of her journey. Her emotional development is charted in the music, from the longing of the exile to enter a lost Paradise, to her pity for the suffering humans, to her ecstatic joy when her third gift is accepted and heaven's gate opens to admit her.

Each level of being is characterized in music: the immortal sounds of the Islamic heaven, heard through the half-open gate; the rivers and woods, valleys and hills of the ancient world in its original beauty, and in its affliction by man-made and natural catastrophes. Four soloists and a vocal quartet, chorus and orchestra create a vast musical canvas. Each character has a different vocal style: the Narrator (mainly divided between alto and tenor, with smaller parts for soprano and baritone); the angel at heaven's gate; the conqueror from Gazni and the young hero who defies him; the dying youth and his devoted bride; the innocent child and the vicious criminal. Schumann creates new parts for the vocal quartet and a divided chorus of men's and women's voices. He expands hints from the text, dramatizing the battling conquerors and Indians of part 1 and the dancing genii of the Nile in part 2. He invents additional characters for delightful treatment, lightening the somber tone of the episodes, a chorus of houris in part 3 and a chorus of peris who long to join their sister in her quest. The full chorus joins forces in grand finales to each section. A fugal hymn to freedom ends part 1; a lullaby for the lovers in their sleep of death ends part 2; the Peri's joy at her admittance to heaven ends part 3, with the Peri's voice soaring ecstatically above the chorus.

The premiere of *Paradise and the Peri* took place in Leipzig on December 4th, 1843, with a second performance on the 11th. Schumann conducted both performances, his first experience of conducting. The fine singer Livia Frege, a pupil of Wilhelmine Schröder-Devrient and a close friend of the Schumanns, sang the part of the Peri. According to Clara, the soloists, the quartet and the full chorus all sang "with body and soul."

Paradise and the Peri was acclaimed at once by audiences and critics, and was performed more than fifty times in the next few years in European cities and at festivals. Greeted with enthusiasm by audiences and musicians, it established Schumann's reputation as a master, worthy of a place alongside Mendelssohn. Yet in time it dropped out of the repertoire. By the end of the century it was considered sadly dated, as was Moore's *Lalla Rookh*, popular in Schumann's time and later virtually unread. In our own time, Moore's "oriental romance" has little appeal for an age skeptical of all moralities, Islamic, Christian, and secular. Schumann's romance is full of soaring melodies and superb choral passages, intensifying those elements of the poem that still speak to modern sensibility: resistance to tyranny; love and loyalty overriding self-interest; the longing for immortality of a creature half human, half divine. Schumann's *Peri* has recently been rediscovered as an enchanting musical realization of a poem with serious themes, very much of its time, but highly pleasurable if one exercises that suspension of disbelief advocated by Coleridge and essential to the appreciation of much Romantic poetry and music.

THE RUSSIAN TOUR

The triumph of *Peri* softened the prospect of a concert tour of Russia, to which Schumann had reluctantly agreed. Long cherished by Clara, the plan had been discussed for months. Traveling would have to start in January in order to arrange concerts in St. Petersburg and Moscow in early spring. There were no rail links beyond Berlin. Stagecoaches would have to be arranged along the way, going farther northeast each time, into the brutal northern winter. From Berlin they would travel forty-eight hours by coach to Königsberg, in eastern Prussia, stopping in Lithuania (Tilsit and Tauroggen) en route to the North Sea port of Riga, capital of Latvia. Clara would arrange concerts in Mitau and Dorpat in neighboring Estonia, returning to Riga for the forty-eight-hour coach trip to St. Petersburg, arriving there in mid-February. After a month in St. Petersburg, they would proceed to Moscow, again by coach. Even after rail links had been established, it would have been a daunting prospect.

Clara knew that her competitors Thalberg and Liszt had toured the Russian cities to rapturous enthusiasm. She was twenty-four years old, ready for any challenge, determined to take advantage of her youth, her stamina, and her remarkable gifts. She hoped to earn enough money to enable Schumann to devote himself exclusively to composition, and she dreamed of establishing his reputation in Russia. Her party piece was to be his popular Piano Quintet, and his *Spring* Symphony would be offered to Russian impresarios. Clara prepared a program of favorite virtuoso showpieces, with short works by Chopin and Mendelssohn, certain to delight audiences. She had triumphed in Vienna and again in Copenhagen. If she had had another six months, she would have made her name in Paris. In Russia she and Schumann would triumph together, a unique artistic pair. They had friends or acquaintances in each city who would smooth their way.

The only obstacle she faced was the reluctance of her beloved Robert. But he too was young—only thirty-three—and despite occasional spells of ill health he was at the height of his powers. In his imagination, he could, like the Peri, soar to the farthest reaches of the known world. In real life he clung to the security of his own pleasant lodgings on Inselstrasse, his two little girls, afternoon walks with Clara to the Rosenthal gardens or longer excursions to a country inn at Connewitz, returning for his usual evening beer at Poppe's tavern. His attempt to establish the *New Journal* in Vienna had been a disaster. He was comfortable only in his native Saxony: the familiar triangle of Leipzig; the artistic court city of Dresden to the east, and his quiet family home of Zwickau to the south, with Schneeberg, where his brother Carl maintained the family publishing business, just twelve miles away. Gone were his and Clara's dreams of starting married life in a grand capital city—Vienna, Paris, or London. Home was busy, bourgeois Leipzig, where Schumann was known and respected, and Clara could entertain fellow musicians at domestic soirees and perform in the Gewandhaus at any time she chose.

Clara went to their friend Mendelssohn in tears, begging for his support for the Russian tour. She wrote to him later: "My husband speaks now seriously about our trip, and I know whom to thank for this. When I think of the morning when I came to you in despair I am ashamed. I think I must have seemed very childish to you, and I'll never forget how kindly and patiently you listened to me." Schumann spent an evening with Mendelssohn in which they discussed "everything," including the Russian tour, Clara's commitment and Schumann's reluctance. On January 20th, Carl and his second wife, Pauline, came from Schneeberg to collect the little girls, who would spend the next months with their uncle and aunt. Mendelssohn had left Leipzig for Berlin at the end of November. Clara and Robert set off for Russia two months later, leaving Leipzig on the 25th of January.

The first stop in their journey was Berlin, where they visited Clara's mother and spent time with Mendelssohn and the young Danish composer Niels Gade. Mendelssohn wrote to colleagues in St. Petersburg and Moscow, introducing the Schumanns in glowing terms as "two very dear friends and two of our very best German artists . . . No one is more deserving than they are. . . . He has composed outstanding pieces, his last work [*Paradise and the Peri*] made a great stir; one expects even greater things from him. His wife is first among our [female] German pianists, possibly the greatest now living."

Writing in French to the famous violinist Alexei Lvov, who was a personal adjutant to Tsar Nicholas I, Mendelssohn was even more specific: "No one could be more worthy than Madame Schumann—the only [pianist] who can interpret Beethoven at the piano as you can on the violin." He wrote in the same vein to Count Matvei Wielhorski, who hosted musical soirees in the family mansion in St. Petersburg, as Mendelssohn's sister Fanny had done for years in Berlin. At the same time he wrote in English to his London publisher, Edward Buxton, urging an English publication of *Paradise and the Peri:* "I have read and heard this new work with the greatest pleasure . . . I think it a very important and noble work, full of many eminent beauties. As for expression and poetical feeling, it ranks very high. The Choruses are as effective and well-written as the solo parts are melodious and winning." This was a significant tribute from the composer of *St. Paul,* the oratorio that Schumann had praised on its premiere for "its masterly musical perfection, its noble melodies, the union of word and tone, speech and music, that cause us to gaze into the whole as into a living depth." Masterly craft and noble, poetical feeling were the common aims of both composers, realized in his earliest compositions by Mendelssohn and now achieved after long struggles by Schumann.

Mendelssohn also presented Clara with a manuscript of pieces from his fifth book of *Songs Without Words,* which he dedicated to her. The first piece opens with the "Clara" theme Schumann had used in his A Major String Quartet, a descending fourth (similar to the descending fifth of the quartet) singing "Clara" in the private language known to Mendelssohn. Clara's favorites in the book were the "Spring Song," one of Mendelssohn's happiest ideas, and the "Venetian Gondola Song." She played both frequently in later concerts, in preference to the equally charming but more personal piece that opens the collection. Mendelssohn sent his brother Paul to the coach station to help arrange the Schumanns' further travels; and Mendelssohn and Gade both came to see them off on their departure, at seven a.m. on January 29th.

Johanna Christiane Schumann
(c. 1767–1836), Robert Schumann's mother.
Oil painting by L. Glaeser, 1810

August Schumann (1773–1826),
Schumann's father. Oil painting by
L. Glaeser, 1810

Marketplace of Zwickau, from a postcard of 1900

Robert Schumann, age sixteen.
Anonymous miniature, 1826

Zwickau pastoral. Watercolor by G. Taubert, 1840. "What I loved best was
to go for walks alone and relieve my heart in nature."—Robert Schumann

Clara Wieck, age
sixteen, playing her
own Piano Concerto.
Lithograph by
Julius Giere,
Hanover, 1835

Friedrich Wieck (1785–1873).
Anonymous oil painting, 1830

Caricature of Paganini's Vienna concert of 1828.
Drawing by Johann Peter Lyser

Concert Hall in the Leipzig Gewandhaus, after a drawing by B. Strassberger.
Several of Schumann's major works were first performed here.

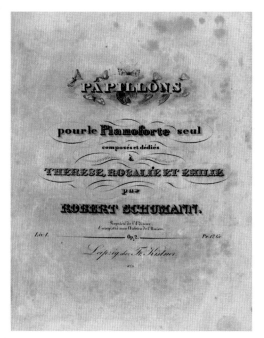

Title page of *Papillons*, April 1832, dedicated to his sisters-in-law. Schumann's first publications used French titles, in the style of the time.

Title page of *Carnaval* (composed in 1834–35). Includes musical portraits of the *Davidsbündler*, real and imagined: Florestan and Eusebius, Chiarina (Clara), Chopin and Paganini.

Signed title page of Piano Sonata, op. 11, "dedicated to Clara by Florestan and Eusebius." Schumann's name did not appear on the score of the first edition.

Chopin. Drawing by George Sand, 1845. "Try to conceive such perfection, a mastery which seems unconscious of itself." —Schumann on Chopin playing his own compositions

Mendelssohn, age twenty-one. Detail from a watercolor by James Warren Childe, 1830. "He is the finest living musician in the world."—Schumann

Liszt, age twenty-five. Oil painting by Jean Gabriel Scheffer, 1835–36. Liszt was the first major artist to recognize Schumann's originality.

Clara Wieck, age seventeen.
Drawing by Elwine v. Leyser,
Maxen, 4 December 1836

Friedrich and Clara Wieck,
with Clara's friends Emilie and
Elise List on the right. Drawing
by Pauline Viardot Garcia

"Der Dichter spricht" (The Poet Speaks), final piece of *Kinderszenen* (1838),
a defining self-portrait in music. With Schumann's markings: "Sehr langsam" (very
slow) at the top and a correction in the first bar of the final stave

Robert Schumann, age thirty-six, and Clara Schumann, age twenty-seven. Signed lithograph by Eduard Kaiser, with dedication to Schumann's Zwickau friend Emanuel Klitsch, Vienna, January 1847

Manuscript draft of "Ich bin dein Baum," opening bars. Courtesy of
Heinrich-Heine-Institut Düsseldorf, Akz-Nr. 2005.5005/13. First publication

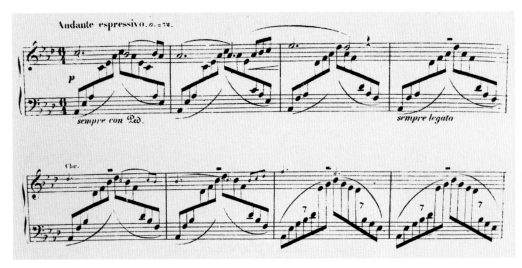

Piano Concerto, op. 54, bars 156–163

Schumann's draft of Friedrich Rückert's love poem "Ich bin dein Baum" as a
duet between soprano and tenor, sketched in January 1841, was set aside and
reused note for note as a duet between piano and solo clarinet in the Piano Concerto, op. 54. The tender words of Rückert's poem still resonate in the concerto.

Schumann, age thirty-nine. Enlargement of daguerreotype by
Johann Anton Völlner, Hamburg, March 1850

The Schumann children. By W. Severin, Düsseldorf, 1854. From the left: Ludwig, Marie (with Felix on her lap), Elise, Ferdinand, Eugenie. (Julie was living in Berlin with Clara's mother.)

Clara, age thirty-four. Watercolor drawing by Jean-Joseph-Bonaventure Laurens, 16 October 1853

Title page of *Lieder für die Jugend*, 1849. Design by Ludwig Richter, a Dresden artist well-known to Schumann

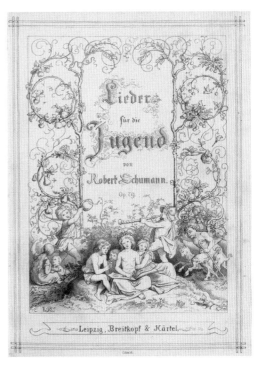

Brahms, age twenty-one. Silver pencil drawing by Jean-Joseph-Bonaventure Laurens, October 1853 (misdated 15 September). Made at Schumann's request. Two years later, in Endenich asylum, Schumann asked Brahms to bring him this treasured picture.

Joseph Joachim and Clara Schumann playing music together.
Photograph of a pastel by Adolph von Menzel, December 1854

Düsseldorf Piano Trio: Julius Tausch, piano; Wilhelm Joseph v. Wasielewski, violin; and Christian Reimers, cello. Caricature by Reimers, 1850, with the theme of Schubert's Trio in E-flat, op. 100, below

Schumann, age forty-four. Drawing by Jean-Joseph-Bonaventure Laurens, October 1853. Underneath his portrait, Schumann has inscribed the poignant violin theme which opens the slow movement of his Piano Trio in D Minor, op. 63.

Manuscript of a theme supposedly dictated by angels, with the beginning of a first Variation, on which Schumann was working when he suffered a psychotic breakdown in February 1854

The final letter Schumann wrote to Clara from Endenich, dated 5 May 1855. The opening sentences read: "On the first of May I sent you a spring greeting; but the following days were very agitated; you shall discover more from my letter which you shall receive by the day after tomorrow. A shadow lies within, but the other things it contains, my beloved, will make you rejoice." Clara wrote under the date: *"Letzter brief"* (Last letter).

It was an encouraging start to the tour, promising a welcome reception in their first staging post, Königsberg. They then toured the chief cities of the Baltic countries, Lithuania, Latvia, and Estonia, which were under Russian control but included large German-speaking populations. From the major port of Riga, they at last set forth to St. Petersburg. Altogether they were to spend four months on tour, chiefly in St. Petersburg and Moscow. The records of their tour consist of brief notes made by Schumann, later expanded by Clara, documenting each stage of their travels, the people they met, the places they stayed, concerts given and attended, the food (usually unpalatable), the palaces and art collections, the vast squares and monuments of Petersburg and Moscow. Schumann made notes on the Russian custom of separating men and women at formal dinners, smoking even in company with women, bowing low on meeting friends, "shameful" behavior during concerts and plays (tea drinking and constant talking). He set down in order the distances covered and the cost: the trip from Leipzig to Berlin, 118 miles, took six and a half hours by train—it was a trip Mendelssohn frequently made, as did Clara, on visits to her mother—and cost 10 thalers; passage from Berlin to Königsberg took forty-eight hours, and cost 51.4 thalers; the mail coach to Tilsit, on the border of Prussia and Lithuania, 75 miles, took twelve hours; then on to Tauroggen, Riga, Dorpat, back to Riga, and the longest trips—from Riga to Petersburg (390 miles) and from Petersburg to Moscow (445 miles).

The distances covered during the Russian tour were extraordinary, as were the discomfort and the boredom of endless hours of coach travel. But they both enjoyed the stimulation of new sights and new people. Clara organized concerts and performed in each city, struggled to find a decent piano, and varied her programs depending on the musical forces available. She balanced works by Schumann—the Piano Quintet, occasionally one of the *Fantasy Pieces* and if a singer was available, two or three songs ("Der Nussbaum," "Die Lotosblume," "Mondnacht")—with virtuoso variations by Henselt and Thalberg on popular opera themes. The initial tour of the Baltic countries meant traveling back and forth between cities, as concerts were arranged. The additional travel probably contributed to a week-long illness that Schumann suffered in Dorpat, the last city they visited before departing from Riga for Petersburg.

Despite the hardships they experienced—bitter cold weather, filthy hotels, out-of-tune pianos—Clara was able to arrange trial runs of concerts for the great cities of St. Petersburg and Moscow. Once they had arrived in Petersburg, Clara soon established herself as the "queen of pianists" Mendelssohn had described to his friends. Count Wielhorski, who had met the Schumanns in Leipzig, arranged private soirees where Schumann's *Spring* Symphony was performed, and Clara played Beethoven sonatas and other favorite works. But they soon found that the aristocratic audiences for music were far more interested in famous artists than in the quality of the music. Even their friend Pauline Viardot-Garcia, touring at the same time, gave in to popular taste, performing only lightweight Italian arias in her public concerts.

Although Schumann had at last made his name in Germany, in Russia his music was unknown, his name as a composer was hardly recognized, and he soon withdrew into the silence for which he had always been noted. He was a shy, distant figure at social occasions, increasingly unhappy at his role as the companion of a celebrated artist. The common language at aristocratic soirees was French. Clara had taken weekly lessons during her months in Paris, and although she was not a fluent speaker, she could understand her hosts. Schumann was comfortable only in German, and his usual shyness was exacerbated. He was reduced to standing in a far corner, puffing at his cigar, the insignificant husband of the charming pianist who was the center of attention wherever she appeared.

He remained isolated and depressed in Moscow, despite visits to the Kremlin and picturesque cathedrals. He mainly occupied himself with writing a long poem, "Die Glocke von Iwan Welikii" (The Bell of Ivan the Great Bell Tower). The legend had special resonance for Schumann. In part one of his poem, which Schumann dates "1735," an artist is fired with the ambition to create a great bell to be placed on the highest tower in Moscow, a monument to God which would also ensure the artist's fame. With great ceremony, the bell is hoisted to the top of the highest bell tower in the Kremlin, named for Ivan the Great. But a piece breaks off, the great bell falls deep into the ground, and the artist is mocked for placing his vanity above service to God. In part two, dated "1836," the tsar recognizes the artist as worthy of respect for his ambition despite the failure of his work. He orders the broken bell to be recovered and installed at the foot of the high tower, where it murmurs softly in response to the chiming of Moscow's many bells. (Both dates are roughly accurate for the casting of the great bell and for its restoration.) Schumann then compares the artist's ambition and his failure to the career of Napoleon—hero of France, conqueror of Europe, defeated by the people of Moscow, and later marooned on Elba until his death. Schumann dated the complete poem in the combined Russian and German forms: "Moscow, 13/25 April 1844." It is an interesting work, although it confirms the obvious truth that Schumann's genius lay in music rather than poetry. But the poem also provides insight into his character and his melancholia. He identified imaginatively with the ambitions of the Russian artist and the defeat of his vision. He too cherished vast ambitions, and he feared disaster even as he summoned all his energy to create the masterpiece that would define his lasting achievement.

Schumann and Clara arrived back in Leipzig on the 24th of May, exhausted, exhilarated, relieved to be at home. Schumann summarized their takings, which came to about 4,700 thalers, a substantial contribution to their finances. They left for Schneeberg to find the little girls well and happy, stayed with Carl and Pauline for a few days, and returned to Leipzig to pick up the threads of their former life.

Yet nothing was quite the same. Given the profits of the Russian tour, and income from investments, carefully itemized in the household books, there was no financial reason for Schumann to continue work on the *New Journal*, which had become burdensome to him. In June, he handed editorial responsibilities to Oswald Lorenz. Despite the strains of the Russian tour, Clara hoped to arrange a tour of Belgium and England—another ambitious plan, which had to be postponed indefinitely when Clara discovered in early July that she was again pregnant.

Schumann fought off recurrent spells of ill health during the summer, turning restlessly from one project to another. He thought again of writing an opera based on Byron's *Corsair*, and sketched an overture and a few scenes. He taught a few lessons at the Leipzig Conservatory, where Clara was also invited to teach. According to later reports, Schumann's lessons consisted of listening quietly as his students played for him, and nodding appreciatively now and then. Mainly self-taught, and resistant to academic theory, he was not a born teacher of others, and his heart was elsewhere.

"Chorus Mysticus" *(Faust)*

A new project had been occupying Schumann's thoughts for some time—a setting of scenes from Goethe's *Faust*. He finished sketching three scenes at the end of August, writing in his diary that he was sacrificing his last powers to the task. He set the work aside, turning later to what would have been the final scene, the "Chorus Mysticus" that welcomes the spirit of Faust as he ascends to heaven. The final chorus of *Faust* was a natural extension of the heavenly choruses of *Peri*, but in a far more serious, tragic vein. This, too, Schumann left incomplete. The task he set himself was monumental, probably unachievable. The subject was to haunt his later years, complicated by his fears of inadequacy as he struggled to set Goethe's greatest work to music.

Schumann was drawn to the elements of Goethe's epic poem that spoke to his own ambition, his grievous faults and his struggle to overcome them—the weaknesses of his youth, his sexual lapses. In a way he was continuing the themes more lightly touched on in *Peri*, especially in the final scene, as the Peri is welcomed into heaven. But he had to postpone completing the work each time he returned to the task.

In the second week of September, hoping that a holiday would restore his spirits, Clara and Schumann took a vacation in the Harz Mountains, and the change of scene seemed to help. Returning to Leipzig on the 18th, Schumann wrote in his diary: "Now let heaven give me health and strength to return to work!" But his general condition worsened. In early October Robert alone traveled to Dresden, where he had an acute week-long attack of what he now referred to as his "nervous affliction." Along with a range of disabling symptoms, he suffered continuously from insomnia for eight nights. His condition was later described by Dr. Carl Helbig, the Dresden doctor he consulted: "As soon as he concerned himself with anything of a mental nature, he trembled, felt faint and cold in the feet, and was in an anxious state, with a particular fear of dying . . . He had a fear of high mountains and buildings, all metal objects, medicines, a fear of being poisoned. He suffered badly from insomnia, felt worst in the mornings." Schumann also recorded disturbances of sight and hearing; when he heard music, it "cut into him" like knives.

With Mendelssohn occupied in Berlin, life in Leipzig seemed less and less attractive to Schumann. The journal he had founded and edited for ten years had no further claim on him. He must have been bitterly disappointed to discover that his young friend Niels Gade had been asked to take Mendelssohn's place as conductor of the Gewandhaus Orchestra. Schumann had evidently not even been considered for the post. Dresden was a flourishing artistic center, with an active but undemanding musical life. Both Schumann and Clara had friends in the city and in the nearby countryside. Now that the families were reconciled, Wieck's presence in Dresden was no longer threatening, and might offer a form of support. Schumann had written regularly to Clara's father during the Russian tour, addressing him as "Papa." The decisive factor was probably the hydrotherapy for which the city was famed. The only useful advice Schumann had had from the doctors he consulted was one or another form of sea baths or mineral baths, still a common treatment for anxiety, or what used to be called a "nervous breakdown."

Before leaving for Dresden, the Schumanns attended a soiree at which Mendelssohn's Octet was performed. They were delighted by the playing of the twelve-year-old violinist Joseph Joachim, who was to prove a staunch friend in later years. Clara played the most technically difficult of Beethoven's piano concertos, the *Emperor*, at the Gewandhaus. On the 8th of December the Schumanns gave a farewell matinee at which Schumann's Piano Quartet was premiered, with Clara at the piano; she also performed Beethoven's *Waldstein* and *Appassionata* Sonatas.

A week later Schumann and Clara moved from Leipzig to Dresden, taking up residence in the garden flat of Waisenhausstrasse 6, near the Old Market, a fifteen-minute walk from the famous Brühl Terrace overlooking the Elbe. In the royal capital of Saxony, a city they already knew well, home of the ducal palace and the grand opera house, they hoped that Schumann would recover his health.

12

COLLAPSE AND RECOVERY

Dresden, December 1844–1847

The move to Dresden marked yet another major change in Schumann's life and work. After his marriage to Clara in 1840, his career had taken a new direction. Supported by Clara's ambition for him and her direct experience of concert audiences and managers, he was ready to make his name in the traditional forms of the great masters. He had turned first to symphonies, followed by string quartets and chamber music for piano and strings. Next came the prospect of oratorio, with Bach and Handel as models, leading to the "new genre" represented by *Paradise and the Peri,* his first major success.

In his composition of symphonies and chamber music, Beethoven's achievement towered over Schumann as a limitless resource and challenge: nine symphonies, sixteen string quartets, and virtually every other form of chamber music—piano trios, violin and cello sonatas, a quintet for piano and winds. Schumann knew Beethoven's only opera well; he had compared the overtures to *Fidelio* at length in his journal. He knew Beethoven's piano concertos, his violin concerto, his vocal works, his thirty-two piano sonatas.

Beethoven composed in all these genres with total authority, and he had transformed them with each new series of works. Schubert, working in Vienna in Beethoven's shadow, had also composed symphonies, piano sonatas, string quartets, two superb piano trios, and more than six hundred songs, his best-known legacy. Although many of Schubert's works remained unpublished until long after his death, Schumann had completely absorbed the works in print, and he reviewed the works published after Schubert's death as they appeared. Strangely, until he, too, was consumed by a songwriting fever, Schumann considered Schubert's songs less significant than his instrumental works. Reviewing their works regularly in his journal, Schumann regarded Beethoven as masculine, Schubert as feminine, much as Florestan and Eusebius represented divided and complementary natures. Bach alone he saw as a complete man, the source of all music. And it was Bach to whom he turned in his greatest need.

After Schumann fell seriously ill in the summer and fall of 1844, the doctors he consulted attributed his nervous collapse to overwork—specifically, to his intensive work on the "Chorus Mysticus" of *Faust*. In Dresden, Dr. Helbig prescribed complete rest from all mental activity, especially musical composition. In effect this led to a radical change in Schumann's approach to the writing of music and to his sense of his own contribution to the art.

So it seemed to Schumann himself, writing notes toward an autobiography, yet another example of his stock taking: "I used to write most, almost all, of even my shortest pieces in inspiration, many composed with unbelievable swiftness—my Symphony no. 1 in B-flat Major in four days, as was a *Liederkreis* of twenty pieces; the *Peri* too was composed in a relatively short time. Only from the year 1845, when I began to imagine and to work out everything in my head, did a completely new manner of composing begin to develop."

Although Schumann suffered from long spells of illness in 1845, he was determined to keep working, to cure his suffering through his own efforts. Disregarding Dr. Helbig's insistence on complete rest, he turned to his usual resource in times of stress, the works of Bach: *The Well-Tempered Clavier,* the Preludes and Fugues for organ, and *The Art of Fugue,* a comprehensive exploration of every possible form of fugue and canon. Schumann's study of counterpoint was an instinctive effort to calm his persistent agitation of mind and body. He sensed that the strict musical forms of canon and fugue might counteract the chaos, disorder, and confusion of his mind.

The relatively simple requirements of canon, with a theme repeated at regular intervals, and the more elaborate forms of fugue evidently helped to calm his anxiety. The mathematical challenge was like solving a puzzle, another exercise known to calm the nerves.*

Six Fugues on B-A-C-H; Six Canonic Etudes

It was natural that Schumann would combine his contrapuntal studies with compositions of his own. This is when his "new manner of composing" began. He walked about rather than sitting at the piano or his desk, "working out" music in his head. But inspiration remained central to all his compositions. It is the inspirational element—the play of fantasy, improvisation—that comes across most powerfully in his later as in his earlier works.

In February he composed two fugues in D minor, adding two more in March, noting "fugue passion" in his household book. In April he began a joint study with Clara of Cherubini's *Treatise on Counterpoint and Fugue*.

Clara, too, studying alongside Schumann, composed three preludes and fugues, published as her op. 16. They show her gift for melodic themes and effortless development, but they stay well within a conventional Romantic idiom. Schumann's Four Fugues, op. 72, are far more experimental. A unified set, they are closely related by key and organized in contrasting tempo and mood, moving from the first two, in D minor, to a strange, melancholy fugue in F minor, ending with a cheerful fugue in F major. Schumann considered these pieces to be more than mere formal exercises. He saw them as "character pieces," the same term he used for Bach's fugues. They were as poetic as songs with or without words, works of art expressing contrasting states of mind and feeling.

Schumann had suggested to Clara just after their marriage that they work through all forty-eight preludes and fugues of *The*

---

* Schumann's instincts have been confirmed by modern studies of the effect of music on the brain. It seems possible that music can encourage damaged neural connections to re-form or to be bypassed, possibly triggering a chemical affecting the emotional state of the patient.

Well-Tempered Clavier in order, taking a new prelude and fugue each day. Now it was Bach's *Art of Fugue* which claimed his attention. Bach inserted in his final fugue a four-note theme inscribing the musical letters of his own name: B (B-flat), A, C, H (B-natural)—a form of musical play very dear to Schumann. In early April he composed the first of his Six Fugues on B-A-C-H—the musical letters of the composer Schumann revered above all others. Two fugues were finished in April; four more in September and October. The full set was published the following year as Six Fugues on the Name BACH, for Organ or Pianoforte with Pedal.

The challenge was immense, very much in the spirit of Bach's *Art of Fugue*. Each fugue began with the same initial subject, ingeniously varied by altering rhythm and register, with countersubjects gradually introduced. Schumann responded to the limitations of a four-note theme much as he did to the four notes of "Asch" in *Carnaval*. The four notes spelling "Bach" constituted an even more alluring challenge, moving by semitones around B-flat, thus inevitably (and gratifyingly) chromatic.*

All but one of the six fugues are in B-flat; the melancholy Fugue no. 3 is in its relative, G minor. There are no marked key changes, but a new variation of the theme in no. 4 invites an even higher level of chromaticism, leading to a greatly extended development. A series of sustained climaxes gives this central fugue an intensely Romantic character. Fugue no. 5 offers relief in a *lebhaft* staccato piece, returning in Fugue no. 6 to the baroque seriousness of the opening fugue.

When Bach introduced the musical version of his own name in *The Art of Fugue*, he initiated a variation that he left unfinished at his death. It was said at the time that Bach died with his pen in hand. By taking Bach's final theme as the subject of his own *B-A-C-H* fugues, Schumann was continuing Bach's unfinished labor and bringing it to a satisfying conclusion of his own. The work is composed with

---

* The four notes spelling BACH are only one whole note below the opening subject of the great C-sharp Minor Fugue of book 1 of *The Well-Tempered Clavier,* which Schumann must also have had in his mind.

the same care for organization that marks Schumann's song cycles and piano suites. The substantial fugues that open and close the set provided a satisfying frame. The set as a whole explores all the possibilities of a fugal treatment of the simple four-note theme. Each set of two fugues has its own character and form, with the final fugue, the longest (in time), a grand summation of the whole.

Schumann wrote to a friend that he believed these fugues would be regarded as his most enduring work. They are demanding pieces, formally correct, but intensely poetic. For their grand style Schumann probably had not only Bach's fugues in mind, but also Mendelssohn's Six Preludes and Fugues, about which Mendelssohn had consulted Schumann a few years before. Although he knew Bach's works intimately, Mendelssohn composed his preludes and fugues in his own Romantic idiom. Schumann's works make a suggestive companion study. Limited to fugues alone, without introductory preludes, they observe the form closely, but with an expressive freedom marking them as distinctly "Schumannesque," just as Mendelssohn's works are unmistakably "Mendelssohnian."

In late April 1845, Schumann noted with delight the arrival of a special sixteen-foot pedal which was to be attached to his own piano, two octaves long and worked by the feet, like an organ pedal. The pedal piano, as it was known, was not new. Bach owned one, as did Mozart. The adapted instrument offered a three-staff alternative to the usual treble and bass staffs of most keyboard music. This meant that the canonic or fugal subject and its variations could move freely from one register to the next and down to the lowest register, provided by the pedals, for added support and sonority. Schumann tried out the possibilities of his new toy with a set of "sketches" for pedal piano. He soon moved on to Six Etudes in Canonic Form, works which have remained in the piano repertoire even after the disappearance of their original inspiration.

Canons follow a simpler form than fugues, with the themes repeated note for note by each voice as it enters, a fifth, an octave, or another interval higher or lower. But as usual, Schumann develops the form in his own way. Like the *B-A-C-H* fugues, the canons were composed in pairs. The first two, in A minor and its relative major,

C, observe the canonic form fairly strictly. Nos. 3 and 4 are developed with greater freedom and inventiveness. No. 5 is in a charming staccato B minor, with no. 6 a contrasting, reflective adagio in B major. The canonic themes are usually written on the upper staffs, for the piano keyboard, with the pedal providing harmonic support, only occasionally picking up the canonic theme. The entire set is in turn tender or melancholy, always expressive. The studies have been performed and recorded on organ, but they are far more pianistic, with bass accompaniments to the canonic lines coloring their lyricism. They were given new life by Georges Bizet, who arranged them for piano four hands in 1873, and by Debussy, who arranged them for two pianos in 1891. Both composers (along with Fauré and Ravel) were among Schumann's most devoted advocates in France. Bizet's *Jeux d'enfants* and Debussy's *Children's Corner* were inspired by Schumann's *Kinderszenen,* as was Ravel's *Mother Goose,* originally composed for piano duet.

The fugues and canons Schumann composed at this time were therapeutic, a source of private pleasure, an extension of his love of counterpoint. In periods of relative health, he also wrote for the public. In June and July he added two movements to the Phantasie for Piano and Orchestra, which he had composed in 1841, the year after his marriage. It had been his happiest time, when he was most inspired, most productive. He failed to find a publisher for the Phantasie when it was first composed, but it now served wonderfully as the first movement of a new piano concerto.

Piano Concerto in A Minor

The Piano Concerto in A Minor is one of Schumann's most popular works, a favorite for pianists and audiences. It has the charm of his early piano writing, enhanced by the continuing dialogue between piano and orchestra. Although Schumann revised the earlier one-movement Phantasie in a few places, he retained its lyrical, improvisatory feeling. It opens as if announcing a virtuoso display, perhaps following the heroic example of Beethoven's *Emperor* Concerto—a piano flourish introducing the principal subject, proposed by the woodwinds. But Schumann deliberately eschewed the shallow virtuosity of concertos by his contemporaries. Marked Allegro affettuoso, the woodwind theme is quiet, tender, free from display. The piano repeats the theme in its own lyrical voice, after which it accompanies the strings in a new development, with the feeling of a free, spontaneous impulse.

Both in its original one-movement form and as a full-length concerto, the work was written for Clara and for her special gifts as a pianist—lightness of touch, singing tone, complete technical fluency in the service of instinctive musicality. The A-minor key has special associations with Clara, and the opening theme also seems to be singing her name, echoing the first three notes of the descending scale common to Schumann's piano sonatas and the C Major Fantasie. The theme returns in an Andante in A-flat major over a new arpeggiated accompaniment, answered in canon by a solo clarinet. It is as if the pianist is saying: "Let us hear how my lovely theme changes in this form, in virtually the same notes, but with an altogether different feeling." The theme then returns in an Allegro recapitulation in A major, another demonstration of its emotional range. Schumann was still painting "Clara" in every conceivable way, writing piano works in her keys (A minor, A-flat major, A major), reinventing her themes, singing and even spelling her name. Unlike the troubled agitation of the Fantasie in C—Schumann's "long lament for Clara," composed during their separation—Clara's portrait in the Piano Concerto is suffused with the happiness of their marriage. In its original form, it is a work of youth, his and hers, joined at last in the most enduring of unions, engaged in delightful dialogue, each responding to the other, as pianist and orchestra converse, confirming each other's thoughts, providing additional comments, new ideas.

A draft setting of a Rückert canon casts interesting light on the composition of the earlier Phantasie for Piano and Orchestra and its A-flat-major Andante section. In January 1841 Schumann had copied out a dozen poems by Friedrich Rückert from a much larger collection called *Liebesfrühling* (Springtime of Love), a radiant affirmation of the mutual love of the poet and his young wife. Schumann proposed that he and Clara each compose song settings of the poems, to be published together. The Rückert texts appealed to Schumann as the image of his own happy marriage. When he was putting together the Rückert poems for Clara to study, Schumann drafted a canon for soprano and tenor of one of the poems, "Ich bin dein Baum" (I Am Your Tree). Drafted in March 1841, the canon was probably intended for the joint collection of songs by husband and wife, but was set aside with only thirty-six bars of the duet and four bars of a piano accompaniment written down. In May 1841, when Schumann began work on the Phantasie for Piano and Orchestra, he used the opening bars of the canon for the Andante section of what was later to become the first movement of the Piano Concerto. The tender words of the poem underlie the duet between piano and clarinet that opens the Andante section: "I am your tree, O gardener, whose faith holds me in love's bonds and sweet tenderness; I am your gardener, O tree of faith."

The image of tree and gardener, mutually dependent, loyal, faithful, perfectly suited the vows Schumann and Clara had sworn to each other, to be faithful unto death. The words were unnecessary; the music said all.

To turn the one-movement Phantasie into a piano concerto required two more movements. Schumann had already done something of the kind for the earlier Fantasie in C, when he decided to turn it into a three-movement homage to Beethoven. He began the revision in June by composing a buoyant rondo to serve as a final movement. For its opening theme he wrote an upbeat A-major variation of the poignant A-minor theme of the original one-movement Phantasie. The development of the new rondo gives full rein to Clara's gifts, with arpeggios flying up and down the piano, and *fortissimo* octave scale passages. Each time a phrase is repeated, it adds new meaning, new coloring. It often seems as if it is not the composer but the pianist who is improvising, unwilling to let go of a joyful sequence, a delicious melody. At the end, the composer outdoes himself and his beloved pianist with an extended *brillante* conclusion, calculated to send an audience into rapturous applause. Schumann wrote an interlude which became the second movement, skillfully linking the first movement and the third, appropriately called Intermezzo. Its lyrical poignancy could have been credited to Eusebius in his most intimate mood. Clara loved the concerto, which showed off every aspect of her musicianship. She soon arranged its premiere in Dresden and played it again at the New Year's concert in Leipzig. It remains to this day a joyful expression of love between a supremely gifted composer and an artist of the first rank, delighting listeners at the time and ever since.

In August Schumann felt well enough to consider attending a Beethoven festival in Bonn. He wrote to Mendelssohn after a long silence, suggesting that he and Clara might visit Mendelssohn in Frankfurt, en route to the festival. His letter reflects the fragility of someone slowly recovering from a dark period.

> Dear Mendelssohn,
>
> Perhaps we'll see one another soon . . . Do you think of us still in friendship? Might we visit you? Ah, I have much to tell you—what a terrible winter I had, how a complete nervous illness, bringing with it an assault of terrible thoughts, brought me to the edge of despair . . . and that things are looking better, and music also beginning to sound within . . . and that I hope to be entirely healed soon. But of all this I will bravely keep silent [a reference to his reputation for remaining silent in company]. We would like to know what you have been working at. We know about Oedipus, the organ sonatas, and a new oratorio. [This was *Elijah*, Mendelssohn's crowning achievement.] I can show you very little—I've held back. But inwardly I feel I must not remain still as a musician—a glimmer sometimes kindles inspiration. I long to recover my full powers soon, and to be able to work with new vigor.
>
> Farewell, my honored Mendelssohn, and tell me soon with a word whether you still think of me kindly.

Mendelssohn wrote back at once, expressing deep concern and assuring Schumann of his enduring esteem and affection.

> It was a great joy for me at last to see your dear well-known hand again, and to hear from you that you still think of me in our old friendship! I hardly need to tell you in words how I sympathize with everything you achieve in the world and in music . . . And so the news of your serious illness . . . greatly moved and troubled me, for I thought of you cheerfully working away, as I was working happily away . . . and to think of you in reality suffering such illness . . . Thank God that you tell me you are feeling better—that is the main thing . . . I hope above all that we can see each other, and speak together. Let us not fail to meet.

A recurrence of illness meant abandoning all thought of attending the Beethoven festival on the Rhine. Schumann described his symptoms in his diary: "Tendency to dizziness. Fear and unrest mainly in hands and feet—jerking in the limbs—not much appetite—weak pulse, easily excitable—pains at various points in the head—not strong but causing anxiety." Instead, Schumann and Clara traveled to Weimar and Rudolfstadt, paying homage to Goethe and Schiller. They returned home sooner than they had planned.

Clara knew that her presence was the key to Schumann's continued well-being. But there were unavoidable separations. In October she agreed to give the first performance of a new piano concerto by Henselt at the Leipzig Gewandhaus, under Mendelssohn's direction. Schumann remained in Dresden with the children, too unwell to join her. She wrote to him the day after she arrived in Leipzig:

> My dear Robert,
> Now let us both sit beside each other! How are you, my dear one? How painful it was to say goodbye yesterday—it was long before I could calm myself, and I came here feeling so melancholy . . . I found a bed all made up for me here, but I was alone, and hardly slept all night, always thinking

of you. Oh, Robert, what is my life even for an hour without you? Nothing! I love you so indescribably—you must hear this from me again and again.

Clara ends the letter: "I can only grieve to think of you and your solitude, and surely you also long a little for—your *Alter* [old friend]." She continues with good advice: "The weather is so wonderful! Do not work, you can work in bad weather! Do as I say, my dear Robert, and think that you do this for me and for your children."

Clara's letter crossed with one from Robert: "My dear Klara, If you were only with me again! I had not thought myself so weak, I am so used to you now, you are missed everywhere, and by the children too. Come back soon—you are my support, my joy." The next day, after he received Clara's letter, he responded to her advice: "I cannot work—all peace is gone, and I look for you in every room—You are my peace" (quoting the Schubert song "Du bist die Ruh").

They exchanged similar anguished letters each time they were separated, even for a day or two. Schumann longed unbearably for Clara during her absence; Clara was all too aware of his vulnerable state. Much of the music composed in Dresden reflects Schumann's dependence on Clara, his need for her, his fear of losing his ability to work, his determination not to be felled by his recurrent anxiety.

Symphony in C

Even while he was fighting his illness by composing fugues and canons during the first months of 1845, Schumann began to have "symphonic thoughts." At the end of the year, these turned into "symphoniaca" and "symphonic fever," those familiar signs of intensive work.

In the distance he heard C major in horns and trombones. And so a new symphony took shape. On the page, the distant motif became the introduction to the first movement of a C Major Symphony. A horn call sounds over a melancholy sequence of sixths in steady motion in the strings, while the call of horns and trombones announces something new on the horizon ... perhaps returning health. The evocative introduction resembles the introduction to the

D Minor Symphony, now abandoned, also featuring horns signaling above a sequence of slowly moving sixths. Although Schumann had set the D Minor Symphony aside, perhaps he was unwilling to relinquish its opening bars, so he reused or adapted them. As in his B-A-C-H fugues, what seems to be repeated is actually varied in a subtle way, and the sequence of sixths in the C Major Symphony, under the combined horn/trumpet/trombone summons, has a new direction, far more tragic in C major than the similar sequence was in D minor.

Schumann's notes suggest that he was writing as quickly as he had in the past, working joyfully, day after day. The first movement was "almost ready" on the 17th of December; the second-movement Scherzo was sketched on the 18th and 19th; the tragic Adagio espressivo begun on the 21st, and the Allegro molto vivace finale sketched on the 25th and 26th. The symphony was "just about ready" on the 28th. It had been fully sketched in about two weeks. A month's pause followed, with orchestration begun on the 12th of February, 1846, soon after the birth of a first son, Emil. (Sadly, he was never robust, and lived only for a year and a half.) Significant works heard in performance at around this time included Beethoven's Missa Solemnis, Mozart's *Magic Flute*, and Wagner's *Tannhäuser*.

Mendelssohn visited in late March, worried about his friend and colleague. In July, Schumann and Clara went to the island of Norderney, famous for its many spas, for three weeks of sea baths. They left Dresden for Leipzig, where Schumann spent time with Mendelssohn, recording in his diary: "his 'Robert' "—the first name was a sign of their new intimacy, although it did not move on to an exchange of "Du." He and Mendelssohn discussed *Tristan and Isolde*, an epic poem by the dramatist and novelist Karl Immermann, as a possible subject for opera. (Wagner anticipated them, as he did with the Nibelung saga, also considered by both Schumann and Mendelssohn.) Robert and Clara went on to Hamburg, where they heard Jenny Lind as Donna Anna in *Don Giovanni*, their first meeting with the "Swedish Nightingale," who was to become a close friend. They traveled next to Bremen, reaching Norderney on July 28 for a daily course of sea baths, in which Clara participated. Schumann recorded being dreadfully bored by the therapeutic regime. They left Norderney three weeks later, arriving back in Dresden in late August. Schumann wrote in his diary: "now onward [i.e. back to work], with God's help." Their new lodgings were more capacious, better for work—which meant putting the C Major Symphony into final form. Schumann worked steadily on the orchestration in September, finishing the symphony in October.

According to his first biographer, Wilhelm Joseph von Wasielewski, who knew Schumann well in his last years, the C Major Symphony is "more mature, masculine and powerful, more profound than the B-flat and D Minor Symphonies of 1841." Schumann wrote in a more personal vein to Mendelssohn: "I sketched it out while suffering severe physical pain; I may well call it the struggle of my mind, by which I sought to beat off my disease." Of Schumann's four symphonies, it remains the most problematic, with some conductors and critics regarding it as his greatest work, others regarding it as seriously flawed.

The first movement is agitated, even distraught in feeling. The solemn, tragic introduction could be read as an indication of Schumann's mental struggle at the time. The Allegro picks up the call of the horns and trombones, as a rhythmic "cell" which soon becomes unrelenting. The few passages of relief seem compelled, as if the strain were simply too great to be continued. Then the hammering rhythm starts up again, is repeated, ascending step by step, until the body (the orchestra) can ascend no higher, must pause at the summit, and descend. The second-movement Scherzo is equally driven, with relief provided by two contrasting trios. Then inspiration takes over, and the third-movement Adagio is one of the most moving of Schumann's slow movements, heartbreaking, almost unbearable. The lyrical theme is repeated in every guise, by each instrument and group of instruments, given new coloring, ever greater pathos. It is a cry of the soul, never resolved, sustained to the end. It seems to be an unmediated expression of the suffering Schumann was experiencing.

Schumann wrote to Mendelssohn that it was only in the finale that he began to feel like himself. Marked Allegro molto vivace, it transforms the agitated thematic material of the opening Allegro into an optimistic conclusion, cheerfully diatonic, signifying harmonic reconciliation and returning health.

In response to Schumann's account of his troubled year, Mendelssohn assured the ailing composer repeatedly of his high regard for his fellow artist and friend, for the man and his musical works. Mendelssohn instinctively recognized aspects of Schumann that resonated with his own experience—his need for recognition, his perpetual insecurity. Clara, driven by ambition for the husband she revered, underestimated his weaknesses. She knew he was one of the most original composers of the time, the equal of Mendelssohn and Chopin, superior to Liszt, Berlioz, Wagner, and the shallow virtuoso composers she had often performed to general acclaim. She could not understand why the wider world was so slow to recognize his genius.

Writing frequently to Schumann, Mendelssohn ended each letter with the hope that Schumann was better. He trusted that Schumann still thought of Mendelssohn "in unchanged friendship." In his letters Schumann harks back to their early meetings, as if in his weakened state he is trying to hold on to the past. He writes: "Really, couldn't we write to one another from time to time without a specific reason? If our friendship were wine, then it would now be a good vintage (ten years ago today we were in the Rosenthal)." Mendelssohn echoes Schumann's words, as if soothing an invalid: "Yes indeed, I agree with you, it should not be tedious business alone that makes us write." He hopes that Schumann can attend the rehearsal in which Clara was to play the Henselt concerto: "then perhaps in the afternoon we can play chess in the Rosenthal as in December—ten years ago!"

Mendelssohn did everything in his power to promote Schumann's works. He scheduled a revival of the *Spring* Symphony in October, thanking Schumann for "the great many hours of joy" it had given him again, "as if for the first time." Schumann was too ill to attend, but wrote to Mendelssohn, imagining the performance, ending his letter: "If only I might stand before you in person tomorrow evening with my faults and clumsy manners, but also with a heart that wishes for your affection above all others."

Mendelssohn responded: "Thank you (and so heartily!) for your dear, dear letter . . . for everything you have ever said and written to me, but above all thank you for remaining true to me!"

When Schumann added two movements to create his Piano Concerto in A Minor, Mendelssohn urged Clara to set a date for a Leipzig premiere, which took place at the New Year's concert in 1846. He suggested to Clara that she include one of Schumann's works along with the short pieces by Mendelssohn and Chopin that usually made up her solos at Gewandhaus concerts. He asked about a possible performance of Schumann's setting of scenes from Goethe's *Faust;* Schumann explained that the pages were still lying on his desk.

Finally Schumann told Mendelssohn that his C Major Symphony was finished and ready for performance. Mendelssohn scheduled its premiere for the 5th of November, 1846. He hoped to pair the symphony with Bach's Triple Concerto, with Clara as one of the pianists. But a third pianist was not available, and he revised his plans, substituting Rossini's *William Tell* Overture, always popular with audiences.

The premiere of Schumann's new symphony was a disaster. Mixed reviews in the Leipzig newspapers blamed deliberate mismanagement on Mendelssohn's part. The response to the *William Tell* Overture was so enthusiastic that Mendelssohn repeated it. Critics claimed the audience was so exhausted by the time Schumann's symphony was performed that they were completely unable to appreciate it.

Mendelssohn scheduled a second performance, inviting Clara to perform his own G Minor Piano Concerto after the interval. Meanwhile, Schumann revised the symphony extensively. Mendelssohn arranged two rehearsals, and the performance ten days after the premiere, on the 16th of November, was warmly received. The reviewer of the *New Journal for Music* wrote a long, appreciative account, singling out Mendelssohn's conducting for special praise. But Leipzig's daily newspapers had been attacking Mendelssohn in anonymous letters charged with anti-Semitism. One correspondent asked if the reason for repeating the *William Tell* Overture was "outer" or "inner," implying that Mendelssohn was (in Jewish fashion) indulging his vanity. A second writer proposed that the main reason for the repeat was "purely 'Mosaic'"—implying that like all Jews, Mendelssohn was motivated by self-interest. Schumann wrote anonymously in defense of the performance, praising conductor and orchestra in the highest terms.

Many years later, mutual friends, including Ferdinand Hiller and Ignaz Moscheles, expressed surprise that Schumann was hardly mentioned in Mendelssohn's published correspondence. Evidently Mendelssohn had little sense of camaraderie for the fellow artist who worshipped him. Estrangement seemed confirmed by the publication of a letter Mendelssohn wrote to his close friend the London diplomat Karl Klingemann, who had asked Mendelssohn to recommend a student to Clara Schumann. Mendelssohn wrote back that he was unable to do so. "Her husband has behaved very ambiguously to me (or worse than that)—and has circulated a truly hateful story about me—about which I shall say no more—which has damnably cooled my former zeal to help him on . . . More in person."

The "ambiguous" behavior probably refers to the anti-Semitic attacks in the Leipzig newspapers, which Mendelssohn must have attributed to Schumann or to a Schumann claque. Hence his anger at the fellow composer whom, as he wrote to Klingemann, he had done so much to help. And hence the absence of references to Schumann in the correspondence later published by Mendelssohn's family, which was coedited by Klingemann.

Were there possible grounds for Mendelssohn's suspicion of the friend to whom he had sworn undying friendship? Perhaps there had been an incident, though nothing specific is mentioned in Mendelssohn's letters or Schumann's diaries.

Mendelssohn might also have had personal reasons for his quick anger. Friends commented on his extreme irritability and touchiness in the last year of his life. Ferdinand Hiller mentioned a similar estrangement, for unspecified "social" reasons. In a letter written only a few months before his death, Mendelssohn told Klingemann that he was his only true friend—a sign of Mendelssohn's feeling of isolation at the time, when he was convinced that his mission in life would never be achieved. He was frustrated by the continuing bureaucracy in Berlin, and consumed by the difficulties of revising *Elijah*. Its central figure is a prophet crying in the wilderness, whose despairing aria, "Es ist genug," recalls Bach's *Passion* music. Prince Albert, attending the premiere in Birmingham in April, detected a self-portrait of the composer in the searing work.

For Mendelssohn, who ended his intimate letters "Remain true to me," disloyalty was unforgivable. Yet just as he refused to write to the press to clear his name, he was too proud to accuse Schumann of the offense of which Schumann was probably unaware. It was a sad ending to what had become an intimate friendship between the two leading composers of the age. Schumann continued to regard Mendelssohn as his ally against a musical establishment intent on wrecking everything they both had fought to achieve.

On November 26, a week after the second performance of the C Major Symphony, Schumann and Clara left home for a major concert tour of Prague and Vienna. They hoped that in addition to Clara's concerts, Schumann's *Spring* Symphony and *Paradise and the Peri* would be performed. The two older children, Marie and Elise, traveled with them for the first time. They went first to Prague by post wagon, then by train to Vienna, where Clara had triumphed years before as a young prodigy in white, a golden bow in her dark hair. Schumann must have pushed aside unhappy memories of his time in the Austrian capital, when he had struggled in vain against intrenched bureaucracy. But Vienna was still its own world, subject to fashion, fickle and hostile to ambitious provincial newcomers—which included Schumann, whose music was still relatively unknown there. Clara, though only twenty-five, was no longer the "shepherd child" praised by Grillparzer; she was now a mature woman dressed in sober black, worn out by childbirth. The Viennese cafés no longer served *torte à la Wieck*. Schumann's music and Clara's playing both met with a lukewarm response from audiences and critics. The happiest time they had was with Jenny Lind, whom

Schumann described as a complete artist; he had never before heard his songs sung with such natural understanding. She spoke of Mendelssohn as "the purest and most refined of all artists." Mendelssohn had spoken of her to Schumann in similar terms.

The famous young singer and Clara became friends at once, and when Lind offered to join in Clara's fourth and final concert, the hall was sold out and the audience ecstatic. She sang Schumann's "Der Nussbaum," and he wrote in his diary that he would never forget her wonderful rendition of the song. But "Der Nussbaum" and one of his early Fantasy Pieces ("Traumes Wirren"), which Clara played, were the only works by Schumann performed. Prague was far more receptive to the artist couple; a well-received concert there featured the Piano Quintet and two groups of his songs. From Prague the Schumanns went to Berlin, where he conducted *Paradise and the Peri* and they spent time with Mendelssohn's sister Fanny Hensel. Mendelssohn was still in Leipzig, having conducted what would be his last Gewandhaus concerts. He was soon to leave for England and the premiere of *Elijah*. The high soprano solo of the Angel who calls on the despairing Elijah to "arise" and stand before his Lord was composed with Jenny Lind in mind.

Schumann and Clara returned home in March, exhausted after four months of travel. Schumann remained under medical care, taking mineral baths as prescribed. There was no thought of returning to Leipzig. Schumann pursued the idea of a *Kränzchen*, a small musical circle of friends, possibly including Wieck, who had become a frequent visitor, and Ferdinand Hiller. Schumann dreamed of setting up a series of subscription concerts on the model of Leipzig's Gewandhaus concerts. As his health improved, he began to think again of writing chamber music.

Piano Trios

In June, Schumann composed the first of two piano trios, with Clara's special qualities as a pianist always in mind. A year before, Clara had composed a Piano Trio in G Minor, which was later performed on its own and alongside Schumann's; her work has recently re-entered the piano-trio repertoire. As Schumann's three string quartets were indebted to Mendelssohn's earlier example, and dedicated to him, so his new piano trio reflected Schumann's love of Mendelssohn's two piano trios, composed only two years before, and often performed by Clara. In his own D Minor Piano Trio Schumann echoes the opening bars of Mendelssohn's D Minor Trio, note for note, as if one friend is paying tribute to the other in his own style.

Like Mendelssohn's trios, Schumann's works have entered the repertoire, adding new dimensions to the groundbreaking piano trios of Beethoven and Schubert. Both trios reflect the "fugue fever" of Schumann's first year in Dresden, with a liberal use of canonic imitation distributed among the three instruments. Unlike Mendelssohn's piano trios, composed with his usual care and close revision, Schumann's works were written at speed. At the time and even in our own day, they are sometimes seen as flawed, marred by repetition. But they are works of great energy and beauty, with memorable themes, slow movements of heart-wrenching poignancy, lyrical writing for violin and cello over dramatic piano accompaniments. Each trio is ingeniously constructed, with an array of interrelated themes, their connections not always obvious on first hearing. They reveal a composer working out his own material with the skill acquired from close study of the masters. As with so many of Schumann's works, they require from performers a sensitive combination of Romantic feeling, freedom, tenderness, and an understanding of Schumann's special forms of musical structure.

Schumann departs from his models almost at once. In the D Minor Trio, midway in the opening movement, there is suddenly a mysterious sequence in which violin and cello softly play a slow theme close to the bridge, over high *pianissimo* piano triplets, *una corda* (with the soft pedal down). The effect suggests the "voice from afar" in the *Davidsbündlertänze* or the eighth *Novellette*, with the suggestion of a chorale realized when the piano plays the theme in solemn chords toward the end of the movement. The passage signals that nothing is going to be quite the same. A demonic scherzo picks up the rhythmic second theme of the first movement, driving it to excess, as if in memory of the frantic sleigh rides of the Russian tour. It yields to a slow movement that is one of Schumann's most original and disturbing compositions. It seems a new departure in its sustained dissonance. Built on a wandering string melody, it is really a violin recitative, with cello support, over harmonies that have no obvious progression, no clear resolution. A middle section relaxes into a recognizable key, but soon yields to a réworking of the fluid, unresolved opening section. Schumann is suddenly writing music of the future. Even now, after the experiments of Anton Webern and Alban Berg, it is a tragic, profoundly unsettling movement, and one wonders what audiences of the time made of it. Yet the trio as a whole is beautifully constructed, its themes intricately related one to another. The long opening phrase of the slow movement imitates in its shape and rhythm the opening theme of the first movement, supported on its first appearance by a perfectly recognizable harmonic sequence. Similarly, the buoyant D-major finale—an exuberant proof of the composer's knowledge of the rules of harmony—is also a recognizable variation of the same theme.

The trio was presented to Clara on her birthday and played through with friends. But her favorite was the Second Trio, in F major, composed during the autumn. Schumann himself described it as "friendlier" in spirit, and in its structure and "working out" it is more immediately comprehensible than the D Minor Trio.

The first movement, in the "friendly" key of F major, is exuberant, exciting, a declaration of returning confidence. In case there might be any doubt about the impetus informing the trio, a gentle piano accompaniment in C major introduces a theme that closely echoes the second song in the Eichendorff *Liederkreis,* "Dein Bildnis wunderselig / Hab' ich im Herzengrund" (Your wonderful image is enshrined in my heart). It was a private message to Clara, played in canon by the strings over broken chords in the piano, returning once more and repeated at the end of the movement. It is central to the trio much as the quotation from Beethoven's *An die ferne Geliebte* is central to the C Major Fantasie. The andante opens with a variant of the same theme in D-flat, now continuing its downward motion over a tender piano triplet accompaniment. The song is echoed again in the third movement, and another variant appears in the finale, affirming that Clara's image is central to the composer and to every aspect of his music.

The Andante movement is one of Schumann's most inspired lyrical creations—a reminder that joy and sorrow are inextricably paired. One poignant theme follows another, each intensely expressive, the three voices now accompanying one another, now urging a new thought, reminding one another of their earlier conversation, coming together in a new development, a new key, a new rhythm, developed and fully realized, until the players return to their first thoughts. The effect is of an intimate conversation overheard, three close friends supporting one another in shared melancholy, shared longing. The Andante is followed by a more hopeful version of similar thoughts, a dancelike variation in the minor form of the same key. A falling fifth seems to sing "Clara," another echo of the Eichendorff song quoted in the opening movement and varied in the Andante. A final movement restores sanity and good humor, proof that all may yet be well in this most imperfect of worlds.

It was at about this time—during the summer and autumn of 1847—that Schumann finally began to receive substantial signs of public recognition. After he sold the *New Journal for Music*, the editor, Franz Brendel, his former assistant, wrote a series of essays comparing Schumann and Mendelssohn, arguing that while Mendelssohn represented the best of the past, Schumann was forging an original style appropriate for the new age. The essays were flattering to Schumann, but their influence was chiefly limited to musical circles in Leipzig, where both Schumann and Mendelssohn were well-known figures, and Schumann's music was frequently performed in public concerts and private soirees.

In July 1847, the Zwickau organist Johann Kuntsch, Schumann's first teacher, invited the Schumanns for a two-week festival in Zwickau celebrating the composer and his artist wife. They were greeted in Schumann's hometown with a torchlight parade and an evening serenade. Two days of concerts, one in the open air, featured Schumann's new C Major Symphony and his Piano Concerto, with Clara at the piano, also a "Song of Farewell," setting a poem by Rückert for chorus and winds. (The text of the poem, also set by Mendelssohn, is a farewell to everything the poet loves—uncannily prescient.) The concerts were enthusiastically received, and Schumann was celebrated in the Saxon town of his birth as one of their own. According to the report in the *New Journal*, four thousand people assembled to praise the noble pair. It was a true "people's festival," lasting well into the night. But the wider world was still slow to respond.

Mendelssohn's beloved sister Fanny died suddenly of a stroke in May 1847, aged forty-one. It was a blow from which Mendelssohn was unable to recover. He sought refuge in Switzerland with his wife, Cécile, their children, and his brother Paul's family. His anguish found expression in his F-sharp Minor String Quartet. It is music of startling modernity, a dramatic contrast to the sunny charm of his earlier works in its unremitting intensity, its prolonged dissonance. In November, only a few months after Fanny's death, the composer who had enjoyed the adulation of music lovers throughout Europe died after a series of strokes, aged thirty-eight.

When he heard the news of Mendelssohn's death, Schumann was devastated. He traveled at once to Leipzig to be one of the pallbearers, as Mendelssohn's coffin was borne to the train for the final trip to Berlin. He was to be buried next to Fanny.

Soon afterwards, Schumann set down his memories of his first meetings with Mendelssohn in 1835, when the new music director had taken up his post in Leipzig. Schumann consulted his diaries to record Mendelssohn's conversation, his thoughts about life, music, and marriage, his performances on piano and organ and as a conductor, his occasional fits of temper, his many virtues as an artist and as a man. Apart from Schumann's relationship with Clara and her redoubtable father, his friendship with Mendelssohn had been the most profound and rewarding of his adult life. He had no idea of the bitterness with which Mendelssohn had turned against him.

He expressed his loss a year later in a song without words in Mendelssohn's style, which he published in his *Album for the Young*, entitled *"Erinnerung"* (Remembrance), with the date of Mendelssohn's death—7 November 1847. It makes a touching companion piece to the song that opens the collection of *Songs Without Words* that Mendelssohn dedicated to Clara, at a time when both composers were at their peak.

13

RETURNING HEALTH, HIGH AMBITIONS

Dresden, 1848–August 1850

Schumann had many masks, and his true self was multilayered, always in process of discovery. He presented himself in different ways in his confessional letters to Clara before their marriage, in his heartfelt letters to Mendelssohn, in his intimate diaries. He was seen in different ways by family, friends, and colleagues, as their reports at the time and later testify.

When Schumann applied for a doctorate from the University of Jena in 1839, desperate to present himself as a suitable husband for Clara, he summarized his artistic life as he wanted it to be seen by the professional world. In the self-portrait he had offered to Gottlob Wiedebein ten years earlier, he described himself as an untutored youth writing purely from his heart. As a candidate for a doctorate, he compared himself favorably to Mendelssohn, a composer attached to the past, and to Chopin, a truly original composer. Schumann, in contrast, straddled the past and the future. Like Mendelssohn, he studied the past as a foundation for his own work, but he was also original—implicitly describing himself as a figure superior to the most prominent musicians of the age. His account of his studies shows considerable rewriting: "In 1828 I entered the Leipzig University, chiefly for the purpose of hearing Professor [Wilhelm Traugott] Krug's philosophical lectures. In 1829, I went to Heidelberg, attracted there by Thibaut's fame as an excellent musical connoisseur and a bold thinker. Here I began to busy myself exclusively with music . . . For greater culture I returned to Leipzig in 1830, completed my study of composition under Heinrich Dorn, then director of music there, and published my first compositions." He describes his founding and editorship of the *New Journal for Music* and concludes: "I have published twenty-two compositions, some of which have been played in public by Liszt, Clara Wieck, Henselt, and others." The doctorate was awarded, entitling Schumann to be addressed henceforth as "Doctor," a convention that Mendelssohn, also awarded an honorary doctorate, observed meticulously.

Schumann thought of putting together notes toward an autobiography in 1846, when his life had changed in so many ways. He was now a respected artist, head of a household, husband and father. This was to be a history of his artistic life, his true self. His notes in the household book include a report of a phrenological examination, which, like most pseudoscientific fads, confirmed his own view of his chief strengths and weaknesses. His gifts lay in music and poetry; he was driven by high-minded ambition to achieve in these fields. He was truthful and loving, modest and loyal. He was a great reader, had much good will toward the world, was good-natured through and through. His chief weakness was "anxiety, preventing his happiness."

Posterity has also assessed his life and work at its various stages, with the Dresden years often seen as his Biedermeier period, suggesting a significant decline in his powers. The implication is that his early romantic enthusiasm and originality as a young man pouring out his inmost feelings in poetry had given way to the bourgeois complacency of a family man, determined to make his name known in conventional musical genres. The term "Biedermeier," devised as late as 1855, was adopted as a description of the petit-bourgeois home life characterizing the period better known in Germany as the Vormärz, the relatively stable time leading up to the European revolutions of March 1848. But Schumann's life was never determined by prevailing trends. It is true that he loved being at home with Clara, and his home life centered more and more on the young children, Marie, Elise, and Julie (born in Dresden in March 1845). But it was always a working life for Schumann and also for Clara.

"Biedermeier" suggests the cozy domesticity of *Hausmusik*, which hardly applies to the piano trios of 1847 or to the C Major Symphony, which preceded them. Nor does it apply to the projects that occupied Schumann throughout late 1847 and beyond.

Genoveva; Manfred; Scenes from Goethe's "Faust"

The major works of Schumann's last years in Dresden were hugely ambitious. For years he had been thinking of writing an opera, considering several possible subjects. Wagner had been director of Dresden's opera house since 1843. He never became a close friend of Schumann's, but he was a regular visitor, and Schumann was deeply impressed by his works. He read *Tannhäuser* in score and heard it in performance—a work that was to change music history. Here was a German opera that brought to vivid life the all-absorbing themes of sin, repentance, and salvation in a Romantic medieval setting. These themes are embodied by the minstrel Tannhäuser, torn between the sensual delights of the Venusberg and the pure love of the faithful Elisabeth. In her virtue and loyalty, Elisabeth represents womanhood in its most sacred aspect. Her fate realizes the Wagnerian themes of love and death, Eros and Thanatos, forever joined together.

The success of *Tannhäuser* made Schumann even more determined to write an opera of his own. His immediate inspiration was a play by the well-known dramatist Friedrich Hebbel, *Genoveva*, which retells the legend of Genevieve of Brabant. The original tale dates back at least to the seventeenth century, with parallels in medieval legends. Genevieve, the virtuous young wife of the heroic Siegfried, Count Palatine of Trier, is wrongly accused of adultery when her husband is away on a military mission. Siegfried's trusted majordomo, secretly consumed by lust for Genevieve, takes revenge on her for rejecting his sexual overtures and engineers a plot that convinces Siegfried on his return to condemn his wife to death. She is saved by a compassionate servant and spends six years in the wilderness, nursing her infant with the help of a roe.

An ardent reader of Shakespeare's works, Schumann would have identified Hebbel's Genoveva with the loyal Hermione in *The

Winter's Tale, condemned to death for adultery by her jealous husband, Leontes. (Schumann saw the actress Rachel as Hermione, and considered *The Winter's Tale* as a possible project for an opera.) The figure of the virtuous wife, the victim of male ego, power, and possessiveness, is a familiar theme from medieval to Romantic times. In the introduction to his play, Hebbel explained that he saw the central character not as the innocent Genoveva but the steward Golo, a good man tortured by lust, torn between his loyalty to the count and his illicit passion for the count's wife. Schumann found Hebbel's approach congenial, and wrote to the playwright asking whether he would consider turning his play into an opera libretto. He could hardly contain his excitement when the famous writer visited him later that year. But Hebbel declined to write the text, and the libretto became the first of many problems besetting Schumann's first and only opera. He invited the poet Robert Reinick to adapt the play, but was unhappy with the result, and went back to an earlier version of the tale by Ludwig Tieck. In the end Schumann made his own version, omitting several episodes usually considered central to the tale, including Genevieve's infant, her six-year exile in the wilderness, and the fact that while she has been vilely mistreated by humans, including those who should be most loyal to her, it is a creature of nature, the roe, who saves her life.

For Schumann, as for Hebbel, Golo's conflicting passions lay at the heart of the drama. He is an erring man tortured by sexual guilt, suffering the punishment of conscience—"agenbite of inwit" in James Joyce's phrase—an ideal Romantic subject. But although Schumann worked at the musical setting with skill and dedication, the opera was a failure on its first performances, and revivals have been few and far apart.

Schumann began work on the overture and first act in December 1847, a month after Mendelssohn's death. The opera took shape alongside several other activities during the first six months of 1848. Schumann's friend Ferdinand Hiller had left Dresden to take up a post as music director in Düsseldorf, bequeathing the amateur men's chorus he had founded to Schumann. Schumann's work on major projects, including *Genoveva*, was interwoven with compositions for the men's chorus and for a mixed chorus he himself founded. Among these compositions was a group of three revolutionary songs inspired by the February revolution in Paris and the March revolutions in Vienna and Berlin. Composed in April, the songs were arranged for choir with (optional) winds, trumpets, and trombones—a design in itself announcing revolutionary sympathies. These revolutionary songs followed a similar group Schumann had composed a year earlier, in response to news of uprisings in Switzerland in November 1847, and published as his op. 62. The poets he set at that time were well-known favorites from earlier times, Eichendorff, Rückert, and Klopstock, and the settings were sensitive and thoughtful rather than incendiary.

The poems Schumann set in 1848 were by poets already famous in radical circles, known and feared for their dangerous beliefs. The settings were a call to arms, and Schumann knew that it would be unwise to publish them. Their tone was similar to that of the *Communist Manifesto*, circulating in 1848: "Workers of the world, unite! You have nothing to lose but your chains!" "Schwarz-Rot-Gold" (Black-Red-Gold) by Karl Marx's friend Ferdinand Freiligrath celebrated the colors of the revolutionary flag raised in Berlin, with the stirring lines: "Freedom is the Republic! And again the Republic! Gunpowder is black, Blood is red, Gold flickers the flame!" "To Arms," by the radical politician Titus Ullrich, attacked the powerful enemies of freedom, the oppressors, the Empire that could be overturned if only the oppressed rose as one. The poem raises the specter of the ghost that is haunting Empire (like Marx's image of the specter of communism) and urges people: "Remove the mask from your face! The witching hour tolls." The "Song of German Freedom" by Josef Fürst opens with warlike rhetoric: "The Victory is yours, my heroic people!"—wishful thinking, since the rebellions in German cities were soon put down, with minimal concessions to popular demands for reform.

Schumann's settings realized the radical spirit of the poems, cheering on the revolution. They remained relatively unknown until 1913, when the *Revue de Paris* published them as "Three Choruses of Robert Schumann, for the Revolutions of 1848." Schumann's choral society performed them in Dresden. These small choral societies (*Liedertafeln*) often served a political role, nurturing dreams of German unification under constitutional rule, with protection of civil rights and press freedom—reasonable demands rejected by the princely rulers of the small German states.

This was but an interlude, though one that engaged Schumann's sympathy for the ideals of the French Revolution. The 1848 mottos were still "Liberty, equality, and brotherhood," and the revolutions were against the same monarchies, which had been restored in 1815. Like many other artists, Schumann hoped the uprisings marked the beginning of a new age. Meanwhile, he continued to work on *Genoveva*, with its very different moral. The servants who rebel against Genoveva and the count are the villains; the treacherous Golo is a bastard of low birth, his mother a servant who doubles as a witch. Virtue resides with the aristocrats. Count Siegfried rescues his unjustly disgraced wife and is reconciled with her as the populace celebrates, an echo of the final act of Beethoven's *Fidelio*, when the imprisoned Florestan is saved by the arrival of the king's minister Don Fernando.

Schumann completed the four-act opera in August, but a series of delays meant that its premiere, in Leipzig, did not take place until June of 1850. The violinist Wasielewski, as a member of the Gewandhaus Orchestra, was closely involved in the Leipzig performances. He judged that the text was "flabby and weak," although the music was "incomparably superior." The reasons, he suggested, were innate in Schumann's disposition: "He could not renounce his lyric nature"—in short, "he was not born for the stage." Wasielewski was affected by the standards of the time; he felt that the opera should have focused on the innocent Genevieve of the original tale rather than on the troubled soul of Golo. On the whole, posterity has endorsed his view, although the opera has had its admirers. The conductor Hermann Levi tried to revive it several times, praising its "abundant musical content" as well as its dramatic richness. In 1893, George Bernard Shaw reviewed the first staged performance in England and dismissed the plot as "utter bosh." The music, he wrote, only reached Schumann's high standard in two or three scenes.

Most critics agree that the opera is static, its plot unconvincing, and its characterizations weak. Though Schumann devoted most of the year to it, it is hard to see *Genoveva* as the success Schumann was eagerly anticipating. The overture has entered the repertoire, though it is seldom performed, and there are some striking scenes: Golo torn between his lust and his guilt; his duet with the innocent Genoveva as he attempts to seduce her; Genoveva praying for strength from the Cross; her final duet with Siegfried, when she pardons a remorseful husband. But although Schumann wrote beautifully for the voice, he was unable to give life to one-dimensional characters. He had no real feeling for the simplicity of the legend or for its heroic setting. Germanic mythology was far better left to Wagner, who was composing one opera after another, putting all his energy and imagination into his conception of the "total work of art," writing his own verse libretti and giving sustained musical expression to the themes of love and death. Schumann recognized Wagner's genius even as he criticized his lack of craftsmanship. ("He is incapable of writing five measures without parallel fifths," he wrote to Mendelssohn, who agreed.) With *Genoveva* Schumann was attempting his own version of a through-composed work. But his one and only opera never caught on with a public avid for grand spectacle.

Schumann turned next to a setting of Byron's "dramatic poem" *Manfred*. From his early youth, Schumann had been drawn to Byron, the Romantic hero for so many Europeans of his generation. Schumann's father had made his own translation of *Childe Harold's Pilgrimage*; Schumann himself set a poem from Byron's *Hebrew Melodies* in his first song cycle, and added three more songs later. Byron's poetry remained a source of Romantic excitement long after his death in Greece. Schumann knew that Byron endowed his fictional heroes with his own life and character, from Childe Harold, whose adventures in Europe and the Orient closely resembled Byron's own travels, to the Corsair, a free spirit living a life much to Byron's taste. Count Manfred, weary of life, seeking his death, could be seen as another self-portrait. These fictional characters were all autobiographical to some degree; they represented Byron's love of personal and political freedom. *Manfred* also had at its center a disguised reference to Byron's incestuous love for his half-sister, Augusta—regarded as his chief offense by the English upper classes.

Count Manfred appears first in the high Swiss mountains, an exile haunted by sexual guilt, a Faustian figure impatient of ordinary human limitations. Like Faust, he calls spirits from the deep and communes with them. Summoned by Nemesis, the spirit of his beloved Astarte appears, and as Manfred pleads with her to speak to him, she forgives him with a brief, repeated "Farewell." Despite the pleas of a kind father confessor, Manfred is ready to accept his death without the consolations of religion.

Schumann conceived of his musical setting as an overture with incidental music dramatizing significant moments in the poem, along with solo arias and spoken verse. Precedents included Beethoven's incidental music to *Egmont*, Mendelssohn's incidental music to *A Midsummer Night's Dream* (a late addition to the overture composed in his youth) and his *First Walpurgis Night*. When Liszt suggested a performance of Schumann's *Manfred* in Weimar, Schumann insisted that the work was not an opera, a *Singspiel*, or a melodrama, but "a dramatic poem with music," which he considered "completely new and unprecedented." This was how he felt about each work as it matured and reached final form. In the full version of *Manfred*, he was offering a form that has never managed to attract audiences or performers in significant numbers. The Overture to *Manfred*, however, has entered the repertoire as one of Schumann's masterpieces. In its varied moods it portrays the complexity of the doomed Byronic hero, his love for Astarte and his guilt, his longing for death, his impatience with religious pieties. Even if it had no title and no program, the overture would stand as a work of intense expressiveness. The incidental music, though rarely performed, is also of high quality. The problem lies with the spoken verse, unconvincing in German translation and dated in Byron's original English.

Byron's Romantic poem constituted an ideal subject for Schumann as he was leading a comfortable life with his beloved Clara, ticking off each night of sexual intercourse in his household book with a marginal sixteenth note. There is no hint in Schumann's diaries or letters of this time that he suspected his recurrent illness might be connected to his earlier syphilitic infection. Although the bacterial nature of syphilis was not discovered until late in the century, the course of the disease was common knowledge at the time. Mental asylums were filled with victims suffering a defining element of the final stage of syphilis—general paralysis of the insane, or GPI. At some level Schumann might have feared the worst. What is unquestionable is that the figure of the solitary nobleman, Byron's alter ego, guilty and despairing, spoke to him in a profoundly personal way, inspiring some of his greatest music.

As he was putting the final touches to *Manfred,* Schumann went back to the work that had consumed his last months in Leipzig, precipitating a severe breakdown of his health. He had returned to *Faust* in early 1847, writing a few scenes and then abandoning the project. When he resumed work on *Faust* in 1849, it took shape as a series of key episodes from Faust's life, from his seduction of Gretchen to his death and transfiguration. While Clara was making a vocal score of the earlier setting, Schumann turned once more to the last section of Goethe's text.

Schumann's melancholy, his nervous ailments, his disturbing sense of his own mortality, fed into his obsession with the final scenes of Goethe's great work and its climactic "Chorus Mysticus." He had turned repeatedly to Goethe's works—the early novels, *The Sorrows of Young Werther* and *Wilhelm Meister's Apprenticeship*; the erotic poems of the *West-Eastern Divan*. The sprawling verse epic of the two parts of *Faust*, composed at intervals over the whole of Goethe's long life, represented the ultimate challenge.

Goethe's epic poem is on a different plane from Moore's oriental romance. Yet *Paradise and the Peri*, composed at a time of joy and high spirits, anticipated Schumann's struggles with *Faust*. He gave the central figure of the half-human, half-divine Peri a distinctive voice, expressing in lyrical song her longing to enter the Paradise from which she has been excluded, her instinctive sympathy for human suffering, and her ecstasy when she is at last admitted to a sensual Eastern heaven. The moral of the poem is that the repentance of an erring soul is "dearest to the gods." The plot includes human guilt and penitence, angelic pity and divine forgiveness.

Similar themes dominate the final scenes of Goethe's *Faust*. Faust's lover Gretchen is guilty of the murder of her mother and her infant, but she is sincerely penitent. She has been forgiven by the Virgin Mary, the loving mother of Christ, and is translated to heaven by "eternal Love." From her new place among the saved, she greets the soul of Faust, cleansed of its earthly dross, purified by death. Whatever religious beliefs Schumann held, his belief in the redemptive power of love was at the heart of his moral and spiritual being. Clara was his better self. Her love for him, all-accepting, all-forgiving, was his salvation. She enters into his song cycles as they chronicle the course of a poet's love; she serves as a model for the Peri, the virtuous Genoveva, and the spirit of Manfred's lover Astarte. She enters too into the climax of Goethe's epic poem, as Gretchen welcomes the immortal soul of Faust to the realm of eternal bliss.

The final scenes of *Faust* have parallels to Dante's journey in *The Divine Comedy*, as he is led through several levels of heaven by the love of Beatrice, who repeatedly summons him upward. For Goethe, too, the saving virtue is love human and divine, identified with compassion and forgiveness. It is the power of love, symbolized as the *Ewig-Weibliche*—the Eternal Feminine—that assures immortality to the erring mortal.

The "Chorus Mysticus" is a sequence of four rhymed couplets, a coda to the entire work—a riddling summation of the whole.

Alles Vergängliche	*All that is mortal*
Ist nur ein Gleichnis;	*Is only a semblance;*
Das Unzulängliche,	*That which is inadequate*
Hier wird's Ereignis	*Here becomes real;*
Das Unbeschreibliche,	*The indescribable*
Hier ist's getan;	*Is here accomplished;*
Das Ewig-Weibliche	*The Eternal Feminine*
Zieht uns hinan.	*Draws us upward.*

These couplets are preceded by the appearance of the Virgin Mary, Mater Gloriosa, through whose divine agency the repentant Gretchen enters heaven. In the "Chorus Mysticus," Christian iconography takes on Platonic echoes. The myth of the cave, in Plato's *Republic*, proposes that the world we know is a realm of shadows, semblances, ephemeral, insubstantial, a brief interval between the eternal realm from which we come and the eternity to which we aspire, and to which we are drawn by the power of Eros, or love. In the *Symposium*, Plato's best-known dialogue, the "wise woman" Diotima describes the universal longing to know eternal truth and beauty, which leads the seeker to experience each successive stage of love, sexual, intellectual, and divine. Diotima could be speaking in Goethe's famous final couplet: "The Eternal Feminine"—that is, Eros, the love of beauty—"Draws us upward." For Plato, the love of beauty starts with the love of boys; for Goethe's Faust it is love of the childlike Gretchen, followed by the desire for Helen, the most beautiful of women. Finally the "Eternal Feminine" is represented by the Virgin Mary, all-loving, all-compassionate, all-forgiving. Goethe draws freely on Platonic imagery and Christian iconography, in his eclectic scheme drawing no distinction between them.

The final paradoxes of the "Chorus Mysticus" resonated strongly with Schumann. He gave the couplets in turn to each vocal line of an eight-part quartet and chorus, repeating the words in canon and finally in a grand fugue—the most profound of all musical forms, he believed. There was no need to interpret the words, to explain the mystery. His aim was to set the sequence of paradoxes in the most compelling way possible. Each couplet is given new treatment as the chorus progresses, and recalled in increasing intensity as the chorus reaches new heights of affirmation, with the final couplet gloriously ending in praise of the enduring power of the "Eternal Feminine"—love, beauty, the artistic principle—to lead the human spirit toward its ultimate desire and destination. The only equivalent is Beethoven's setting of Schiller's "Ode to Joy"—and to love and brotherhood—in the Ninth Symphony.

Schumann was not alone in his obsession with the work that Goethe himself struggled with for so many years. Berlioz was composing his *Damnation of Faust* when Schumann was drafting the "Chorus Mysticus," and Liszt was to follow with his *Faust* Symphony. But for Schumann, the *Faust* project had special importance. Goethe's *Faust* was the culmination of a lifetime's work of the greatest poet of the age. The challenge for a composer was not simply to set a difficult, sprawling text, but to rise to the complexity of the epic work and its profound vision of human life. In contrast to the sensuous Islamic heaven of the Peri, the immortality that welcomes the cleansed soul of Faust is ascetic and humane, an Enlightenment vision, with elements drawn from myths of all times and cultures. For Schumann, the challenge was immense, and he was unable to consider the task finished to his satisfaction.

The scenes he completed in 1849 told the story of Gretchen, Faust's seduction of the innocent girl; her prayer to the Madonna; and her horror in the cathedral after she has unwittingly poisoned her mother, obeying the cynical instruction of Faust and Mephistopheles. She suffers the judgment and condemnation of the townspeople, as they chant the Dies irae in Latin, ignoring her cries for help. Schumann followed Goethe's text of the three key scenes from part 1: Gretchen in the garden; her prayer to Mater Doloroso; Gretchen in the cathedral. His dramatic settings are equal in power to the finest sections of *Paradise and the Peri* and to his earlier setting of the innocent love and ultimate despair of *Frauenliebe und -leben*. He had set three scenes earlier, presenting Faust's final delusion of power as he is seduced into executing a vast agricultural plan, to the gloating of Mephistopheles, and dying in an ecstasy of false hope. These scenes, too, are of high quality. It was not until 1853, when he wrote an overture for what was finally presented as *Scenes from Goethe's Faust*, that Schumann considered the work finished. The "Chorus Mysticus" and the third part (Faust's transfiguration) were performed in Dresden, with Schumann himself conducting. Liszt, as music director in Weimar, was eager to stage a performance for the Goethe centenary, and he copied the parts from Schumann's manuscript; there was also a performance in Leipzig. But Schumann was never to hear the entire work performed, and it was not published in full until after his death.

Toward the end of his Dresden years, Schumann was at last receiving sufficient recognition to allay his perpetual insecurity. He wrote to his friend Hiller that his music was being recognized throughout Germany. Liszt's performances of his dramatic works at Weimar contributed to his sense of achievement. There were still rebuffs—the opera house at Dresden declined to produce *Genoveva*; his publishers haggled over the fees for his works. But *Paradise and the Peri* was performed in cities across Europe, and even in New York. The *Spring* Symphony and the Piano Quintet were always popular. Wilhelmine Schröder-Devrient sang *Frauenliebe und Leben* in full at a private soiree, and individual songs appeared regularly in concert programs by Jenny Lind and others.

Album for the Young; Waldszenen

Schumann's notes in 1846 describe accompanying Clara to the train station when she went to Leipzig to hear Jenny Lind in concert. He and six-year-old Marie saw Clara off at the train, then wandered hand in hand in the woods, where they captured a butterfly, releasing it soon afterwards. Schumann noted: "Happy childhood—one relives it again in one's children." He thought of writing a book of childhood melodies—the first hint of a congenial project that took form in the autumn of 1848 as *Album for the Young*.

The *Album* was conceived as a handbook for Marie, who was already taking piano lessons. Short pieces in simple binary form explore basic technical problems in a painless way, starting with simple five-finger exercises in C, moving on to one or two sharps or flats, gradually introducing legato and staccato touch, arpeggios, melody and accompaniment exchanging places in right and left hand, different rhythms. The music imitates the natural sounds of birdsong and horn calls and evokes the changing seasons. Charming titles invite the young child to imagine a scene or a mood. These are little "character pieces," gradually increasing in difficulty. A second book of pieces was composed for older children.

Schumann next composed a cycle of short pieces for piano, *Waldszenen* (Forest Scenes), which could have served as a third *Album for the Young*, perhaps for young adults. The pieces are in the poetic mood of the final pieces of *Album for the Young*, reminiscent, too, of *Kinderszenen* and some of the *Davidsbündlertänze*. The composer could be telling a series of magical stories to a child. The first piece suggests stepping into the woods, followed, in later pieces, by encounters with hunters, a haunted spot, flowers, a strange "prophet bird," and other woodland scenes. The cycle ends with a "Farewell" to the forest—like the "End of the Song" in the *Fantasiestücke*, op. 12, or "The Poet Speaks" at the end of *Kinderszenen*. "The Bird as Prophet," with its magical call, evokes the myth of a bird whose language can be understood by humans with special gifts, like Cassandra in the *Iliad*, or Siegfried in the Nibelung tales. It was one of Clara's favorite pieces, and one imagines her playing it to Marie, Elise, and three-year-old Julie, with Schumann standing by the piano, as in their portraits.

Album for the Young was followed by "Advice to Young Musicians," originally designed for publication with the *Album*. It went instead into the *New Journal* and was reprinted in Schumann's later *Collected Writings* as "Musical Rules for Home and Life." Here Schumann set down his thoughts about musical training, drawing upon his own hard experience: "Learn the fundamental laws of harmony at an early age. Do not be afraid of the words 'theory,' 'thorough-bass,' 'counterpoint,' etc—they will appear friendly enough to you when you are familiar with them. *The Well-Tempered Clavier* should be your daily bread. . . . Rest from your musical studies by reading the poets. Exercise often in the open air! Listen to all folk songs; these are a treasure of lovely melodies. Honor the old but bring a warm heart to what is new. . . . Study is unending."

Some maxims relate to Schumann's recent activities—for instance, the importance he now attached to writing for chorus and orchestra, and his interest in folk song not only as a source of lovely melodies but as a different way of composing, with dance rhythms and simple harmonies suggesting an unspoiled past, natural and unsophisticated. Gypsy songs, Scottish and Irish ditties, traditional tunes sung by shepherds and sailors all had their own attraction, and entered into Schumann's compositions of this period.

Album for the Young was a commercial success, which Schumann followed a year later with *Song Album for the Young*, pedagogical in design but thoroughly Schumannesque in feeling. These albums were in the tradition of Bach's pedagogical works, simple pieces for his wife Anna Magdalena and his son Wilhelm Friedemann Bach.

When revolutions broke out across Europe in 1848, gaining ground in one city after another, Schumann was exhilarated at the prospect of liberalization and reform. He noted with joy the unrest in Berlin and Vienna, powerful centers of reaction. But when revolutionary violence erupted in Dresden a year later, in May 1849, the actual disorder, the sight of dead bodies lined up in the hospital courtyard, were as alarming to Schumann and Clara as they were to most law-abiding citizens. When a neighborhood security brigade went from house to house looking for able-bodied men to defend the city, they left quickly by the garden gate with Marie, leaving the younger children with the housekeeper, and took refuge with their friends in Maxen. Schumann was only thirty-eight, though his portraits show a middle-aged man, serious and portly. His sympathies were with the insurgents, as his "songs of freedom" had demonstrated the year before.

But one cannot imagine Schumann wielding a gun or taking an active part in the uprising, as Wagner did, serving as a lookout on the barricades. Schumann's diary notes on the revolution reflect his distress: "horror upon horror" on the 6th of May; and on the 10th: "the image of a terrifying revolution." Clara went back to Dresden with a local woman to collect the remaining family. After a few days, they left Maxen for the quiet spa town of Kreicha, where Schumann composed four pieces known to his circle as the "Barricade Marches." Marked *with strongest energy* in the first march and *with power and fire* in the fourth, their tone of heroic defiance included an unmistakable quotation of the "Marseillaise." Schumann wrote to his publisher Friedrich Whistling that the Four Marches were "rather republican in spirit. I couldn't think of a better way to channel my excitement—they were written with genuine ardor." The Four Marches, like the revolutionary songs composed in 1848, express strong liberal sympathies; but since they contained no words, it was safe to publish them. Schumann had quoted the "Marseillaise" in his *Faschingsschwank aus Wien* in 1839, defying censorship in the city of Metternich. His setting of Heine's ballad "The Two Grenadiers," a lament for the victims of Napoleon's ill-fated Russian campaign, ended with a full quotation of the "Marseillaise." Schumann's political sympathies took early musical form in the "March of the *Davidsbündler* Against the Philistines," which ends *Carnaval*. The jubilant march announces the war against the musical establishment that Schumann was launching at the same time in his *New Journal for Music*. And one of his last works, the overture to Goethe's epic poem *Hermann and Dorothea*, set in the aftermath of the French Revolution, used the "Marseillaise" as one of its chief themes. Most of the poets whose works he set had radical sympathies—not only Burns, Byron, and Heine, but Friedrich Rückert, the ballad poet Ludwig Uhland, and others. August Heinrich Hoffmann von Fallersleben, whose innocent children's verses Schumann set to music in *Song Album for the Young*, was expelled from Prussia for his ironically named *Unpolitical Poems*.

Despite his liberal sympathies, which she shared, Clara knew that Schumann had to be protected. It was safer for him to read about events from afar and to express his sympathies in music. By the time he and Clara returned to Dresden, the insurgents had been routed, and Frederick Augustus II, king of Saxony, was back in place.

Konzertstück for Four Horns and Orchestra; chamber music; *Song Cycles*

The last years of Schumann's time in Dresden were remarkably productive, even though he continued to suffer from bad days, regularly noted in his household book. He wrote several part songs for his choral society, and a variety of small-scale instrumental works. The range and quantity of his compositions during this time reflect his "*Advice for Young Musicians*," and his own self-imposed training. He urged the importance of knowing every instrument, not just one's own; he advised musicians to take every opportunity of hearing the organ, seeing opera, listening to folk song; he recommended reading a score as if you can actually hear it in performance, a skill Schumann had mastered when he was reviewing new works for his music journal.

He was now a fully accomplished musician who could write virtually on any subject, for any combination of musical forces. Many of the works composed at this time, unlike his earlier works, reveal little of the masks or the man. This is especially true of the choral works for the *Liedertafel* he had inherited from Ferdinand Hiller. Some of these works, written for amateur singers, are deliberately restricted in harmonic and rhythmic complexity. Others are marked by Schumann's distinctive inventiveness, notably a *Ritornelle* setting seven short poems by Rückert in canonic style, each canon ingeniously varied, and the whole forming an engaging a cappella cycle. Recent studies suggest that these choral works are well worth reviving.

Schumann also composed several delightful instrumental works at this time, for one or two solo instruments with piano, each work a mini-cycle of interrelated pieces. Despite a few early lessons on violin and cello, the piano was Schumann's only instrument. But his orchestral writing had familiarized him with strings, winds, and brass, and he relished the different qualities of sound produced individually and in combination. His new compositions explored the special strengths and character of each instrument. In February of 1849, he produced three *Fantasiestücke* for clarinet, unusual in form, which treat similar thematic material in increasingly rapid tempi, as if to demonstrate the relationship of tempo to musical meaning. Soon afterwards he composed an inspired Adagio and Allegro for the new valve horn and piano, in the same A minor/A major keys as the clarinet pieces. In April he composed five pieces "in folk style" for cello, each piece in a different "folk" character. In December, he wrote three lovely Romances for oboe as a Christmas present for Clara, also in A minor and A major. He added three magical *Märchenbilder* for viola and piano in 1851, and in 1853 a set of *Märchenerzählungen* for clarinet, viola, and piano. Although the published scores specified alternative instruments—cello instead of horn, viola instead of clarinet, violin instead of oboe—each work was composed with a particular instrument in mind. They are among his most charming compositions, enhancing the core repertoire of each solo instrument. Nowhere more than in these short cycles is Schumann's conception of music as poetry—*Dichtung*—more relevant. Their titles suggest literary forms of storytelling—romances, fairy tales, fantasy pieces. They are meant to be played poetically by the solo instrument in partnership with the piano, songs without words, open invitations to the imagination of performer and listener.

It is a mistake to consider these works as "merely" *Hausmusik*. Each set of pieces is different, an example of Schumann's writing at its most engaging. New departures for Schumann, they bear comparison with his early sets of pieces composed for piano alone, *Fantasiestücke,* op. 12, and *Drei Romanzen,* op. 28. They are composed for professionals rather than amateurs and have proved ideal for concert performance. It would be an unusually large living room that could easily accommodate the virtuoso works for horn or clarinet.

Schumann also composed one remarkably original piece which has entered modern repertoire—*Konzertstück* for Four Horns and Orchestra, op. 86, an exhilarating work that has special appeal for the modern orchestra. The orchestras in Schumann's time would have been stretched to find four horn players skillful enough to master the complexities of the solo parts. Schumann was intent on exploring the sonorities of the new valve horn and its range, alone and in combination, and he was probably indifferent to any realistic prospect of performance.

During 1849, Schumann turned again to songwriting—a period sometimes known as his second "Year of Song," although critics disagree about their quality. Certain songs are on the level of the greatest 1840 songs and have entered the repertoire of many singers. "Mein schöner Stern!" from the Rückert *Minnespiel*, op. 101, sets a poem that perfectly expressed Schumann's recurrent melancholy. It is a heartfelt, intensely moving address to the shining star: "I beg

you, O do not let your radiance be dimmed by my dark clouds—rather
dispel my darkness with your light!"

Among the many works composed in 1849, two groups of Spanish folk songs are of special interest. They were taken from *Volks-
lieder und Romanzen der Spanier* (*Spanish Folk Songs and Romances*),
translations by the poet Emanuel Geibel of the original Spanish
texts. *Spanisches Liederspiel* is a cycle for four voices, with piano
accompaniment. As Schumann's title suggests, the songs are linked
by themes and musical motifs in a game of love, alternating despair
and joy, both emotions given a Spanish coloring. A second cycle,
Spanische Liebeslieder, arranges the accompaniment for four voices as
a four-hand piano duet—a scheme that Brahms was to follow in his
Liebeslieder Waltzes. Schumann was trying new combinations, new
ways of setting words on a variety of themes, many of them familiar from his early choices of poetic texts: joy and melancholy, love
gained and lost. Both Spanish cycles are arranged ingeniously, alternating male and female voices in solos, duets, and final quartets,
and linking the songs by key (the *Liederspiel* opens in A minor and
closes in A major; the *Liebeslieder* take G minor/B-flat as their tonal
center). Both cycles have a Spanish character, provided by dance
rhythms and occasional suggestions of a guitar accompaniment. In
the *Liebeslieder*, the four-hand piano duet has an independent role,
introducing the first half with a preview of later motifs and providing an "Intermezzo" before the second half, a sharply accented
"national dance." In the published work, the original Spanish title
or opening words introduce each song, and the texts celebrate the
passions of the south—love freely given and returned, in a Spanish
landscape lightly sketched (mountains, valleys, the river Ebro, the
"folk" engaged in their usual pursuits). Schumann had only a pass-
ing acquaintance with authentic Spanish folk songs, and his settings
are his own response to the subject matter, which obviously appealed
to him. Even when the lovers sing of their grief, these songs seem
relatively lighthearted, in contrast to the despairing emotions of the
1840 song cycles. The songs are of variable quality, perhaps because
Schumann was writing not from his heart but from his interest in

the "folk" character of the poems and the attractions of the life portrayed, so different from the unrelieved anguish of much German lyric poetry.

The Spanish cycles were followed by a group of songs for children, in the spirit of *Album for the Young*. Simple, tender, affectionate, they express a side of Schumann's nature that sustained him through his bouts of illness and melancholy—his delight in his children, his ability to enter into their play. It was a quality Clara remembered well from her own childhood, when Schumann had joined her in games, charades, and fairy tales, engaging for their "doubles" to meet at the gate of St. Thomas Church.

The *Song Album for the Young* was drawn from Schumann's favorite poets and from *Des Knaben Wunderhorn* (The Youth's Magic Horn), the German folk poems collected by Achim von Arnim and Clemens Brentano, later given memorable musical form by Brahms and Mahler. The opening group were from a set of children's poems by Hoffmann von Fallersleben, best known for the song "Deutschland über Alles"—at the time a protest against the reactionary politics of local German princes determined to hold on to their power. The songs included a "Gypsy Song" by Emanuel Geibel, two poems from *Des Knaben Wunderhorn*, one each by Hans Christian Andersen and Eduard Mörike, two from Schiller's *William Tell*—like most of Schiller's plays, a work with a strong political message. The songs affirm the delights of innocence, the joys of nature, the renewal of life with the arrival of spring.

Another group of songs for adults was inspired by Schumann's rereading of Goethe's *Wilhelm Meister's Apprenticeship*. Schumann sympathized with many aspects of the novel, including Goethe's reflections on human life, on the need to cultivate one's talents to the full and to lead a useful life. At the heart of the novel is the story of the Harper and the Neapolitan orphan Mignon. The Harper is a destitute, ageless Italian minstrel who appears at the tavern in which Wilhelm Meister is taking refreshment. Mignon, who attaches herself to young Wilhelm as his devoted assistant, turns out to be the Harper's illegitimate child. Both the Harper and Mignon are natural poets, and their songs are scattered through the novel, an inspiration for composers. Schubert set several of the poems in versions Schumann would have known.

Schumann set all nine of the poems in the novel as a connected cycle, beginning with Mignon's melancholy lament about her lost infancy in the south of Italy, "Kennst du das Land." He placed this poignant song last in *Song Album for the Young* and first in the *Wilhelm Meister* cycle. His setting, a perfect realization of Goethe's touching poem, makes a fascinating comparison with Schubert's version. In Schubert's setting, the piano accompanies the singer in simple chords, as she asks the question "Kennst du das Land wo die Zitronen blühn?"—"Do you know the land where the lemons bloom?" Schumann typically precedes the opening lines with four bars of a melancholy piano motif setting the mood, and repeated all through the song as if in counterpoint, the composer's voice responding to the child. When Mignon's song becomes more agitated, Schumann, like Schubert, sets the piano's triplets against Mignon's semiquavers, but with more intense effect; and Mignon's melody, too, is more intense, rising to a higher note with the dramatic answer to her opening question: "*Dahin*"—Let us go there! If there was any suspicion that Schumann's powers were declining in 1849, Mignon's song demonstrates his continued genius for setting poetry that speaks directly to his imagination.

He also composed a fifteen-minute *Requiem for Mignon* for soloists, chorus, and orchestra, in the style of the *Scenes from Goethe's Faust*. The themes were another variation of those dominating *Genoveva, Manfred,* and *Faust*: sexual guilt and remorse, innocence betrayed. The Harper is an aged, unworldly man, driven to madness by the violent passions of his early life. Mignon is an innocent child, happily dressing as a boy, growing up to young womanhood. In her death and transfiguration she is robed in white, garlanded with a golden wreath, a winged angel. The Harper, like Manfred, is determined to take his life. The songs of the Harper range over other themes close to Schumann's heart: the nature of art and poetry ("I sing as the bird sings . . . The song is its own rich reward"); compassion for the poor and the lonely ("Who has never eaten his bread in tears . . . he knows you not, you heavenly Powers."). The quality of these songs is consistently high, as if Schumann had at last conquered his initial resistance to the greatest writer of the age.

On October 17, 1849, Chopin died in Paris, aged thirty-nine. Fifteen years before, Schumann had greeted him as "the most noble, proudest spirit of our age." He died of tuberculosis, a broken man, bitterly estranged from George Sand, tended by his devoted sister Ludwika, who had come from Warsaw to be with her dying brother. The streets of Paris were lined with thousands of admirers as his funeral cortege made its way to the Church of the Madeleine, where Mozart's Requiem was performed. Schumann noted the date in his diary and tried to arrange a concert in Chopin's memory, but he could not persuade the Dresden church authorities to grant permission.

As he was recovering from the nervous attack that had felled him in 1845, Schumann began to think of resuming a salaried position, possibly in Dresden, although nothing suitable materialized. He wrote discreetly to friends in Vienna, asking whether he might be considered for a post that fell vacant; he also wrote to friends in Leipzig, hoping for a post there. Nothing came of his tentative overtures. In the autumn of 1849, Ferdinand Hiller, who had been music director in Düsseldorf for five years, accepted a similar position at Cologne. Reassured by a letter from Schumann, in which he expressed confidence in his ability to direct, Hiller recommended his friend for the Düsseldorf post. Hiller was one of the few friends whom Schumann addressed as *Du*—an intimacy he shared with Niels Gade but had never achieved with Mendelssohn.

Schumann was tempted but hesitant. He asked Hiller for details of his responsibilities, his salary, the possibility of taking time off. He wanted to be sure of a role for Clara. He had an additional concern, he told Hiller, after reading about Düsseldorf in an old geography book. "There I found mentioned as noteworthy: 'three convents and a lunatic asylum.' To the first I have no objection if it must be so; but it was disagreeable to me to read the last . . . I am obliged to avoid carefully all melancholy impressions of the kind. And if we musicians live so often on sunny heights, the sadness of reality cuts all the deeper when it lies naked before our eyes. At least so it is with me and my vivid imagination." This was a heartfelt admission, which he could trust his friend to understand. It was a key to his emotional state at this time, which included worries about his nervous symptoms—dizziness, insomnia, tinnitus. An aural affliction strikes at the very being of a musician. With Beethoven's deafness vividly present to Schumann, the possibility of damage to his most precious sense was alarming. His responsibilities as father to five young children also weighed on him. Two sons had been born in Dresden: Ludwig in January 1848, Ferdinand in July of 1849. Schumann was not eager to move, but his discreet attempts to secure a position at Dresden or Leipzig had come to nothing. Hiller assured him that the mental asylum was no longer there and tried to allay Schumann's other fears. The fact that his friend would be close by at Cologne reassured Schumann.

Although he had misgivings about accepting the Düsseldorf post, the Rhineland held many attractions. Though predominantly Catholic (unlike "enlightened" post-Reformation Saxony), it was one of the most beautiful and poetic regions of Germany. Musical forces in Dresden, apart from the court chapel and the opera house, were amateurish. Schumann's social circle was small, although he and Clara had become friends with painters like Eduard Bendemann and Julius Hübner, who were both prominent in Dresden's artistic life. Still, Mendelssohn had been unhappy about his first appointment in Düsseldorf, and there was no reason to think matters had improved substantially. No German city, not even Berlin, could compare to Leipzig in the quality of its musical life; but Leipzig was out of the question. It seems not to have occurred either to Schumann or Clara that a full-time position as music director would be completely unsuitable for Schumann. He had experience of conducting his own works, but was neither expert nor comfortable in the role. The decisive factor was probably the prospect of an annual salary, which would relieve the pressure on Clara to earn money from concertizing. On the other hand, while Schumann was considering whether or not to take up the post, he and Clara left for a concert tour of Bremen and Hamburg, where they spent time with Jenny Lind. After she assisted in Clara's concerts, they returned home with a profit of eight hundred thalers—a hundred thalers more than the year's salary offered by Düsseldorf.

Despite his doubts, Schumann accepted the appointment, with the proviso that he would not take up residence until the end of 1850, leaving time for the Leipzig premiere of *Genoveva*. This took place finally in June, with three performances and a mixed response from critics. Schumann was already at work on other projects, and he hoped confidently that *Genoveva* would eventually take its place in the operatic repertoire.

In August there was much music, a farewell dinner, a farewell concert. On the first of September the family left Dresden, arriving two days later in Düsseldorf. Schumann was forty, Clara a week short of her thirty-first birthday. They had every reason to hope that many years of fruitful collaboration lay ahead.

14

MUSIC DIRECTOR IN THE RHINELAND

Düsseldorf, September 1850–Summer 1853

When Schumann and Clara arrived in Düsseldorf, they were welcomed at the train station by their friend Ferdinand Hiller and members of the civic music committee. Later that evening the town choir serenaded them at their hotel. All augured well as the family settled into spacious lodgings on a cobblestone street near the old town center and the river. There was an official banquet and a gala concert of Schumann's music, opening with the Overture to *Genoveva*, and featuring part 2 of *Paradise and the Peri*. Hiller must have put great effort into preparing the concert, especially *Peri*, given the large choral and orchestral forces required, and the demanding solo part of the Peri.

Schumann had taken a steamboat down the Rhine in his youth, and the great river had magical associations for him. He dramatized its famous myths in his early song cycles. In the Eichendorff *Liederkreis* he portrayed the Lorelei, the siren who lures travelers to their death:

You know me well, from its towering rock
My castle looks silently deep into the Rhine;
It is already late, already cold,
You shall never again leave this forest.

Another Eichendorff song describes the old knight of the castle asleep in his watchtower as a wedding party sails by on the sunlit Rhine.

In his *Liederkreis,* op. 24, Schumann set Heine's words:

With friendly greetings and promises
The river's splendor beckons me;
But I know how, gleaming above,
It brings its inner death and night.

The contrast between the surface beauty and the darkness below was part of the river's fatal attraction.

Schumann turned to Heine again in *Dichterliebe:* "In the Rhine, the holy river, / There is reflected in the waves / With its great cathedral / The great and holy Cologne." With its magnificent Gothic cathedral still unfinished, Cologne was only twenty-one miles south of Düsseldorf, forty-five minutes by train. It was Schumann's first destination after arriving in Düsseldorf. Although their musical forces could not compare with those of Leipzig, Düsseldorf and Cologne alternated as hosts of the Lower Rhine Music Festival, often conducted in the past by Mendelssohn.

Schumann's responsibilities included weekly rehearsals with choir and orchestra, preparation of Beethoven's Mass in C for performance in the St. Maximilian Church, and the first subscription concert of ten, scheduled to run from October 1850 to May 1851. The October program was typical of Schumann's programming, opening with Beethoven's *Consecration of the House* Overture and continuing with Clara performing Mendelssohn's G Minor Piano Concerto and Bach's Prelude and Fugue in A Minor, Schumann's own setting for chorus and orchestra of Rückert's "Adventlied," and ending with the premiere of a dramatic oratorio by his friend Niels Gade. Although Schumann had seldom conducted works other than his own, at first his inexperience did not cause major problems. He soon brought in as assistant concertmaster Joseph von Wasielewski, whom he had first known as a student at the Leipzig Conservatory. Wasielewski became a regular sonata partner for Clara, and, eventually, Schumann's first biographer.

Cello Concerto; *Rhenish* Symphony

Despite the demands of his new appointment, within a few weeks Schumann began work on one of his most attractive works, the Cello Concerto in A Minor—Clara's key, again. Clara's name appears throughout the concerto in the falling figure sounding "Clara," especially in the tender slow movement, and more playfully in the last movement. The concerto is perfectly written for the cello's singing quality and its power to move the heart. While the A Minor Piano Concerto was composed as a dialogue between soloist and orchestra, the soloist in the Cello Concerto improvises on one theme after another, all tinged by melancholy, with the orchestra mainly a discreet accompanist. Schumann made sensitive use of the cello's special qualities in his chamber music, especially in the Piano Quartet, with its haunting cello solo in the slow movement. The year before writing the new concerto he had explored the cello on its own in his Five Pieces in Folk Style, with the cello imitating the stomping rhythms of peasant dances. The Cello Concerto is very different, virtuosic but also intimate and lyrical. The cello becomes a profoundly expressive solo voice, like a human voice but with a wider register and a more dramatic range of sonority, conveying meaning in music with no need for words.

Schumann sketched the piece in about two weeks as three closely linked, continuous movements, under half an hour in performance. One novelty, adding to the feeling of a single sustained work, was a short accompanied cadenza in the final movement instead of an unaccompanied cadenza for virtuoso display, commonly placed in the first movement of a concerto. Although Schumann scheduled many of his own works in his Düsseldorf concerts, the Cello Concerto was not included, and he never heard it performed with orchestra. Christian Reimers, the orchestra's first cellist and a good friend, played it through with Clara at the piano. Reimers also became a favorite trio partner for Clara, with Wasielewski often playing the violin.

A visit to Hiller in Cologne inspired the major work of these first months, a new Symphony in E-flat, which came to be known as the *Rhenish* Symphony. It is a glowing tribute to the Rhineland, its people, its country pleasures, and its great cathedral. Although conductors have their own favorites of the four symphonies, the *Rhenish* is often considered Schumann's masterpiece. It provides a compelling argument against the widespread assumption that his powers of invention and organization were in decline during his last years.

The symphony was composed and orchestrated in a month, starting in early November 1850. Dispensing with the usual slow introduction, Schumann begins his third symphony directly with a tribute to Beethoven, born in Bonn, the most famous musical son of the Rhineland. The opening theme hints at the E-flat-major-triad theme of Beethoven's Symphony no. 3, the *Eroica*, with the arpeggiated triad given a Schumannesque treatment, ascending joyfully, breaking up the rhythm, transforming itself from a rising fanfare into a lyrical songlike descent, natural, distinctive, and memorable. It is as if all Schumann's knowledge of past masters and his own experience of writing for orchestra have liberated his imagination, enabling him to create an entirely new work with assured mastery of orchestral forces and symphonic form.

This Third Symphony is more compressed and more closely organized than the others, unfolding naturally from one movement to the next, with themes ingeniously interleaved to suggest various aspects of Rhineland life. The second-movement Scherzo (originally entitled "Morning on the Rhine") echoes Beethoven's *Pastoral* Symphony with a simple, warmly accented motif suggesting a country dance, interwoven ingeniously with a rapid string motif which reappears in later movements, transformed in tempo and mood each time it makes a new entrance. An "extra" movement (the fourth of five), marked "ceremonial," evokes the soaring spaces of Cologne cathedral in its rising choralelike polyphony, with echoes of Bach and earlier religious composers. It was originally given a full descriptive heading: "In the character of a procession for a solemn ceremony," a reference to the elevation to cardinal of the archbishop of Cologne, Johannes von Geissel, in late September. But Schumann wished to avoid a programmatic reading of the work, and the single word "ceremonial" (*feierlich*) frees the music to convey its own meaning. The four horns are given special weight throughout the symphony, with a distinctive role in the "ceremonial" movement, supported by trumpets and trombones. The joyful finale relieves the earlier solemnity, celebrating instead the optimistic, pleasure-loving nature of the Rhinelanders, known to be fond of wine, music, and dance. But toward the end of the movement, the brass choir enters with a reminder of the cathedral and its profound spiritual heritage. Schumann delights in setting each theme in combination with the others, deepening meaning as the theme takes on new rhythm and emphasis. He is now completely at ease in managing the brass choir, reveling in its quasi-religious sonority—"religious" in an ecumenical sense, uniting the concert hall and the cathedral.

Fairy Tales on a Grand Scale; Ballads for Declamation

Inspired by the change of scene and the successful completion of a new symphony, Schumann next composed two full-scale fairy tales, *The Pilgrimage of the Rose*, for soloists, chorus, and piano (later orchestrated), and *The King's Son*, a ballad by Ludwig Uhland, set for soloists, chorus, and orchestra. Moritz Horn, a Leipzig lawyer turned poet, had sent his *Pilgrimage* to Schumann, explaining that his libretto was written after hearing a performance of *Paradise and the Peri*. Schumann was charmed by the idea of setting the fairy tale—a sign not of impaired health but erratic literary judgment. To modern sensibility, the plot is even more dated than Moore's oriental tale. The "pilgrimage" is undertaken by a rose magically transformed into a young woman, who seeks love, marries, and dies giving birth to a child. "Rosa," as she is called, is transformed into an angel, who gives her infant a magic rose to ensure her future happiness. Schumann wrote to Horn suggesting that he compose lyrics for an angelic chorus to end the work. "The progression—rose, maiden, angel—seems very poetic to me, and besides, it hints at the doctrine of transmutation of being to a higher state, which we all cling to so fondly." In these fairy tales, as in the far more serious treatment of Goethe's *Faust*, Schumann liked to provide a happy ending to the suffering of lovers, the innocent and the damned. The angelic choruses that end his choral works serve a consoling function similar to that of the upbeat allegro finale of a sonata or symphony.

Uhland's medieval ballad, "The King's Son," appealed to Schumann in the same "poetic" way. He gave it a grand setting for a simple ballad. In brief, the favorite third son of the old king sets off bravely by ship to found his own kingdom. His ship is destroyed in a sudden storm, but he is rescued by mermaids, finds a lovely bride, and settles down with her in his kingdom under the sea—another happy ending, which Schumann celebrates with a grand chorus. Both fairy tales were performed widely at the time, though modern performances are rare. A third fairy tale, *The Page and the King's Daughter,* draws on similar themes. In love with the king's daughter, the page is murdered by the king's servants, who throw his body into the sea, where it is discovered by sea nymphs and their Meerman. The Meerman creates a golden harp from the page's head, with which he serenades the king's daughter on her wedding day as she is being forced to marry a nobleman. When she hears the Meerman's song sounding in the distance, the princess falls dead. Love is confirmed in Romantic fashion as the lovers are united in death.

Schumann also composed overtures for works of impeccable literary quality, Schiller's *Bride of Messina,* Shakespeare's *Julius Caesar*, and Goethe's *Hermann and Dorothea.* He entertained thoughts of a full-length oratorio about Martin Luther, possibly a trilogy, exchanging detailed letters about the project with Richard Pohl, a young admirer and potential librettist. He wrote to Pohl that the oratorio should be on a popular level, comprehensible to farmer and burgher alike: "And so I shall try to make my music not 'artistic,' complex, contrapuntal, but simple and strong, working through rhythm and melody . . . for Luther was 'a great man of the people.'" It is impossible to guess whether Schumann's *Luther,* had it been written, would have been a heroic failure, like *Genoveva,* or the crowning glory of his career, on the level of Mendelssohn's *St. Paul* and *Elijah*.

Schumann seemed to be highly energized at this time. A year after arriving in Düsseldorf, he organized a small choral group more to his taste than the large municipal choir, to read through music of the past as well as his own choral works. He was writing songs for solo and mixed voices, including a cycle setting poems by Elisabeth

Kulmann, a prolific young poet who had died at the age of seventeen. With their sentimental texts, the songs have almost vanished from performance. One critic calls them "haunting"; another takes them as "painful evidence of a mind in deterioration." Another late cycle of songs, the *Gedichte der Königin Maria Stuart* (*Poems of Mary, Queen of Scots*), has fared better. Schumann believed that the poems were written by the Scottish queen as she was facing her death, condemned by her cousin, Queen Elizabeth I. The tragedy was familiar to Schumann from Schiller's play *Maria Stuart,* a sympathetic portrait of the doomed queen. The poems dramatize her plea to her heartless cousin, her despair, and her final prayer in prison. Schumann's settings have a melancholy beauty, and many singers have revived them in performance.

Schumann also set three ballads for "declamation with piano accompaniment"—two poems by Friedrich Hebbel, the admired playwright of *Genoveva,* and one by the radical English poet Shelley, whose poems had been translated into German in 1844. Hebbel's poem "Fair Hedwig" was set in 1849 and published as Schumann's op. 106. Next came Shelley's "The Fugitives" in 1852, and Hebbel's "Ballad of the Heath Boy" in 1853. The verses of all three ballads defend youth against age, innocence against oppression. They were to be recited dramatically against an appropriate musical background.

The innovation was a natural extension of Schumann's continued exploration of words and music in combination and separately. He had included words spoken to music in the scenes of *Manfred,* following Beethoven's precedent in the dungeon scene of *Fidelio* and the incidental music to *Egmont.* Setting a complete narrative for declamation was new. Schumann wrote to the bookseller and composer Carl Debrois van Bruyck: "It is a kind of composition that has not existed before; thus we so often have to thank the poets above all for seeking out new paths in art." In Schubert's settings of Goethe's famous ballads "Erlkönig" and "Gretchen am Spinnrade," well known to Schumann from his student days, the drama is in the words, while the music realizes the terror, the fate, the anguish of the speaker. In Schumann's earlier ballads, too, the words are primary—

for instance, in his settings of Heine's "The Two Grenadiers" and "Belsatzar." In the three ballads for declamation, the piano accompaniment is composed as support for the spoken drama. The music is nonetheless eloquent, as "prelude" and "postlude," with intervening musical passages, reinforce the imagery and plot of the narrative. This is especially true of the longest and most ambitious of the ballads, "Fair Hedwig," the tale of a simple girl, an "angel" of no known origin, like Goethe's Mignon, whose steadfast devotion wins over a noble knight. Schumann was proud of the experiment, anticipating *Sprechstimme* or *Sprechgesang*, (spoken song), later used to great effect by Arnold Schoenberg and Alban Berg.

One way of looking at the late songs, including the *Maria Stuart* cycle, was proposed by the singer Dietrich Fischer-Dieskau, among others. The suggestion is that Schumann was writing in a completely new way, aiming for simplicity rather than melodic expressiveness. But Schumann's "new way of writing" did not require a break with the past. His mind was working feverishly at one project after another, with no perceptible loss of mastery. But his subjects were of variable quality, which affected their musical treatment. In his songs, as in his instrumental and choral works, he relied increasingly on a musical language of his own, readily available as and when he needed it. His late works lack the extraordinary originality of the extended piano works of the 1830s and the song cycles composed during the months before his marriage. As he himself often explained to Clara and others, those early works were directly inspired by his love of Clara and its troubled course. They set a high standard, virtually impossible to match. He wrote his late works quickly, without close revision. The general impression is not so much of a great mind in decline as of a more casual and variable approach to composition. The real test has to do with the works not of 1851–1852 but of autumn 1853: the Violin Concerto, composed for Joseph Joachim, who thought it unworthy of Schumann, and the *Gesänge der Frühe* (*Songs of Dawn*) for piano, one of the last works Schumann composed before his final breakdown.

Schumann's first season in Düsseldorf seemed to go well, at least to outward appearances. As the second season approached, problems arose, manageable at first, but increasingly distressing for Schumann and Clara. They were disturbed by the constant noise of traffic on the cobblestone road and moved to a quieter street, which also proved unsatisfactory. The noise was particularly unsettling for Schumann, who was suffering from attacks of tinnitus. They eventually moved to a large town house on Bilkerstrasse, close to their first lodgings, only ten minutes' walk from the famous "bridge of boats" spanning the Rhine.

It gradually became clear that there was a mismatch between Schumann's high musical expectations and the easygoing Rhinelanders, who enjoyed their amateur status. Members of the music committee were accustomed to consulting closely with their music director. Schumann simply made up his own programs, very much in the pattern Mendelssohn had established in Leipzig. Each concert featured a major work by Beethoven, usually a symphony or a concerto, and works by Schumann or Mendelssohn, including the first performance of Mendelssohn's *Italian* Symphony, published only after his death. Mozart and Weber were also featured, and new works by Niels Gade and Ferdinand Hiller. No light entertainment was on offer, no Rossini, no virtuoso variations by Herz or Hünten.

There are several sources of evidence for the problems that led to a final break between Schumann and the town officials who had welcomed him so warmly. The record in his household book was in his usual telegraphic style. On August 25, 1851: "Conference with the *Gesangverein* [choral committee]. My hot temper." Two weeks later: "Conference in the afternoon. Storm with Wortmann. Serious thoughts about the future." (Wilhelm Wortmann was the assistant burgomaster and an official on the choral committee.) Six months later: "Stormy conference—Quarrel with Tausch." (Julius Tausch was the young rehearsal pianist who was asked to conduct in Schumann's place.) The word "shameless" occurs frequently in reference to the music committee, the town council, Düsseldorfers in general.

Clara kept a full record of the conflict, charging the music committee with malicious intrigues against Schumann. Wortmann was singled out as an enemy, as was Tausch, a fine pianist, an all-round musician, and a good composer. Tausch had been a promising student at the Leipzig Conservatory, and on Mendelssohn's recommendation he moved to Düsseldorf as a teacher. He served Schumann well as rehearsal pianist and substitute conductor, working regularly with the choir. After Schumann's serious illness in the summer of 1852, Schumann asked him to conduct the first two subscription concerts of the season, paying Tausch out of his own salary.

Clara's first private comments concerned preparations for a performance of Bach's Mass in B Minor. "The ladies and gentlemen do not show up for rehearsals, they make no secret of their aversion to hard work. The people here respect neither art nor conductors!"

Wasielewski provided a more judicious account in his biography, with further details added in a biography by Frederick Niecks, whose father had served in the Düsseldorf orchestra. Niecks himself remembered as a child seeing Schumann walking in the public gardens, head down, oblivious to his surroundings, his mouth pursed as if whistling.

The first sign of trouble came with a review of a subscription concert. The performance was ragged, and the new music director was blamed. At rehearsals, musicians complained that Schumann failed to give them the beat and hardly commented when things went wrong. His behavior was not new. Earlier accounts suggest that he was not comfortable even when conducting his own works; a performance of *Paradise and the Peri* in Berlin had been fairly disastrous. Mendelssohn's friend the playwright Eduard Devrient described visiting Schumann in Dresden and spending an hour with him in total silence, much to Devrient's annoyance. Wagner, who was anxious to have Schumann's approval, said that when he spent time with Schumann, as he often did, the composer could be silent for hours at a time. (Schumann complained to friends that Wagner talked incessantly.) Even when Schumann was a student, fellow students remarked on his silence in company. His dreamy nature, his tendency to absent himself, were in sharp contrast to his fluency not only in his musical compositions but in his extensive correspondence.

It should have been obvious that he was totally unsuited to be the music director of a civic orchestra and choir. The contrast with Ferdinand Hiller, his friend and predecessor, was painfully clear to the music committee. Schumann was short-tempered, quick to take offense, qualities going back to earlier times, as he himself knew. He had wryly apologized to Mendelssohn for his "clumsy manners." But there was no reason for the Düsseldorfers to overlook his idiosyncrasies. He had been recommended as a great composer who would add luster to the city and its musical life. Instead, he was destroying the progress made by Hiller and his equally conscientious predecessor, Julius Rietz. The music committee and the town officials who had appointed Schumann agonized over the situation, hoping that in time matters would improve.

Meanwhile, Schumann continued composing, arranging four-hand versions of his orchestral works with Clara's help, and carrying on with his working life. One of the happiest events of 1852 was a two-week-long festival of his music in Leipzig. Three Gewandhaus concerts featured his recent works: the *Manfred* Overture, *Pilgrimage of the Rose*, and the *Rhenish* Symphony. His chamber music and songs were performed in private gatherings and public concerts. His diary records his joy at being recognized at last in the musical center which had been the scene of his happiest and most productive years. It was the city of Bach, the home of thriving music publishers, many of them now vying to publish his music. He was welcomed by old friends with daily visits, shared meals, and evening entertainment. The concerts attracted musicians from near and far: Karl Emanuel Klitzsch, from Zwickau; Moritz Horn; Joachim; Clara's half-brother Woldemar Bargiel; Liszt, who played four-hand music with Clara simply for pleasure; Niels Gade. Schumann's works were enthusiastically received, and audiences were delighted by Clara's performances of works by Chopin and Mendelssohn. At the final concert Schumann was given a laurel wreath. But the festive trip ended with an attack of nerves, a sign of difficulties to come.

Schumann suffered another health crisis later that summer, marked by hyperventilation and shortness of breath. After rehearsing his Overture to *Julius Caesar* with the orchestra, he noted: "Sad weakening of my strength. Extremely exhausted." He tried bathing in the Rhine each day. A holiday with Clara at the spa of Scheveningen, in the Netherlands, failed to provide relief. His last diary note before leaving Düsseldorf for the spa was "Miserable days." His first note on returning to the new lodgings on Bilkerstrasse, after three weeks of treatment, was "Miserable state." It was not until the end of September that he noted: "Better state on the whole." He was correcting the parts for *Pilgrimage of the Rose*, working on a piano reduction of *Manfred*, correcting his revised D Minor Symphony. But the summer of 1852 marked a turning point from which there was to be no recovery.

It has become common to regard the music Schumann composed in Düsseldorf as his late style, on the analogy of the familiar division of Beethoven's works into early, middle, and late periods. It is hard to identify a middle style for Schumann, although his major works parallel distinct shifts in his circumstances. It could be argued that the Leipzig years, starting around 1830, represent his early style, devoted in the first ten years to works for piano alone; in early 1840 to a "Year of Song"; and after his marriage, in turn to symphonies, chamber works, and oratorio (*Paradise and the Peri*). The Dresden years (1845–1849) would represent his middle style, marked by a change from improvising at the piano to "working out" music in his head. The Dresden period begins with the study of counterpoint and the writing of fugues and canons, moves on to the Piano Concerto and the C Major Symphony, with its opening movement reflecting his troubled emotional state at the time. In his last years in Dresden, he turns to opera and grand choral works, followed by a second "Year of Song" in 1849. The Düsseldorf years (1850–1854) would represent his late style, sometimes described as a move toward increasing simplicity. This division has gained wide acceptance among critics, many of whom also argue that the late style reflects a weakening of creative power, linked to Schumann's breakdown in February of 1854.

It is true that Schumann always seems to be moving on, trying new experiments, creating his own variations on established genres. But he often returns to his earlier passions. He wrote songs throughout his life, and in his early years tried virtually every form that later defined an intensive period of composition—symphony, chamber works, choral works.

The Düsseldorf years are the problematical ones, for in this short period, from September 1850 to February 1854, Schumann's works are variable in quality. His late *Fantasiestücke* for piano, op. 111, hardly bears comparison with the enchanting *Fantasiestücke*, op. 12, of 1837. Yet the later "Fantasy Pieces," too, have qualities of their own, inviting reinterpretation by pianists who have already performed and recorded the earlier masterpieces. As lovers of Schumann's music have often discovered when they look at his late compositions, on close reading they reveal qualities of feeling and artistry as compelling as many of the earlier works. What seems to be missing is the effortless inventiveness of the early works, the apparently inexhaustible play of inspiration.

Violin Sonatas; Piano Trio in G Minor

Three works composed in the autumn of 1851 provide strong evidence of Schumann's undiminished creative powers at this time. The violinist Ferdinand David, concertmaster in Leipzig and Schumann's close friend, had been much taken with the *Fantasiestücke* for clarinet. He wrote to Schumann asking whether he might not write something equally fine for violin and piano. A year later, in September 1851, Schumann sketched a Violin Sonata for Piano and Violin in A Minor, followed soon by a Piano Trio in G Minor, and within days by a Grand Sonata for Violin and Piano in D Minor, in which David's name is ingeniously inscribed as a principal theme, announced boldly as four *forte* chords on the notes: D-A-F (for V)-D. The three works, all sketched and finished quickly, are among Schumann's finest compositions, and after a long period of neglect, they have entered the repertoire in performances and recordings. This group of three bears comparison with Schumann's works of 1842, the three op. 41 string quartets, all in linked keys, the Piano

Quintet in E-flat, essentially a string quartet in conversation with piano, and the Piano Quartet, also in E-flat. The two Piano Trios of 1847 were also closely related. In each case Schumann was composing in a single wave of inspiration, trying in each set of interlinked works new variations of melody, rhythm, and form, new ways of relating each movement to the others.

The A Minor Violin Sonata is a sustained *cri de coeur,* impassioned throughout. Schumann said it was written when he was very angry at certain people—probably the Düsseldorf orchestral committee and the musicians who complained about his conducting. Anger is hardly conveyed by the sonata, which is lyrical from its opening bars through to the end. Perhaps Schumann was escaping from his uncomfortable relations with the Düsseldorf music committee by turning to his best resource in times of trouble, expressing his true feelings in music. The sighing interval calling "Clara" appears every now and then, forming a natural element in the texture of the music, usually in the voice of the violin, calling to the piano.

The Piano Trio in G Minor seems to carry on directly from the A Minor Violin Sonata. Both opening movements are in 6/8 time, with an arpeggiated piano accompaniment to a turbulent theme tossed back and forth by the strings. The opening motif of the Trio—a rhapsodic, arpeggiated cry by the violin, answered by the cello—echoes the final phrase of the Violin Sonata theme; it is also reminiscent of the strange cry of "The Prophet Bird" of *Waldszenen.* The distinctive motif is repeated insistently by each instrument in turn, giving the movement a driven, unstable character. A poignant slow movement follows, a heartrending dialogue between cello and violin, a song without words over a soft, chromatically rising chordal piano accompaniment. But even here, a new episode recalls the agitated, stormy writing of the first movement. The third movement recalls the two hunting songs in *Waldszenen*—as if the fairy tales of the dark forest were still haunting Schumann's imagination. The final movement is marked *Kräftig, mit humor* (strong, with humor), in a burlesque Florestanian mood, with *sforzando* diatonic chords firmly establishing G major as the "humorous" conclusion to one of Schumann's most elegiac works.

Even in the more conventional movements of the Violin Sonata and the Trio in G Minor, the writing in interludes is jagged, angular, unsettled, and unsettling. It could seem like a new development for Schumann, a "late style," as some critics have suggested. It could also be a reflection of his agitated feelings at the time, with public criticism reinforcing his own insecurities, his sense of failing powers. Increasingly taciturn, often withdrawn, he could not speak about these feelings except in his music, where his strong sense of structure enabled him to shape the musical content. The resulting compositions have great beauty and poignancy, even as they express his fears and anxieties.

The Piano Trio was dedicated to Schumann's friend, the Danish composer Niels Gade, whose surname Schumann had used as the theme of a "Nordisches Lied" in *Album for the Young*. Perhaps it was as a gesture to Gade that he chose the key of G minor; indeed the musical letters G-A-D-E can be discovered in measures 6 to 8 of the first movement, G-A-D in the piano bass notes, followed by a single E in the cello. But the theme is well disguised, meant simply as a private message to a friend.

The piano trio was followed almost immediately by a Grand Violin Sonata in D Minor, dedicated to Ferdinand David, with David's name broadly inscribed in notes in the opening chords of the slow introduction, again in the opening violin notes of the following allegro, and varied throughout the sonata. Schumann said that he wrote the Second Violin Sonata because he was dissatisfied with the first. He considered the Second more "friendly," and from its opening chords spelling "David" it is ebullient, rhythmically assertive, with bravura passages for the violin, and at times an improvisatory feeling. Schumann seems to be cheering himself up with a "friendly" game, playing with the four-note theme. But the intense lyrical beauty of the A Minor Sonata seems closer to Schumann's inner spirit. Perhaps he felt that its melancholy was too personal, too revealing. Both violin sonatas are closely written, their themes contrasted and interwoven, and they are often performed today. The G Minor Piano Trio too has been revived recently, after a long period of neglect.

—⊶⊷—

Four *Märchenbilder* (*Fairy Tale Pictures*) for viola and piano were composed for Wasielewski in three days in March 1851, and were dedicated to him; he played them through with Clara soon afterward. They combine the lyricism of the haunting Three Romances for Oboe, composed in 1849, with the folk elements marking the Five Pieces in Folk Style for cello and piano, also composed in 1849, and they have been performed to great effect by leading violists of our day. A set of *Märchenerzählungen* for clarinet, viola, and piano, was composed as late as October 1853. The instrumental combination explores the complementary expressive qualities of clarinet and viola; and the slow movement is written in Schumann's most poignant mode. Yet he seems content to repeat himself, to linger over the same melodic line, the rhythmic pattern established at the start of each movement. Determined as he was to continue working, to sit at his piano or his desk, to keep his mind active, he was tiring day by day. His last compositions hint at his physical and mental exhaustion as well as his heroic effort to keep the demons at bay.

It was Joseph Joachim who inspired Schumann's most substantial works for violin, composed in September and October of 1853. Joachim, the seventh child of a Hungarian Jewish family, well trained by leading teachers in Pest (now Budapest), had entered the Leipzig Conservatory as a twelve-year-old prodigy in 1843. Mendelssohn immediately recognized the boy's remarkable gifts and took him to London, where he performed Beethoven's Violin Concerto with his own cadenzas to great acclaim. Schumann's diary for 1845 records "the young Joachim" performing the Mendelssohn Violin Concerto in Dresden, with Hiller conducting. Joachim reappeared in Schumann's life in his last year in Dresden, visiting with Niels Gade and attending the music festival in Schumann's honor held in Leipzig. Schumann became close friends with Joachim at the Lower Rhine Festival in May 1853, when Joachim performed the Beethoven Violin Concerto in the same concert in which Clara played Schumann's Piano Concerto.

Though still in his early twenties, Joachim was now a recognized composer as well as the greatest violinist in Europe, a deeply serious musician, with a profound love of Bach and Beethoven, devoted, like Schumann, to Beethoven's late string quartets. He was also a lover of Shakespeare, and had composed overtures to *Hamlet* and *Henry IV*, with the hope of writing an opera of *Hamlet*. When he first heard Joachim's *Hamlet* Overture, Schumann recognized the young man as a true fellow spirit. At his request, Joachim sent him the score, along with a gift of the Beethoven concerto. Thanking Joachim, Schumann wrote of the present: "It reminds me of the magician who led us with perfect assurance through the mazes of this magic structure, impenetrable to most." Joachim visited Schumann again at the end of August, and played sonatas for violin and piano with Clara. Schumann described his playing as "Wonderful!" On the next day, he wrote: "Joachim astounds everyone"; and on the following evening, "Joachim played music—happy hours."

Schumann was entranced by the young man's playing, by his ambition and dedication. Joachim became one of the inner circle, a devoted friend and admirer of both Schumann and Clara, a supremely gifted fellow musician. Schumann composed a Fantasie for Violin and Orchestra for Joachim in September 1853, which he performed more than once. The Fantasie, lasting only fifteen minutes, was followed in October by a three-movement Violin Concerto, composed, like the Fantasie, with Joachim's effortless virtuosity in mind and his special quality of tone, with dazzling passagework, double stops, and sustained legato lines in the highest possible register. Although he said he loved the slow movement, Joachim found the writing awkward, and he was reluctant to perform the work. Years later, Clara consulted him again about its perceived defects, and with Brahms's agreement she omitted the concerto from her edition of the Collected Works. The Violin Concerto was resurrected in 1937 by two great-nieces of Joachim's, who claimed that they were led to the manuscript, on deposit in the Prussian State Library, by the spirits of Joachim and Schumann. Several leading violinists, including Yehudi Menuhin, welcomed the concerto, and it has had a new life in performances and recordings. It is a virtuoso showpiece for the violin, with a slow movement that in the hands of a great violinist often reduces listeners to tears. Most critics agree that its musical qualities are not on the same level as Schumann's earlier works, even those of the Düsseldorf years, and the orchestral accompaniment is barely sketched. Schumann was fighting an illness which manifested itself in attacks of tinnitus, dizziness, headache, impaired speech. It seems reasonable to assume that he was working on automatic pilot much of the time. Yet there is enough material of genuine beauty, or pathos, in all these works to charm listeners.

In October, Schumann also composed a set of Five Romances for Cello, which Christian Reimers performed several times. Clara felt that the works were unworthy of Schumann's standards, and she decided not to publish them, either separately or as part of Schumann's Collected Works. She held on to the score until 1893, at which point she consulted Brahms. When he agreed that the work was not worthy of publication, she destroyed the manuscript. It seems that Reimers took a copy of the Romances with him to Australia, where he moved soon after Schumann's death. The score may yet be discovered, reassessed, and attributed either to Schumann's mental decline or to a new "music of the future."

During his last years, Schumann was moving in new directions, many of them mentioned in his "Advice to Young Musicians." He was attracted by folk song as a source of "lovely melodies and national character." In his Five Pieces in Folk Style for Cello and Piano, the Schubertian dance forms of waltz, ländler, polonaise, ecossaise gave way to a new "folk" style, with strong rhythms, unusual harmonies, sharply accented offbeats. The work is delightful in performance. Schumann had in mind Bach's insertion of a "quodlibet" based on two common folk songs as the penultimate number of the *Goldberg* Variations; Beethoven too often includes traditional tunes in his works. Schumann himself had made use of the "Grandfather's Dance," or "Theme from the seventeenth century," in *Papillons*, *Carnaval*, and *Carnival Jest from Vienna*. Yet he also indulges his personal motto in the Five Pieces for cello with the lovely introduction of a "Clara" theme midway. In the *Rhenish* Symphony, he told Wasielewski, he was aiming for a popular style, realized in the country dance of the second movement. But this is only one element of several. Counterpoint is employed throughout the symphony, and the polyphony of the "ceremonial" movement suggests a sophisticated musical source, the sixteenth-century *stile antico* of Palestrina and Lassus, whose works Schumann read through with the choral group he founded in Düsseldorf.

His interest in choral writing, praised in "Advice to Young Musicians," goes back to his early married years and *Paradise and the Peri*. Most of his shorter choral works were composed for the choral groups he conducted, first in Dresden, then in Düsseldorf. During this time he published four volumes of *Romances and Ballads* for mixed choir, and several shorter sets for male or female voices, usually unaccompanied or with instrumental accompaniment ad libitum. He had always been fond of fairy tales, legends, and ballads. He set them now as grand, extended works for soloists, chorus, and orchestra or, more attractively, as "songs without words" for solo instruments: the exquisite Three Romances for Oboe and Piano, the *Fairy-Tale Pictures* for viola and piano, the *Fairy Tales* for clarinet, viola, and piano. He was drawn to music for children and images of childhood innocence, like the mysterious Mignon in *Wilhelm Meister's Apprenticeship*, and the young poet Elisabeth Kulmann. In part this coincided with his attachment to his growing family, especially the older girls, all given pet names: Mariechen, Lieschen, Jülchen. *Album for the Young* was written for Marie and Elise, both of whom were taking piano lessons; and on her thirty-third birthday, Clara was presented with a song written jointly by "Marie and Papa." Before putting together the *Album for the Young*, Schumann presented Marie with a handwritten Klavierbüchlein (Little Piano Book), inscribed "For Mariechen's 7th birthday, the 1st of September 1848, from her Papa." The nicely bound manuscript, recently published in facsimile, included simple pieces by Bach, Mozart, Handel, Schubert, and Beethoven, ending with a "Rebus" puzzle—notes that could be read as letters: "Las das Fade, fass das Aechde" (Give up the fads, seize the genuine). It was a principle that Schumann followed conscientiously throughout his life.

Another interest at this time, also going back to his early years, was music of a specifically religious cast—the highest aim of every composer, he told a correspondent. As a child he had set the 150th Psalm for chorus and orchestra. Now he composed two liturgical works, a Mass and a Requiem, intended for performance at one of the large Catholic churches in Düsseldorf but also suitable for the concert hall. He wrote both works very quickly, and he was unable to secure complete performances or publication for either. In later years, Clara was uncertain about whether they should be published. After consulting Brahms and Joachim, she decided to include them in Schumann's Collected Works, and both can now be heard on the Internet. They show little of the experimentation that marks several of Schumann's late works, but they are serious and rather beautiful settings of the traditional Latin texts. Several earlier works included elements that could be considered religious or spiritual: *Paradise and the Peri, Scenes from Goethe's "Faust," Genoveva* (the latter two works include prayers to the Virgin Mary), and "Adventlied," Rückert's poem describing Christ's entry into Jerusalem. Schumann made little distinction between religious and spiritual belief in his life or his music; he was "religious without religion." Bach, a devout Lutheran, was always his master. As music director in Düsseldorf, Schumann scheduled Bach's *St. Matthew Passion* and *St. John Passion* and Handel's *Israel in Egypt* and *Joshua,* all settings of biblical texts. He often said that the only sources needed for moral or spiritual instruction were the Bible, Shakespeare, and Goethe. In their letters and diaries, both Schumann and Clara express a conventional faith in a benevolent God. They had their children baptized but otherwise had little contact with organized religion. They both believed that human beings, especially creative artists, had to shape their lives through their own efforts.

FINAL CRISIS

Düsseldorf, October 1853–February 1854

RETROSPECT

During the Düsseldorf years, Schumann decided to look back over his working career and to put it all in order—his early compositions, his critical writings, his collection of extracts about music by Shakespeare, Goethe, E. T. A. Hoffmann, Jean Paul, and other favorite writers. He referred to the pieces he had written for the *New Journal for Music* as his *Davidsbündlerei*, explaining the term in the introduction to his *Collected Writings on Music and Musicians*, in which he fondly recalled the origins of the music journal:

> Toward the end of the year 1833, a number of musicians—most of them young—met together, as though by accident, every evening in Leipzig . . . partly the result of a desire for social intercourse, as well as for the exchange of ideas about that art which was the food and drink of life to them—music . . . On the stage Rossini reigned, at the pianoforte nothing was heard but Herz and Hünten; yet only a few years had passed since Beethoven, Carl von Weber, and Franz Schubert had lived among us. True, Mendelssohn's star was rising, and one heard wonderful things of a Pole named Chopin . . . One day the thought awakened in these hotheads, "Let us not look on idly, let us also lend our aid to progress, let us again bring the

poetry of art to honor among men!" Then the first sheets of a new musical paper were published . . . One of the party—the musical visionary of the society—who had dreamed away his life until then . . . decided to take the editorship of the paper in his own hands . . . And here I may mention a society, a more-than-secret society, which never existed save in the heart of its founder; that of the *Davidsbund.* It seemed a fit idea, in order to express different views on art, to invent opposite artistic characters, among whom Florestan and Eusebius were the most remarkable . . . This society of *Davidsbündler* wound itself like a red thread through the music journal, binding together truth and poetry.

The tone is that of a man of advanced years remembering his early enthusiasms. It is another self-portrait, recalled from a distance, of a "musical visionary," a dreaming youth. These were qualities he never lost, though they were less perceptible to the wider world and less evident in his music.

At this time he was also revising his early piano works, publishing them in new editions and removing all trace of their original authors, Florestan and Eusebius. The new editions included the early Sonatas, op. 11 ("dedicated to Clara by Florestan and Eusebius") and op. 14; the *Etudes symphoniques;* the *Davidsbündlertänze,* originally signed by "F" and "E," now renamed "Eighteen Character Pieces"; and *Kreisleriana,* with its musical portrait of Hoffmann's distraught Kapellmeister, in some ways a "double" of Schumann himself. These works were also stripped of their more awkward details and regularized, to the dismay of many later performers. The changes to *Davidsbündlertänze,* Schumann's most personal work, were the most extensive—some would say the most destructive. As originally published, the *Davidsbündlertänze* contained secret messages to Clara from "F" and "E," which were now conscientiously removed. Clara had been resistant to the work from the start. She preferred the charm of *Carnaval,* which she often performed. Schumann had put so much of his own life and feeling into *Davidsbündlertänze* that he begged her to think again, explaining that the pieces were the "faces" as opposed to the "masks" of *Carnaval*—that is, the true selves of the composer. These faces are the divided aspects of Schumann himself, in many forms, wild and mild, exuberant and quiet, intimate, declamatory, remembering the past, anticipating the future. Clara, too, appears, although she seems not to have noticed that two of her early works are extensively quoted, and that she signs off each book of nine pieces in her key of C. In his revision, although Schumann removed all clues to the secret messages, he left them embedded in the music.

Schumann always kept meticulous records, and he took stock of his life at regular intervals. In these last years, he felt a new compulsion to put everything in order, for himself, for posterity. Going through his early manuscripts, he selected several short pieces intended originally for *Carnaval,* the *Novelletten,* and *Kinderszenen* and published them in a new collection as *Albumblätter* (Album Leaves). They are a poignant reminder of the ease with which he composed and the touching simplicity of many of his compositions in those early years.

Toward the end of his second year in Düsseldorf, Schumann returned to the D Minor Symphony composed ten years before. He now revised it in ways he believed would enhance its orchestration and overall structure, a matter partly of doubling strings with winds or brass. He also changed the tempo markings for the first and second movements. Now marked *Ziemlich langsam* (quite slow) for both opening movements instead of the original Andante con moto (first movement) and Andante (the second), the slower tempo gives the symphony a deeper, more tragic tone, more portentous. It is probably what Schumann wanted at this point in his life, when all tempos seemed too fast to him. He retained the free form of the symphony, in which each movement leads naturally into the next, so that the whole is one continuous work. He was tempted to call it "Fantasy" or "Symphonic Fantasy," but simply renumbered it as Symphony no. 4, and conducted it successfully at the Lower Rhine Festival in Düsseldorf. It was soon published, and the revised version is still the main source of modern performances.

Both in its original and its revised version, it is a splendid addition to the other three symphonies. All four are often recorded together, and performed frequently in concert series and festivals. Along with Mendelssohn's *Italian* and *Scottish* Symphonies, Schumann's symphonies define the Romantic genre as a distinctive development of well-established classical form, building on past masters but pointing toward the future—just as Schumann hoped. His symphonies served as a major inspiration for Brahms and later composers. Despite reservations about the orchestration and discreet revision by several conductors, they constitute an enduring tribute to Schumann's genius.

The same cannot be said for the ambitious dramatic works for soloists, chorus, and orchestra on which he lavished so much care, *Paradise and the Peri, Genoveva, Scenes from Goethe's "Faust,"* and the late fairy tales. Despite passages of great beauty, these large-scale works require special effort on the part of dedicated conductors and performers, and although they are occasionally revived, they tend to remain interesting curiosities.

Probably the oddest development of the Düsseldorf years was the joy with which Schumann embraced "table tapping" as a means of communicating with the dead. In a letter to Hiller he described his pleasure in the new fashion:

> Yesterday for the first time we succeeded in moving the table. A wondrous power! Just imagine, I asked what the rhythm of the first two measures of the C Minor Symphony was. It [the table] waited longer than usual to answer—finally it began—♪♪♪|♩|—but somewhat slow. When I said: "But the tempo is faster, dear table," it hurried to tap out the right tempo . . . We were all beside ourselves with astonishment. But enough! I was too full of this today to keep silent about it.

Schumann's delight in "table tapping" has been taken as a sign of failing mental powers, approaching delusion. But he was simply responding with his usual enthusiasm to a game that he could share with family and friends. He had recently given dramatic expression to the spirits summoned by Manfred and Faust. Ten years earlier he had given voice to the Peri, half human, half divine, to the angel guarding the gate of the Islamic heaven and to a host of houris. To summon the spirit of Beethoven by tapping out the opening rhythm of the Fifth Symphony came naturally to one so well attuned to the supernatural. It must have enchanted the children, giving them a sense of the special power of their papa.

Schumann loved all games and puzzles, puns and anagrams, chess, dominoes, and billiards, which he had played almost daily when he was in company with Mendelssohn. These were all forms of mental relaxation, as was his study of fugue and canon. At the end of his Düsseldorf years, he paid a final tribute to Bach, the master of fugue, to whom he turned earlier in times of joy, latterly in times of distress. Leaving the original scores unchanged, he composed piano accompaniments for Bach's Sonatas and Partitas for Solo Violin, and soon afterward for the six solo Cello Suites.

Whether or not Schumann was moving in these years toward a new style, there is no doubt that he was suffering from a physical decline, increasingly noticeable to others. In addition to the intermittent physical symptoms he recorded in his household book—headache, dizziness, muscular spasms, aural afflictions—friends described absentmindedness, apathy, and irritability. He hardly spoke in company, even at rehearsals with the chorus or orchestra, or he spoke indistinctly. If he was challenged, he lost his temper or left the room. These quirks of behavior go back to earlier times. During their Russian tour, when he felt insulted at one of Clara's concerts, he said nothing to her, but recorded his annoyance in his diary. In his account of Clara's tour to Copenhagen, when Schumann returned home alone, Schumann wrote that he was so averse to argument that he simply agreed to whatever Clara wanted.

He was usually described as good-natured and amiable rather than short-tempered. But when Liszt made a disparaging remark about Mendelssohn, Schumann exploded. He told Liszt that he refused to hear his late friend attacked, and he stomped out of the room. Liszt countered by saying it was only from Schumann that he would accept such rudeness.

Not long after this episode, Franz Brendel published an anti-Semitic piece in the September 1850 issue of the *New Journal for Music*, "Das Judentum in der Musik" (Judaism in Music) by Wagner, signing himself as "K. Freigedank" (Freethinker). The notorious essay attacked Mendelssohn as the most refined example of a Jewish composer, who nonetheless could never achieve true creative greatness because of the race from which he came—a "mongrel" race lacking a nation or a language, preying on its host country. It is likely that Schumann never saw the piece, which he would have found as outrageous as Liszt's remarks. He had just moved to Düsseldorf when the article was published, and there was a gap in his complimentary subscription. Wieck certainly read the anti-Semitic piece, writing to Brendel: "The article on 'Judentum in der Musik' is the most spirited and striking that I and my friends have ever read on this subject. What will your friend Moscheles etc. [that is, Ferdinand David, Ferdinand Hiller, Joachim, and many other Jewish musicians] say about that?" Moscheles and ten other professors wrote to Brendel asking that he resign from the Leipzig Conservatory.

It was soon after his unthinking attack on Mendelssohn that Liszt offered to perform *Genoveva, Manfred,* and the *Scenes from "Faust"* at Weimar, affirming again that he held the highest possible opinion of Schumann's works. The lines between the "New German" school of Liszt and Wagner and the "reactionary" music of the past, represented by Mendelssohn, were already being drawn. Liszt was anxious to claim Schumann for his own party.

Schumann was apparently indifferent to the politics governing musical allegiances at this time. Perhaps he was too wrapped up in his own problems in Düsseldorf. His quirks of behavior, which had once seemed idiosyncratic, were now troubling even to close friends. His absentmindedness at the podium was obvious not only to the musicians but to audiences and critics. He buried his head in the score and failed to signal entries to musicians. Wasielewski, as concertmaster, had to cover for him, conducting discreetly from the first desk. At a rehearsal Schumann continued conducting after the players had finished; again his friends covered for him. He was only in his early forties, but he seemed to be aging rapidly. His irascibility increased, and when he was confronted with problems caused by his apparent inattentiveness, he dismissed his critics as enemies and fools.

He was supported by Clara, who could not bear to see her husband attacked by people she considered lacking in respect. She had taken a dislike to Julius Tausch on first meeting him, displeased by his looks. Schumann, who relied on him as a substitute conductor as well as rehearsal pianist, turned against him when Tausch accepted the music committee's request that he take over most conducting responsibilities. Schumann wrote to him saying that if he accepted the commission, he, Schumann, would regard him as "ill disposed." Poor Tausch was put in an impossible position. He accepted the role of conductor and was banished by the Schumanns.

"HERR BRAHMS, FROM HAMBURG"

Fortunately, Schumann's life was given new direction by the loyal Joachim, who urged his young friend Johannes Brahms to pay a visit to the Schumanns. The visit followed a five-week summer tour of the Rhine, during which Brahms stayed near Bonn with the Deichmann family, wealthy patrons of the arts. There he met Wasielewski and Christian Reimers, who introduced him to Schumann's music. Johannes, as everyone knew him, was soon ready to make his way to Düsseldorf to meet the famous artistic couple.

The story is well known. On September 30, 1853, a bedraggled young man knocked at the house on Bilkerstrasse and was invited in by Schumann. The household book records on September 30th, "Herr Brahms, from Hamburg"; and on October 1st, "Brahms visits—a genius!" The young man played the opening pages of his First Piano Sonata for Schumann, who interrupted him to invite Clara to join them. Brahms resumed his attack on the piano, emerging from his demonic labors half an hour later.

Schumann welcomed the young composer's works with the same

enthusiasm with which he had greeted Chopin's "Mozart" Variations. Brahms spent much of the next month in Schumann's company, playing through all the manuscripts he had brought with him: piano sonatas, a violin sonata, a string quartet, his double octaves flying from one end of the piano to the other. Clara wrote in her diary: "It is truly moving, to see this man sitting at the piano with his interesting young face, transformed as he plays, his fine hand, which with the greatest ease deals with the greatest difficulties (his pieces are very difficult) and then these marvelous compositions." Later she set a good example to the eager youth, whose articulation was less than perfect. His fingers were short and he probably tended to fake bravura passages, as pianists do to this day.

Brahms came from an extremely modest background. His father was a double-bass player, eking out a living by erratic work in Hamburg's theater orchestra and the town band. His mother, Christiane, seventeen years older than his father, was a simple, uneducated woman, very fond of her gifted son. There was also an older sister, Elise, and a younger brother, Fritz. When Brahms was born, the family lived in three rooms on the first story of the Specksgang Towers, on Anselar Platz in Hamburg, a large tenement housing at least fifty families. They moved frequently, but space was always tight, and money short. His father taught the talented boy to play violin and piano, and at the age of ten he began free piano lessons with a well-known Hamburg teacher, Eduard Marxsen. When the boy left school at fourteen, according to his first biographer, he added to the family income by playing the piano in the seedy taverns and dance halls near the harbor of the thriving port city.

Nothing dampened his love of music—Bach and Beethoven, folk songs and Hungarian dances. He was also passionately fond of literature. Like Schumann, he was a great reader. His favorites were Shakespeare, Goethe, and the *Arabian Nights.*

He met Joachim through the Hungarian Jewish violinist, Eduard Reményi, with whom Brahms had been touring North German towns, playing Gypsy music in bars and taverns. Joachim invited Brahms to spend the summer with him at Göttingen, Brahms's first experience of a university atmosphere. Determined to help his new friend, Joachim gave him introductions to Liszt and Schumann. Brahms was welcomed by Liszt at Weimar, but was uneasy at being enlisted in the "New German" school, with Liszt and Wagner as its chief exemplars. His visit to the Schumanns, soon afterwards, was to change his life.

He was twenty years old, slight of build, beardless, with clear blue eyes and thin fair hair falling to his shoulders. His voice was high-pitched, as if it had yet to break. Schumann and Clara embraced him as a son. He worshipped them both, Schumann as "Mynheer Domine." Within a few days of their acquaintance, Schumann wrote to Joachim in high excitement: "The young eagle has found an old attendant who, used to such young high flyers, understands how to calm the wild beatings of their wings without hindering their powers." At about the same time, Brahms also wrote to Joachim, now his dearest friend:

> What shall I write to you about Schumann, shall I break out in hosannas over his genius and character, or shall I lament that once again people are committing the great sin of misjudging a good man and divine artist so much, and of honoring him so little? And I myself, how long did I commit this sin! Only since leaving Hamburg and especially during my stay in Mehlem [with the Deichmanns], did I learn to know and honor Schumann's works.

Yet even before Brahms came to know Schumann, he signed himself "Johannes Kreisler Junior," in tribute to the distraught Kapellmeister who also inspired Schumann's *Kreisleriana.* The aging master and the young disciple had more in common than they knew.

Soon after Brahms's arrival, Schumann composed an article for his former music journal, greeting Brahms as the herald of a new age. "New Paths" could be seen as a companion piece to Schumann's early review of Chopin's "Mozart" Variations, in which he hailed Chopin as "a genius." Schumann had been equally generous and warmhearted at that time. But the tone of his essay about Brahms is touched with manic rapture. True to Schumann's artistic principles and his sense of his place in history, it includes another self-portrait, marked with signs of the coming tragedy:

> Years have gone by—nearly as many as I had previously dedicated to editing these pages; that is, ten—since I last was heard from in this terrain, so rich in memories. Often, despite intensive productive activity, I felt moved to speak; [for] a new force in music seemed to announce itself, to which many of the emerging artists of recent times bear witness . . . Following their paths with the greatest interest, I thought that there must suddenly appear one who was called to give voice to the highest expression of the times . . . one who, like Minerva, should spring fully armed from the forehead of Zeus. And he has arrived, a youth over whose cradle the Graces and Heroes kept watch. His name is Johannes Brahms. Seated at the piano, he began to reveal wondrous regions. . . . There came a moment of inspiration which transformed the piano into an orchestra of wailing and jubilant voices. If he were to wave his magic wand over the massed powers of the chorus and orchestra, still more wonderful glimpses into the mysteries of the spiritual world will be revealed to us.

And Schumann summoned the *Davidsbündler* to engage once more in battle against the Philistines:

> His comrades greet him at his first step in the world, where wounds may perhaps await him, but also the bay and the laurel. We welcome this valiant warrior. In every age there presides a secret band of kindred spirits. Ye who belong together, close your ranks ever more tightly, so that the truth of art may shine more clearly, spreading joy and blessings over all things.

With hindsight, there are clear signs of overexcitement in the article: extravagant metaphors, the "orchestra of wailing and jubilant voices," the "mysteries of the spiritual world," the secret band, the messianic language. Yet the underlying meaning is consistent with Schumann's lifelong belief in the power of art as a force for good.

Joachim came for a few days, curious to see the impression his friend was making. The party continued, with much music-making. Joachim returned to Hanover, where he was concertmaster of the court orchestra, and he appeared again in Düsseldorf to rehearse his *Hamlet* Overture for a subscription concert on the 27th of October. Neither the rehearsal nor the concert went well, and Joachim suspected that Schumann was suffering from hearing loss. A soiree of chamber music two days later was more successful, opening with Schumann's D Minor Violin Sonata and ending with Beethoven's *Kreutzer* Sonata, performed by Joachim and Clara. Joachim also played his own variations on a Paganini caprice, and Clara performed short works by Chopin, Mendelssohn, and Schumann. In the happy spirit of his *Carnaval* games, playing with the letter-notes of "A.S.C.H.—S.C.H.A.," Schumann proposed that he and Brahms should collaborate with their friend Albert Dietrich on a birthday present for Joachim, a violin sonata using the initial letters of Joachim's motto, "Frei aber einsam"—Free but lonely. This became the FAE Sonata, the first movement composed by Dietrich, the scherzo by Brahms, and an intermezzo and finale by Schumann. Brahms's scherzo, which cleverly conceals the motto FAE in the opening bars of the piano accompaniment, is the only movement frequently played today. Schumann added two movements to make up his Third Violin Sonata, published only in 1927. The work has never achieved the popularity of his first two violin sonatas, although, like virtually all his late works, it has been reinterpreted and acclaimed by lovers of his music.

During Brahms's visit the dispute with the music committee simmered on, interrupting the joyful spirits of the family and their young friends. The town musicians no longer wished Schumann to conduct; and committee members were increasingly pressed to act. The chairman, Julius Illing, and an associate, J. E. Heister, who evidently had tried to pacify the musicians, visited Schumann on the 19th of October to persuade him to hand most of the conducting over to Tausch. Schumann was insulted; Clara was furious. Angry letters were exchanged. Schumann's diary notes, "Shameless people"; and on the 7th of November, "Day of decision." He and Clara talked about leaving Düsseldorf, perhaps for Berlin, perhaps for Vienna, the home of Beethoven and Schubert, where composers were honored properly. Forgotten were Schubert's neglect in Vienna and Schumann's own failure in the Austrian capital. At a subscription concert scheduled for the 10th of November, Schumann and Clara absented themselves, remaining at home. The music committee decided that Tausch would conduct the remaining concerts, and he was appointed music director the following year, after Schumann's contract expired. Schumann's relationship with Düsseldorf's musical forces and the civic authorities was officially at an end, although the mayor arranged for him to be paid for the remaining year of his contract.

In mid-October, Schumann wrote a set of five *Gesänge der Frühe* (Songs of Dawn) for piano. This late work is utterly unlike anything he had written before, both in its unsettling themes and in its unusual, barely resolved harmonic sequences. The opening piece, in what should be the cheerful key of D major, suggests the rising sun illuminating the land. But there is a minor inflection throughout. The following pieces are variations on a hymn to the rising light, and the final piece is a D-major chorale, a solemn prayer echoing the opening piece. Each song has a rising motif, a rising fifth in the first song, a rising fourth in the second. But there is also persistent downward movement, and each song ends with a sad fading away to *piano* or *pianissimo*. The tone is mournful, as if embodying the profound melancholy from which Schumann so often suffered. In their own, very different form, the *Songs of Dawn* complement *Mein schöner Stern* ("My Beautiful Star") in the *Minnespiel,* op. 101, in which the composer prays fervently to the "bright star" to illuminate and dispel his "dark clouds." The manuscript of the *Songs of Dawn* is inscribed "To Diotima," a reference to the wise priestess who discourses on love in Plato's *Symposium*, identifying her with the rising sun and with her power to heal the troubled spirit. "Diotima" is mentioned in the household book on the 15th and

16th of October. Two days later, the *Songs of Dawn* were completed. Schumann described them in a letter to his publisher Friedrich Wilhelm Arnold thus: "They are musical pieces meant to picture the feelings aroused by the gradual dawning and full growth of the morning, but more as an expression of feelings than as a painting."

Opinion is divided on the merit of this late work. Perhaps it is best understood as a last, despairing self-portrait in tones. Schumann is struggling to assert hope with all his remaining strength, as he faces the encroaching dark.

Brahms left to join Joachim in Hanover, and Schumann and Clara embarked on three weeks of concerts in Utrecht, Rotterdam, Amsterdam, and The Hague. In Amsterdam, a concert at the Felix Meritis hall included Schumann's Symphony no. 2, with Clara playing Beethoven's *Emperor* Concerto; Mendelssohn's *Variations sérieuses,* his most substantial work for piano; and two of his *Songs Without Words.* A "Soirée musicale" in Rotterdam opened with Schumann's Piano Quintet, with the Piano Quartet opening the second half. Clara also played Beethoven's *Appassionata* Sonata and her own Variations on a Theme of Robert Schumann, composed the previous summer. The concert tour included Schumann's *Pilgrimage of the Rose,* his *Spring* and *Rhenish* Symphonies, and Clara playing his Piano Concerto and his new Concert-Allegro for piano and orchestra, Weber's Konzertstück, Mendelssohn's G Minor Piano Concerto, and works for piano alone by Bach and Chopin. Although she was in her third month of pregnancy, Clara was in her element, and indefatigable. Schumann's diary records his delight as the tour progressed. In each city they were honored and greeted with enthusiasm. It was one of their most successful tours, despite occasional hints of malaise.

Christmas was celebrated at home with Dietrich, Christian Reimers, and Rupert Becker, who had replaced Wasielewski as concertmaster of the orchestra. On the 19th of January, Schumann and Clara traveled to Hanover to spend time with Joachim and Brahms. For Schumann, the young men were like a reincarnation of his early years and the merry group of music lovers gathered around him in Leipzig. Their deepening friendship with the gifted young musicians marked a new life for Schumann and Clara, celebrated in musical collaborations read through in private, performed in public. The humiliations of the preceding months receded.

"MUSIC IS SILENT NOW"

In early February 1854 Schumann wrote to Joachim in a tone as friendly and affectionate as ever. But his letter struck a strange note from the start:

> We have been gone a whole week without sending you or your companions a word. But I have often written to you in spirit, and there is a secret writing, to be revealed later, between these lines.
>
> And I have dreamt of you, dear Joachim; we were together for three days—you had some heron's feathers in your hands, from which champagne was flowing—how prosaic! but how true!— . . .
>
> Meanwhile I have been working at my "Poets' Garden." It grows ever more imposing; I have added some signposts here and there to prevent misunderstanding—that is, explanatory notes. Now I am deep in the ancient past, in Homer and the Greeks. Especially in Plato I have discovered wonderful passages.
>
> Music is silent now—at least outwardly. How is it with you? . . .
>
> The cigars suit me perfectly. They seem to have a Brahmsian flavor, as usual, somewhat strong, but tasting very well! Now I see him beginning to smile.
>
> I will end now. It is already growing dark. Write to me soon—in words and also in notes!—R. Sch.

Four days after writing to Joachim, Schumann noted in his household book: "In the evening very strong and painful aural attack." A daily record of distress was noted in Schumann's usual telegraphic fashion, alongside records of expenses: a weekly allowance to Clara of fifteen thalers, and smaller amounts for coal, laundry, postage, and beer. On the 11th of February: "Terrible night (hearing and headache)." On the 12th: "Even worse, but also wonderful: the voices sang 'Ein feste Burg' [the Lutheran chorale "A mighty fortress"]." The next day: "Wondrous suffering." On the 14th: "Somewhat better during the day; toward evening very strong (wondrous music)." On the 15th: "A time of suffering: Dr. Hasenclever." (Dr. Richard Hasenclever was called in on the 15th and returned each day; a Dr. Adolf Böger from the military barracks was also consulted.) On the 16th: "No better—old poems gathered together." There are no further entries about his state of mind, just a short list of expenses and, on the 23rd, "The copyist," possibly for the collection of poetic extracts he was putting together for his "Poets' Garden." On the 24th he wrote a letter to his publisher about the *Songs of Dawn,* and on the 26th a note about corrections for a Dutch translation of *Pilgrimage of the Rose,* recently performed in Amsterdam. Both letters were perfectly lucid.

Clara took up the account in her own diary:

Soon after we had gone to bed, Robert got up again and wrote down a theme which he said the angels had sung to him; after he had finished it, he lay down and was delirious all night long, his eyes permanently open and raised heavenwards; he was absolutely convinced that angels were hovering about him and making the most marvelous revelations to him, all in wonderful music; they were calling out to welcome us, and together the two of us would be with them before the year was out . . . Robert spent the entire day at his writing desk with paper, pen, and ink before him, listening to the angel voices and writing down a few words every now and then, but not a lot, and listening repeatedly. During all this time he looked blissful; I shall never forget that look, and yet it broke my heart to see this unnatural bliss just as much as it did to see him tormented by the evil spirits. Oh, all this filled my heart with the most fearful concern as to how it was to end; I saw his mind grow more and more disturbed, but did not yet have any idea of what stood before him and before me . . .

He often had moments at night when he begged me to go from him, because he might do me harm! To calm him I went out of his sight, then returned to him . . . Often he lamented that his mind wasn't right, and he feared it would soon be over with him—then he bade me farewell, and put all his money and compositions in order, etc. . . . Then suddenly at 9:30 p.m. he rose from the sofa and wanted to have his clothes, for he said he must go to an asylum, for his senses were no longer working, and he had no idea what he might do during the night . . . Robert put everything in order that he wanted to take with him, watch, money, note paper, pens, cigars, in short everything with the clearest care, and when I asked him, "Robert, will you leave your wife and children?" he answered, "It will not be for long, I shall soon come back cured." . . . But Dr Böger persuaded him to go to bed, and comforted him until morning. I couldn't stay with him, I had to call for an attendant, staying myself in the room next door . . . Oh, what a terrible morning was to dawn! Robert got up, but he was so profoundly melancholy that I cannot begin to describe it. If I only so much as touched him, he said to me, "Oh, Clara, I'm not worthy of your love." *He* said that, *he* to whom I've always looked up with the greatest, deepest respect . . . Oh, and no amount of soothing words could help.

The catastrophe broke upon them soon afterward. Clara had asked Marie to stay with her papa while she spoke to the doctors. Schumann was making a clean copy of his variations on the theme dictated to him by the spirit of Schubert. Somehow he slipped past the child into the garden, and before anyone realized what had happened, he disappeared. They went out to search for him, but the streets were thronged with carnival revelers, and they could find no trace of Schumann.

He had left the house in his dressing gown and slippers, with no coat or hat. Because it was carnival time, no one thought to stop him or to question his light apparel in the February rain. He made his way through the crowds to the "bridge of ships" across the Rhine, where he gave the toll keeper his silk handkerchief in lieu of coins. He stumbled across, stopped halfway, and threw his wedding ring into the river. Then, before anyone could stop him, he plunged into the river himself.

He was rescued almost at once by boatmen. He struggled with them but was restrained, and when he was recognized by passersby on the shore, he was brought back home, dripping wet, wrapped in blankets. Dr. Hasenclever and Dr Böger between them managed to administer a sedative, changed him into dry clothes, and helped him into bed. They prevailed upon Clara to take refuge with the children at the nearby home of her friend Rosalie Leser. In her fifth month of pregnancy, Clara had to be protected. But it was also for Schumann's sake that she agreed to take refuge with her friend.

What impelled Schumann to attempt suicide? Acute mental illness brings with it unimaginable pain. The mind is out of control, assailed by terrifying thoughts. As the barrier between dreams and waking life is eroded, the ordinary world recedes, and nightmares turn into hallucinations. The anguish can be so unbearable that the patient is driven to take any available means of ending his suffering.

Clara later found a note her distraught husband had left for her: "Dear Clara, I am going to throw my wedding ring into the Rhine, do you the same, as then both rings will be united with each other." He must have written the note just before leaving the house, intending to throw his wedding ring into the river, and then following it himself. It is possible that in his fevered mind, he was seeking not simply to end the life that had become intolerable to him, but to enter that kingdom under the sea pictured in the fairy tales and ballads he had recently set with such joy, the timeless realm in which lovers are joined forever, liberated from the jealousy and spite poisoning their earthly lives.

It is often said that Schumann was taken to Endenich at his own request. It is true that he told Clara he must go to an asylum to be cured. He also told the doctors repeatedly that he must be taken to an asylum. But when he was brought home after attempting suicide, he was in no state to make a decision. It was the doctors who took the next step. When they told Clara that Schumann seemed quieter, she sent him a loving note with a small pot of violets, which triggered extreme agitation. The doctors knew that they would be unable to treat him at home. They arranged to have him admitted to a private mental asylum at Endenich, half an hour from Bonn. Dr. Hasenclever knew the director, Dr. Franz Richarz, and vouched for his excellence. On March 4th, Schumann was taken by carriage to Endenich under restraint, with two warders in attendance. Dr. Hasenclever accompanied them. They stopped twice on the road for a brief rest, and arrived after an eight-hour drive at the clinic where Schumann was to die two and a half years later. His condition was diagnosed at first as "melancholia, with delusions." The diagnosis was later changed to "paralysie générale," or "general paralysis of the insane" (GPI), a progressive condition for which there was no treatment, and which was invariably fatal.

THE MIND STRIPPED BARE

Endenich, 4 March 1854–29 July 1856

Dr. Franz Richarz, the founder and director of the Endenich asylum, was an enlightened physician committed to the progressive psychiatric treatment pioneered by Philippe Pinel in France and John Connolly in England. Pinel recommended careful observation of patients, with daily visits and conversation, so that a detailed case history could be assembled. This was the procedure followed at Endenich. Dr. Richarz also believed in the beneficial effects of rest, diet, fresh air, and exercise.

The asylum was built to accommodate fourteen patients, but had expanded to hold thirty. A separate building was used for acute treatment, where a patient could be controlled twenty-four hours a day, and if necessary restrained. The famous composer was given a room of his own on the first floor, looking out onto a large garden, and he was assigned a special attendant. He was helped into bed, sedated, and strapped down for extra security.

Dr. Richarz told Dr. Hasenclever that for the time being, visits were strictly forbidden. It was necessary to shield the patient from further agitation. This meant no books, no music, no writing materials.

Clara's mother came to Düsseldorf from Berlin as soon as she was told of Schumann's collapse. Brahms arrived from Hanover and offered to stay with Clara as long as he was needed. Joachim followed two days later. Clara felt that her only means of bearing the strain was to resume as much of her usual life as possible, including her teaching. In the evening she and Joachim played Schumann's Third Violin Sonata, the expanded version of the FAE birthday present for Joachim. Clara waited anxiously for news. Wasielewski, now living in Bonn as choral director, had promised to visit the asylum daily and to send reports, but he remained strangely silent.

Until quite recently, the only direct evidence of Schumann's mental state at Endenich consisted of the letters he wrote between September 1854, seven months after he was taken to the asylum, and May 1855: several to Clara (of these, quite a few were lost or destroyed), some to Brahms and to Joachim, and others to his publishers. All the letters sent to Clara, Brahms, and Joachim were shared by the friends. On record also are reports by the visitors who were allowed to observe Schumann unseen or to spend an hour or two with him. Joachim and Brahms both visited Endenich, though they were not always permitted to spend time with Schumann.

It was long suspected that Richarz might have kept records of his most famous patient. In fact he kept a meticulous diary of Schumann's mental and physical symptoms, based on the twice-daily rounds that he took in turn with his colleague Dr. Eberhard Peters. Richarz took this record with him on leaving Endenich in 1859, but embargoed publication by his heirs.

In 1988 the documents came into the possession of the composer Aribert Reimann. After much heart searching, he deposited the sixteen folio sheets, closely written on both sides, in Berlin's Akademie der Künste. The complete medical record was published in 2006 with all the documents relating to Schumann's illness, and a full analysis of its origin and progress.

The medical diary makes harrowing reading. Schumann's entire history fed into his delusions. His lifelong anxieties are charted in the progressive disintegration of his mental and physical faculties, with heartrending intervals of self-awareness. Several times he refers to an unspecified guilt and to his fear that he is going mad. The avenging Nemesis, anticipated in Schumann's early record of his venereal infection, was in full pursuit twenty-three years later.

Within a few weeks of his admission, Schumann was permitting his attendant to help him dress, take meals, rest between meals. The immediate danger, as Schumann's agitation subsided, was that he would sink into melancholia. Richarz and Peters monitored the patient's diet and digestion, encouraged mild exercise, and supervised medication, with all details (including the demeaning application of enemas) carefully recorded. The general practice entailed a careful balance between activity and rest and the removal of supposed poisons from the body.

Clara's mother, Mariane, came to see Dr. Richarz, arriving by train from Düsseldorf. Richarz told her that the patient was quieter and that they hoped to see gradual improvement. She was pleased at the appearance of the asylum, the handsome buildings, the gardens and orchards, the view of the Kreuzberg near Poppelsdorf, the snow-covered mountains beyond Bonn. She asked Richarz to send Clara weekly reports of Schumann's condition. At the end of March, Mariane would be returning to Berlin. She planned to attend her daughter in June for the birth of a seventh child.

Schumann had not asked once about his wife or his children. He was still living in the world of his delusions. His only reference to his wife was a remark he made to Dr. Peters that "his first wife had died and was in Heaven." Peters told the patient that his first wife was in fact his present wife, and that she was still alive. He seemed pleased at this news, but did not pursue the subject.

Wasielewski delayed writing to Clara, hoping for some improvement in Schumann's condition. But he told Schumann's publisher Bartholf Senff that there was little prospect of a cure; Schumann had fallen into a profound melancholia, mixed with signs of insanity. Three weeks after Schumann's admission, Dr. Peters wrote to Clara that Schumann was calmer, but still subject to attacks of anxiety, when he paced back and forth in his room, sometimes kneeling on the carpet in his dressing gown, swaying back and forth, wringing his hands.

The doctors knew that it was too soon to detect signs of progress or to predict whether a cure was likely. The patient's mind was wide open; his darkest fears found horrific expression. He believed fervently that he was a sinner, damned forever. This was not an uncommon delusion, even among the sane. Religion encouraged the belief that all men were damned unless they subscribed to the Apostles' Creed and prayed each night to their heavenly father, his son, or his son's mother for absolution. In Schumann's sick mind, the conviction of sin was overwhelming. He told the doctors he had it on the highest authority that he was damned to burn in hell. He had committed wickedness: he had done many evil things. The doctors conscientiously wrote down the patient's ravings in their notes.

At the beginning of April, Clara wrote to Wasielewski asking if he could arrange to have fresh flowers given to Schumann each day. Perhaps the flowers would remind him of his study at home. The doctors reported that he had plucked some violets in the garden; might these not remind him of his wife?

It was true that Schumann was not as agitated as he had been on his arrival. He slept through the night and submitted to the routine provided: regular meals, a daily walk in the garden, weather permitting. For much of the day he remained in bed, dozing or half awake, muttering to himself, sometimes laughing at the conversations he was listening to in his head. He had a few violent episodes; twice he threw his attendant out of the room; once he struck out at Peters. He had bad nights, when he was in and out of bed several times, pacing back and forth in his room. If he remained free of agitation, Richarz hoped, they might see the beginning of a return to health.

Gradually the doctors noted that Schumann's condition seemed to be more stable. For two weeks, the nights had been calm, with no violent episodes. The patient was courteous and friendly to his attendants. He was beginning to notice the outside world. He commented several times on the flowers in the garden. These were small changes, but they suggested that a healing process was at work. Schumann had not asked about his wife, but he expressed surprise that Dr. Hasenclever had not visited him.

These signs of improvement suffered a setback in May. Dr. Peters wrote to Clara that Schumann was hearing voices again. Clara tried to relieve her suffering by playing Schumann's early music—the masquerade of *Carnaval,* even *Papillons,* which she never played in public. How could the man who created such joyful music be transformed into the tormented figure the doctors described? The same anguished question recurs in her diary and letters to her mother and close friends: how is it possible that her husband has not once asked about her? She tried summoning him—as they had done in their first long separation, before their marriage—by playing his music, arranging to have fresh flowers in his room, rereading his "Advice to Young Musicians," the "Musical Rules for Home and Life" so typical of his kindly nature. She thought of him day and night. Concentrating all her being on his works, his inmost self, would she not be able to reach him, to appear to him as his true, loving wife? Perhaps he blamed her for abandoning him. How terrible it would be if he doubted her love! If she were not expecting a child shortly, she would have no reason to live.

Better news from the doctors reached Clara in June, just before she gave birth to a healthy boy to be named Felix. Robert was no longer hearing voices, his general health and spirits had improved. He was playing dominoes. He asked about his surroundings; he wished to visit the Beethoven monument in Bonn. The signs were encouraging, but progress was slow.

Clara's spirits rose when the news was positive, only to sink again with the next report. Her chief support was the companionship of Brahms, who had taken a room nearby. He played Schumann's music and his own compositions for Clara, including a set of variations on the same theme on which Clara had composed her own variations. Brahms was uniting the three of them musically, in the same spirit in which Schumann had musically inscribed his love for Clara.

Toward the end of July, Clara at last received what she interpreted as a sign of love from her husband. He had picked a small bouquet of flowers in the garden. Fräulein Reumont, a hospital attendant closely involved in Schumann's care, asked Schumann: "For whom are these lovely flowers?" "Ah—you know . . ." Schumann said vaguely. Peters reported on the exchange in a letter to Clara, who also received reports from a few friends who were permitted to observe Schumann, themselves unseen. They confirmed that Schumann looked well, spoke in a friendly way to the doctor, and seemed not very different from his previous self.

Clara had had offers of help from all over Germany and beyond. The newspapers were full of news of Schumann's collapse, and many friends and strangers wrote offering sympathy and advice. Mendelssohn's brother Paul sent Clara a credit note of four hundred thalers with a heartfelt letter, saying it was what his brother would have wished. (It seems that neither his brother Paul nor his wife, Cécile, knew of Mendelssohn's bitter feelings of estrangement toward Schumann.) Clara said she would set aside the gift, but meanwhile she was determined to pay for everything herself—clinic fees, household expenses, the children's schooling. She intended to tour as soon as she recovered from giving birth. Certain pious friends wrote counseling her to pray to Jesus and to accept the will of God. She knew that her only hope lay in activity and service; she had never been in the habit of praying for consolation. It was only in music that she was able to forget her grief.

With Joachim back in Hanover, Clara asked Wasielewski to play the violin at a fund-raising concert in Düsseldorf: trios by Beethoven and Schubert, with Christian Reimers playing the cello. She decided to take the waters at Ostend in August, offering a concert or two at the same time. Marie and Elise were being tutored at home; in 1855 they would be placed in a small private boarding school in Cologne. Clara's mother agreed to take Julie, now seven, to live with her in Berlin. The two boys, Ferdinand and Ludwig, little Eugenie, born in December 1851, and the new infant were still at home, cared for by Bertha Boelling, the housekeeper, who had become a true friend for Clara. There was also a wet nurse and a general maidservant. Brahms took charge of Schumann's household book, recording weekly expenses, and he helped with the children. When Clara moved from Bilkerstrasse to smaller quarters nearby, Brahms took a room in the same house so that he could be in charge during Clara's extensive concert tours.

In late August Brahms paid a visit to Endenich with Christian Reimers. These young men, so devoted to Schumann, were Clara's ambassadors. They told Richarz that she had given birth to a boy in June and was recovering well. She longed to write to her husband, and was awaiting Richarz's permission to do so. Richarz told the young friends that he thought Schumann's illness was not incurable, but that all excitement must be avoided to allow the best chance of recovery.

Peters noted in early September that the patient had asked if his wife and children still existed. Clara was told that she could write to Schumann calmly and in the most general terms. She wrote at once, a letter composed according to the doctor's instructions, short, calm, and loving, sent with a bouquet of garden flowers.

After reading Clara's letter, Schumann wept bitterly, convinced by voices that his wife had suddenly gone mad. He also returned to a persistent delusion that Düsseldorf had been destroyed by floods—the Rhine rising far above its banks. Dr. Richarz assured him that his wife was perfectly well, and Schumann wrote to her by return post. His letter was lucid, but written as if behind glass.

> How happy I was, dearest Clara, to recognize your
> handwriting; thank you so much for writing on just these
> days [their wedding anniversary on September 12th and
> Clara's birthday on the 13th], and [for writing] that you
> and the beloved children think of me still in our old love.
> Greet and kiss the little ones. Oh, if I could only once see
> you and speak to all of you; but the way is after all too far.
> I would like to learn so much from you, how your life is in
> general, where you are living, and whether you still play
> as beautifully as before, whether Marie and Elise are still
> making steady progress, whether they are also singing—
> whether you still have the Klems piano—where my
> collection of scores (the printed ones) and the manuscripts
> (the Requiem, "The Singer's Curse") have been put, where
> our album is, with the autographs of Goethe, Jean Paul,
> Mozart, Beethoven, and Weber, and the letters written
> to you and to me, and the *New Journal for Music* and my
> correspondence. Do you still have all the letters I wrote
> to you, and the love poems I sent you from Vienna, when
> you were in Paris? Could you perhaps send me something

interesting, perhaps the poems of [Christian Friedrich] Scherenberg, some back volumes of the journal and the "Musical Rules for Home and Life"? I feel the lack of notepaper, for sometimes I would like to write a little music. My life is very simple, and I take pleasure only in the lovely outlook to Bonn and if I go there, in the Siebengebirge [Seven Hills] and Godesberg, which you will remember, when in the strongest summer heat, when I was working on *The Page* [*and the King's Daughter*], I was struck by an attack of cramps. I should like to know, dear Clara, if perhaps you have taken care of my clothes and whether you have sometimes sent me cigars. I very much would like to know this. Write to me in more detail about the children, whether they play pieces by Beethoven, Mozart, and from my *Album for the Young*, whether Julie also continues to play, and how Ludwig, Ferdinand, and the lovable Eugenie are developing. Oh, how I would love to hear your wonderful playing once again! Was it a dream that we were in Holland last winter, and that you were received so brilliantly everywhere, especially in Rotterdam, and the torches were brought for us, and how in the concerts you played the E-flat-Major Concerto, the Sonatas in C and F Minor by Beethoven, études by Chopin, *Songs without Words* by Mendelssohn, and also my new Konzertstück in D, so splendidly? Do you remember a theme in E-flat major that I once heard at night, and the variations I wrote for it? Could you send it to me, perhaps with some of your own compositions?

I have so many questions and requests—if only I could come to you and tell you all of them. But if you choose to cast a veil over these things that I have told you about, do so.

And so farewell, beloved Clara, and dear children, and write to me soon!

Your old faithful
Robert

Following the doctors' advice, Clara next sent two letters, one of them mentioning the birth of their son Felix in June. It seemed only right to present this information to her husband. He wrote back immediately.

> Dearest Clara,
>
> What joyful news you have sent me again, that heaven has sent you a fine boy, and in June [Schumann's birthday was June 8]; that dear Marie and Elise played you my *Bildern aus Osten* on your birthday . . . that Brahms—whom you must greet with my friendliest regards—has moved to Düsseldorf—what joyful news! If you would like to know my preferred name, you will guess it—the Unforgettable One! [The infant indeed was named after Mendelssohn.] I am very happy to know that my *Collected Writings* and my Cello Concerto, the Violin Fantasie which Joachim played so wonderfully, and the *Fughetten* have appeared. Could you send me one or another of these, as you so kindly offered to do? When you write to Joachim, greet him from me. What have Brahms and Joachim composed? Has the Overture to *Hamlet* been published, and has he finished another? You wrote to me that you are giving lessons in your piano room. Who are your students now, which are the best? Do not strain yourself too much, dear Clara.

The letter continues:

> Eight o'clock in the evening. I have just come back from Bonn, where I always visit Beethoven's statue, to my delight. As I was standing before him, the organ in the Münster church rang out. I am now much stronger and look much younger than in Düsseldorf. Could I ask you to write to Dr. Peters, telling him to give me some money when I ask for it, which you would repay? Often poor people ask me for alms, and it saddens me not to give them money . . .

Otherwise my life is not as active as before. How different
it was in the past. Do tell me all about our relations and
friends in Cologne, Leipzig, Dresden, and Berlin; about
Woldemar [Bargiel] and Dr. [Hermann] Härtel. . . . Do
you remember . . . the blissful times past, our journeys
to Switzerland and Heidelberg, to Lausanne, to Vevey, to
Chamounix? Then our travels in The Hague, where you
astonished them so, then Antwerp and Brussels, the music
festival in Düsseldorf, where my Fourth Symphony was
performed for the first time, and on the second day my
A Minor Concerto, which you played so beautifully, with
a brilliant response, and the Rhine overture, less well
received. Do you remember, too, how we saw the Alps in
all their splendor, and how you became fearful when the
driver put his horse to a sharp trot? I kept short notes of
all our trips, and also those I made as a schoolboy and
student— . . . it would give me great pleasure if you sent
me a volume of your diaries and perhaps a copy of the love
poems which I sent you from Vienna to Paris? Do you still
have the little double portrait by [Ernst] Rietschel, made in
Dresden? It would make me very happy if you could send
it. I would also like you to send me the children's birthdays,
they are in the little blue notebook. Now I will write to
Marie and Elise, who wrote to me so lovingly. With that,
adieu, beloved Clara. Do not forget me, write soon.

Your Robert.

A third letter was dated 26 September. The tone this time was more
worrying:

What joy, dearest Clara, you have given me with your letter,
the package, and the double portrait. My imagination was
very much disturbed because of several sleepless nights;
now I see you again in your noble and serious bearing.
And you have made me very happy by writing about our

relations, your mother, Woldemar, Pauline, Rosalie in
Nürnburg, and about Julie's musical progress. Also about
Brahms and Joachim and their compositions.

He then goes through each item in Clara's letter, names each of his
own pieces, and ends by asking Clara to write more about herself
and the children.

Dr. Peters wrote to Clara shortly afterwards, suggesting that
she write less frequently, since the correspondence was causing the
patient to become overexcited.

The next letter from Schumann was dated the 10th of October.
Clara, overjoyed to receive each letter, was beginning to worry about
their tone, with so much space given to the details of former concert
tours and holidays, friends and relations, recent works performed
and published. It seemed that Schumann was trying to hold on to
his life by naming its parts. Another letter followed two days later,
thanking Clara for a daguerreotype of herself and Marie, also for
cigars and the fourth volume of *Des Knaben Wunderhorn*. (The first
three volumes had already been sent.) Schumann enclosed a letter
for Brahms, praised Brahms's Variations on a Theme by Schumann,
and also Clara's own variations on the same theme, "which continue to delight me, and to remind me of your wonderful playing
of the variations and other works of mine." He ends: "Write to me
even more about the children, dear Clara. Ludwig continues to find
speech very difficult; I did not know about Ferdinand [also having
speech difficulties]. And write very soon, always with cheerful news.
In old and new love, Your devoted Robert."

The letter to Brahms included a meticulous critique of the variations Brahms had sent to Schumann, commenting enthusiastically
and with perfect musical understanding. There was no reason to
suspect that the writer was suffering from anxiety or confusion.

A letter written on the 18th of October to Clara and the children returned again to the past: "Dear Klara and children, we were
together last Christmas, when I was given the wonderful portrait by
[Wilhelm] Sohn of your Mama. Many friends were also there, like

Frl. Leser, Albert Dietrich, and others . . ." This was preserved as a fragment only; it may not have been sent.

In October, Clara arranged a concert tour in Holland, where she knew she would have large audiences. She performed works by Bach, Beethoven's *Appassionata* Sonata, and a few short pieces by Schumann. She gave a concert each day, returned to her hotel, and wept for hours. Brahms took the mail coach to Rotterdam, surprising Clara in her hotel room, and he spent a week with her. He could not bear the thought that she was working so hard with no one to comfort her, only a woman traveling companion. She arranged concerts in Hanover, Bremen, Hamburg, and Berlin, where she stayed with her mother. Brahms returned to Düsseldorf, serving as postman, sending Schumann's letters to Clara and her replies on to Endenich.

He knew that he was falling in love with his mentor's wife. There was no point in concealing this from Clara, who loved him as a son. He ended a long letter to her with a quotation from the *Arabian Nights,* in which, he said, Prince Kamaralsaman described Brahms's own condition most clearly, ending thus: "Would to God it were permitted me today, instead of sending this letter, to repeat to thee in person that I am dying of love for thee." The prince was dying of love for a distant, unattainable princess, as Brahms assumed that Clara would know. He wrote to Joachim that he often had the impulse simply to put his arms around her; it would seem most natural.

Schumann was increasingly agitated by writing letters, often ending with the plea: "Do not forget me!" His letters to Brahms and Joachim expressed keen interest in their compositions, but also referred more and more to the past. He wrote to Brahms:

> If only I could come to you myself, to see you again and to
> hear you, your wonderful variations, or to hear my Clara
> play them, of whose wonderful performance Joachim wrote
> to me . . . I must thank you, dear Johannes, for everything
> you have done for my Clara; she always writes to me about
> that. Yesterday, as you might know, she sent me two volumes

of my compositions and Jean Paul's *Flegeljahre,* to my
joy . . . You know the surroundings of Bonn; I am always
delighted by Beethoven's statue and the view toward the
Siebengebirge. In Hanover we saw one another for the last
time. Write soon to your devoted and loving

R. Schumann.

In the event, it was Joachim who visited Schumann first, on
Christmas Day. Dr. Richarz permitted him to spend half an hour
with Schumann, talking to him, looking at music together. Joachim
reported that the patient seemed not very different in his outward
manner from the way he had been before, though his speech was
indistinct. He seemed absentminded and his thoughts were occasionally confused. Joachim told Richarz that Schumann spoke to
him of hearing voices and having irrational ideas "of a melancholy
character," but that he knew these were unfounded, even laughable.
He said that he longed for Düsseldorf and would like to return there.

After Joachim left, the patient was heard talking to himself: "It
is indeed noteworthy! . . . No, it is a lie!" Richarz wrote to Clara,
telling her that her husband had been very pleased to be visited by
their friend—another young man selflessly devoted to the suffering
artists, husband and wife.

Brahms followed soon afterwards, and was permitted to spend
a short time with Schumann. But he found Schumann extremely
agitated, so overwrought that he could hardly speak. Brahms wrote
to Joachim: "For the first five to ten minutes he spoke with hor-
rifying haste and fear of what the voices, or else the doctors, had
whispered to him. I didn't understand very much, he was speaking
quickly, with his hand in front of his mouth." Afterwards, as they
talked in Richarz's office, Brahms dropped the pretense of cheer-
fulness. He knew that Schumann read a daily newspaper, and he
was worried about reports of Clara's concert tours. Schumann would
have assumed that she was in Düsseldorf, giving lessons as usual
and waiting for him to return home.

Two weeks later, Brahms appeared at the gates of Endenich with
another letter from Clara and books and music, among them the

revised edition of *Kreisleriana,* the *Songs of Dawn,* and a set of variations, in Schumann's hand, on the theme dictated to him by spirits.
The theme bore an uncanny resemblance to the slow movement of
the Violin Concerto composed for Joachim.*

Brahms showed Richarz a list of topics to be discussed, agreed
to beforehand by Clara, including details of her tours, reports of the
children, accounts of income and expenses, publication plans. He
was to ask whether Schumann needed more cigars and fresh clothes.
Brahms reported on his visit to the woman he now addressed as his
"best beloved friend."

> I was with your beloved husband from two to six. . . . He was
> as warm and friendly as he was the first time, but without the
> ensuing agitation. He showed me your last letter and told me
> how it had delighted him.We talked for a long time about
> your travels. I explained that I had seen you in Hamburg,
> Hanover, Lübeck, and even in Rotterdam. He asked if you
> had been in the same room you were in last year in Rotter-
> dam. I gave him your picture. Oh, if you had seen his deep
> sigh, as tears came to his eyes and he held it ever nearer and
> at last said: "Oh, how long I have wanted to have this!"

Brahms told Clara that he begged Schumann to write to her more
often. "Most willingly," Schumann said. "Each and every day. If
only I had paper." Brahms asked for paper, but the composer was
not happy with the size, or with his pen. Still, he fully intended to
write—if not today, then tomorrow.

Dr. Richarz gave permission for Schumann to walk with Brahms
to the railway station, the attendant walking always a few steps

---

* These variations have recently been resurrected, published, and performed
by Andras Schiff and others as the *Geistervariationen* (Ghost Variations)—the
theme dictated by spirits, the variations composed when Schumann was suffering a psychotic breakdown. Neither Clara nor Brahms saw fit to publish them in
Schumann's Collected Works, although Brahms published the theme alone in a
supplement.

behind. They visited the Beethoven monument and the cathedral. Schumann asked whether his wife walked every day. "In the old days," he told Brahms, "we always walked together." All this and more Brahms reported faithfully. He ended his letter, "With heartfelt greetings from your Robert and from me, your Johannes."

Clara's anguish throughout this period, her loyalty and devotion to her suffering husband, are documented in her diaries and letters. Richarz insisted that she must not visit Schumann, at first because he wanted to keep the patient free from all agitation, later to spare Clara the terrible sight of her husband in the grip of acute psychosis. Her intimacy with Brahms grew closer as he continued to be her chief support. There was gossip about their relations at the time and long afterwards. Neither Clara nor Brahms would have contemplated a sexual relationship while they believed there was even a remote chance of Schumann's recovery. After Schumann's death, relations between Clara and Brahms remained close and tender, with some periods of unhappy estrangement. But strong reasons on both sides urged against a sexual liaison.

In his letters to Joachim and Brahms, there was no mistaking the joy with which Schumann received visits from his young friends, and his eagerness to hear about their music, Brahms's new Ballades, Joachim's viola pieces on Byron's *Hebrew Melodies* and his music for *Hamlet*. Schumann was affectionate, interested, specific about their music and his own. He repeatedly expressed his hope that Brahms would compose large-scale orchestral and choral works. He had written to Joachim in January, before his breakdown: "Doesn't Brahms let drums and trumpets sound yet? He ought always to think of the beginning of Beethoven's symphonies, and try to do something similar. The beginning is the chief thing; once one has begun, the end comes to meet one almost spontaneously." Indeed, this is just what Brahms was later to do in his four symphonies and the *German Requiem,* among the other major works that established his position as one of the greatest nineteenth-century composers.

He paid tribute to Schumann in several of these works, as he did to Beethoven, Bach, Handel, and others. But he followed Schumann's example in making allusions to specific themes by others very much his own, absorbing them into the texture of his work, imprinting them with his own distinctive signature.

Richarz had to decide whether or not to permit Clara to visit Schumann. She told Brahms that she could not bear to observe her husband unseen. It would seem dreadful to her not to be able to embrace him, to hold him to her heart. She said that perhaps she should wait until he was fully cured. No doubt she could read between the lines; it hardly mattered how carefully Joachim and Brahms phrased their reports. She wrote in her diary, and also in a letter to the doctors, "He always speaks of the past, never of the future. Has he no hope? How that grieves me!"

Four months after his first letter to Clara, Schumann wrote to her with new urgency: "My own Clara, I feel as if something frightful were awaiting me. If I were never again to see you and the children—how dreadful!"

In March 1855, both doctors noted worrying symptoms: a cramp in the patient's right hand, weakness in his lower limbs, trembling, a return of the demons. On March 12th the patient had convulsions, with severe headache; his speech was distorted, difficult to understand. Peters reported that Schumann feared again that he was going mad. He said he was being pursued by Nemesis. He told Peters that he used to be an artist; he was accustomed to a very different way of life. Peters observed irregularity in his pupils and their response to light.

The doctors knew that after each period of excitement, it was more difficult for the patient to recover. He was writing furiously every day, sometimes a letter to his wife, mainly long letters to Joachim and Brahms, commenting in detail on their compositions. He was considerably agitated by reading the back numbers of the Leipzig magazine *Signale für die musikalische Welt,* as if he suddenly realized that he had missed an entire year of musical activity. He was also busy composing and playing the piano in the common room, not always in a pleasing way. He expressed joy at receiving letters from his wife and from Brahms and Joachim. There was no doubt that he was in a state of high excitement.

The medical record during the second year of Schumann's hospitalization, from March 1855 onwards, is increasingly pessimistic. Schumann was refusing medication, insisting that it was poison. He repeatedly said that he wished to leave the asylum. He wrote to Brahms: "To be away from here completely! For over a year, since the 4th of March 1854, always the same way of life, the same, and the same view of Bonn. Then where else to go! Think about it, all of you!" He rose each morning at six and sat at the table, writing. He complained that he had no knife to sharpen his pens. Instead of his usual courtesy during the evening visits, he spoke angrily to the doctors, attacking the staff. "They are all scoundrels!" He told Richarz confidentially that when he was in Düsseldorf, he once heard music so beautiful that it must have come from the higher regions.

Brahms visited other private asylums, hoping that a different mode of treatment—homeopathy, magnetism, cold baths—might produce better results. When he described Schumann's history and his continuing symptoms, the doctors said that a change might be dangerously unsettling. Richarz tried to hold out some hope, but the thread was wearing thin.

In May 1855, the grande dame Bettina von Arnim appeared. She was the sister of Clemens Brentano and the wife of Achim von Arnim, collaborators in the folk-song collection *Des Knaben Wunderhorn*. A close friend of Goethe, she had been an *amie intime* of Beethoven, the confidante of the great and good over the past fifty years: a ravaged beauty, with piercing black eyes, a strong nose (Semitic blood somewhere, it was rumored), rouged lips. As a great democrat, she instructed everyone to call her "Bettina." She was accompanied by her daughter Gisela, whom Joachim was courting, hoping that they would marry. Although she had only met Schumann twice, in October of 1853, she knew he was "a good and noble creature." He had dedicated his *Songs of Dawn*, composed shortly before her October visit, to "the noble poetess." She required only a quarter of an hour with the patient in order to know whether or not he was mad.

Clara had written to Peters asking that Madame von Arnim be permitted to visit Schumann. Two weeks after her visit, Bettina wrote a full account to Clara. She described the asylum as a cold, unwelcoming place, empty of all signs of life. Dr. Richarz kept her waiting, before leading her to Fräulein Reumont's room in another building, where she would see Schumann in company with Fräulein Reumont. Schumann soon appeared, and his face lit up when he saw Bettina. He apologized for speaking indistinctly, which he and Bettina blamed on his solitude and the absence of congenial friends. He then spoke warmly about his recent travels and about the compositions of Brahms and Joachim. It was Bettina's firm conviction that he would regain his health if he were removed from the asylum and taken back to his loving family, where he could listen to music and recover his spirits in the arms of his wife. She thought Dr. Richarz was cold, unsympathetic, lacking in all understanding of his sensitive patient.

Bettina's letter contradicted the reports Clara had been receiving from Peters, which suggested a return of earlier symptoms, delusions, anxiety, hostility toward the attendants and doctors. She wrote an anguished letter to Peters, worried that she hadn't heard from Schumann. Perhaps he was working too hard, writing, composing; could he not take walks without the attendant if a friend accompanied him?

Clara had been greatly distressed by a notice that appeared in the *Rheinische Musik-Zeitung* of 4 April 1855, informing the musical world that Maestro Schumann continued to be gravely ill, and his doctors had no hope of his recovery. She asked their friend the publisher Bartholf Senff to place a notice in his journal, the *Signale*, correcting what she believed to be untrue and insulting to her husband. Senff duly inserted a few sentences in the *Signale* of May 3, assuring friends of the distinguished artist of his improved health. He was busy every day, writing, reading, playing the piano; he was corresponding regularly with his wife, and taking the most lively interest in all events.

This notice was reprinted in half a dozen newspapers just as Schumann had taken a turn for the worse. The demons reappeared.

Evil spirits tormented him, stole his possessions, seized his pen when he was writing, prevented him from speaking normally. He talked to himself, argued loudly, making a peroration as if to a large audience. His nights and also his days were increasingly restless. On good days, he walked to Bonn, ate and slept well, and was courteous to his attendant and to the doctors. But the good days were now few and far between.

Close to despair, Clara wrote to her husband on the 5th of May: "Why have I had no word, no sign from you? I have been hoping from day to day, and always in vain! . . . It is fourteen days since the last lines I had from you. I do not know what to think. Are you angry with me, my beloved? Oh, then at least tell me; to know nothing is terrible! Do write to me soon, just a few words! . . . I beg you, my dearest Robert, a word soon to your Clara, eternally yours."

Her letter crossed with one from Schumann: "Dearest Clara, On the first of May I sent you a spring greeting; but the following days were very agitated; you shall discover more from the letter that you shall receive from me by the day after tomorrow. A shadow lies within; but the other things it contains, my beloved, will make you rejoice . . . Farewell, beloved! Your Robert." Clara later wrote on this disturbing note from her husband: "Last Letter."

Richarz saw before them the inexorable course of general paralysis. The doctors would continue to note symptoms but had little hope of treating them. Clara asked to see Richarz at Brühl, some nine miles north of Endenich. She wrote to Joachim, who was staying with the Arnims in Bonn, pleading for his support. Would he meet her in Brühl? To know that he and Johannes were near would give her the courage to face Richarz.

Meeting him in Brühl on the 22nd of May, Clara told Richarz that reports from recent visitors pictured her husband almost as he was before his collapse. It was hard for her to reconcile the accounts of her friends with Dr. Peters's reports. She asked Richarz to be frank with her. Richarz said that Schumann's symptoms represented an interruption in his recovery, which might well resume after the summer had passed. He still hoped for a return to health.

According to the medical diary of this time, Schumann was

sometimes genial and friendly to the doctors. But more often he seemed restless or apathetic ("sunken in himself"). He complained that his head was not right; he spoke again of "demons."

Joachim visited not once but three times within the space of a week in late May. He was distressed to find Schumann agitated and incoherent on his first visit, also on his second. He hoped to take back a better report to Clara if he visited yet again. On his third visit, Joachim was relieved to find Schumann more cheerful and open. They laughed together about Joachim's musical travails and triumphs, and Schumann promised to have his arrangements of Paganini studies ready when Joachim returned with Brahms.

It was clear that weeks of agitation had taken their toll. Schumann was now exhausted, and slept all day or dozed on the sofa. He was making a list of cities and towns in the atlas Brahms had sent to him, at his request. This became his chief occupation. As his mental agitation receded, his bodily symptoms became more pronounced: weakness and jerkiness in his lower limbs, a noticeable tremor, thickness of speech. His birthday was in a few days, on June 8th, but Richarz wrote to Clara to discourage any visits. She accepted his advice that her husband must remain undisturbed, if he was to have any chance of recovering.

Wasielewski went to Endenich in August with Reimers, hoping to pay a short visit to the patient. Richarz said that they could observe him if they liked, but he had agreed with Madame Schumann that visits would be unwise. They watched behind a half-open door as Schumann sat at the piano in the common room, bringing his hands and fingers down heavily and erratically on the keys. The sound was grotesque. Wasielewski thought it was like a machine whose springs are broken, yet some force within the machine still tried to make it work. Reimers, too, was profoundly shocked.

By September of 1855, the medical notes drew a picture of increasing debility, hearing disorders, severe speech impediments, impaired mobility, and a loss of bladder control. The patient's mental symptoms, too, were alarming. He manifested increasing confusion, delusions, memory loss, aggressive behavior alternating with apathy. His mental and physical symptoms were consistent with a single cause, which was now inescapable. Richarz changed his diagnosis from "melancholia, with delusions," to *paralysie générale*. A defining symptom was pupillary inequality, more noticeable each day—*Anisokorie*. When a light was directed at the eye, the pupil did not refract normally, but remained enlarged in one eye or the other, sometimes both. Eventually vision would be affected.

Richarz knew that *paralysie générale*—general paralysis—attacked every organ of the victim, each faculty, each sense: vision, hearing, smell, taste. He knew what to expect. But the illness also had ways of surprising victims and doctors. It fastened onto existing weaknesses of the suffering patient, as the nervous system was eroded, affecting control of body and mind. Hence the convulsive movements of arms and legs, thickened speech, disconnected thoughts, tinnitus, hallucinations.

The doctors increased medication to relieve Schumann's suffering, using copper sulphate and quinine extract. Richarz would write to Clara, to say that in his professional judgment, her husband was incurable. Clara received a letter to this effect on the 10th of September 1855. "To think of seeing him, the most ambitious of all artists, weakened in his mind perhaps, or even more probably, sunk into the most dreadful melancholy—should I take him back again in this state? Or should I not wish to have him only as he was before? Oh, I no longer know what to think; I have thought it through a thousand and more than a thousand times, and it remains always dreadful."

The patient evidently was eager to assist in his diagnosis. He spent one morning writing notes to himself, as if in a diary, all of melancholy import. Among other things he wrote as follows: "In 1831 I was syphilitic and was treated with arsenic." It was as if Schumann had objectively noted his symptoms, and attributed them to the treacherous disease that had attacked him twenty-five years before.

Clara wrote another anguished letter to Richarz. She wanted to write to her husband, but she hadn't the heart to do so; he seemed to have forgotten her and the children. It was six months since she had had word from him.

During his daily call, Peters urged the composer to write to his wife, just one or two lines. "Perhaps in the evening," he said. "I lack the strength to write." Asked the next day, if he would write to his wife, he pleaded again that he was too weak.

As Schumann seemed increasingly agitated, Richarz decided to stop his newspapers and temporarily removed pen and paper. Furious at finding his notepaper gone, the patient wrote on the window with his finger: "Scoundrels! Rogues! Liars!" At night he shouted in his sleep and argued against invisible enemies so loudly that the next morning he was hoarse. Often he would not get out of bed, remaining all day in his dressing gown. The attendant did not know what to do; he said the patient could be quite violent. Yet on some days he was strangely apathetic. Once Schumann asked after his wife. "Where is she? Is she here?" Peters said she was in Düsseldorf, though in fact she was in Berlin, with her mother. Schumann said he intended to write to her soon. His only reading matter now was the atlas he had requested, which he studied for hours. Conceivably he was retracing the travels he had mentioned in his letters to Clara.

The doctors noted Schumann's continued mental deterioration, with occasional lucid intervals. One evening the patient suddenly shouted, "Thief! Scoundrels!" When Peters asked what was wrong, he looked altogether confused and said he felt unwell, he was plagued by idées fixes. He knew his mind was disordered, but he could not clear the mist. He resorted to the atlas, as if the names of cities, towns, rivers provided his only tie to the real world. Removed to the second house, he complained of the smell. He was happy to be back in his room but wandered about in an access of restlessness, pointing to his books and music scores, repeating as if arguing with an invisible enemy, "This one is mine; this one too!" He wrote on the wall with his fingers: "Lies! Liars!" It was as if all confidence in his achievement as a composer had failed. Yet he desperately held on to the remnants of self-respect. When Peters told him that he had been shouting and cursing, he was deeply ashamed and promised to stop.

Ironically, Schumann's music was at last gaining genuine recognition in the wider world. Joachim arranged performances of two of his symphonies and part 3 of *Faust* in his music festival in Hanover;

all received glowing reviews. Clara performed his Piano Concerto and Piano Quintet on her tours, to ecstatic audiences; she also included his *Études symphoniques* and *Fantasiestücke,* op. 12. She was planning a tour of England, where she knew she could earn a great deal of money. She was determined to present Schumann's music in the land that had taken Mendelssohn to its heart. The new editions of Schumann's early piano works were in print, and four-hand piano arrangements of the symphonies and the *Manfred* Overture were now available throughout Germany.

Recognition came too late to allay Schumann's anxiety. In his clouded mind, he was surrounded by enemies, persecuted by evil women. Even if he had been able to read the glowing reviews, they would not have penetrated beyond the surface of his mind. They were powerless against the destructive forces that had taken such deep hold of his being.

A sad letter from Clara to Richarz: She had a Christmas present for her husband—a photograph of Joachim and Brahms. Would it be possible for Brahms to bring the present himself to Endenich? How dreadful she would feel, knowing that her dear husband could not even have a greeting from one friend on Christmas Day. She would enclose a few lines with the present. Her touring left her exhausted, with hardly an hour to herself.

On Christmas Day the patient asked if it was Christmas. He studied the photograph of Brahms and Joachim attentively. He asked for music paper to write something down, which turned out to be a fugue. This was his way of restoring his sense of himself. Would that it could bring respite from his sleepless nights! Clara wrote to him the day after Christmas; he received her letter willingly, but could not be persuaded to write to her in return. His two oldest girls, Marie and Elise, had also written to him.

In February 1856, the Paris newspapers reported the death of Heinrich Heine, aged fifty-nine. He had been living in exile in Paris for many years. The cause of his death was *locomotor ataxia*—another victim of syphilis, the plague of the century. For eight years he had been paralyzed, confined to what he called his "mattress grave." This did not stop him from satirizing the German bourgeoisie and their rulers, exposing the hypocrisy of church and state, puncturing myths of scientific progress with his acerbic wit. The German newspapers said only that the famous love poet died in his sleep in Paris, and was mourned by his devoted wife, Mathilde, and by lovers of poetry throughout Europe.

A long letter from Clara, written directly to Dr. Richarz: She was worried about her husband composing again. Would it not be too much for him? She asked if Richarz could copy out the fugue he had written, perhaps when her husband was walking in the garden, and send it to her. She also suggested ways of helping her husband, methods that she thought might not have occurred to Richarz—cold baths, for instance. A doctor of her acquaintance, who had excellent results in treating nervous illnesses, suggested a cold bath every morning. Another friend suggested a method that also proved beneficial: forty coffee beans placed in a small cheesecloth sack, onto which boiling water was poured, a cup of this infusion to be taken every day. She asked whether she might write again to her husband, and send him her concert programs, which she was sure would please him.

After the next five or six weeks of touring, she hoped to be in Düsseldorf for a fortnight, after which she would be going to England. She asked if she could talk to Richarz in person before she left for England—and she could not help thinking that perhaps she might see her husband just once at that time. For two years the doctors had tried everything possible, without success. Could she not try something herself? She knew that it might be terrible for her to see him—but might it not be helpful for him? She had followed the doctors' instructions faithfully up until now; she did not mean to be unreasonable, but surely her longing to see him was not unnatural.

Clara decided in the end not to go to Endenich. Richarz agreed that Brahms might visit the patient again. Brahms was absolutely determined to see Schumann, having promised as much to Clara.

He found Schumann friendly, well disposed, obviously pleased to see his young friend. But he was trembling, his movements were abrupt and uncertain, and his speech was incomprehensible. Brahms could not make out a single word. Schumann eagerly showed him the atlas, and pages of lists he had arranged alphabetically, starting with towns beginning with A, their rivers, mountains, latitude and longitude.

Brahms could not believe how changed his beloved patron was in the year since he had last visited him. He was like a small child, pointing at things, smiling vaguely at nothing. At last Brahms was able to catch a few words: "Marie," "Julie," "Berlin," "Vienna," "England," nothing more. Possibly he was naming the cities where Clara had been giving concerts. She was now in England. Brahms longed to join her. He invited Clara's half-brother, Woldemar Bargiel, to go with him, for the sake of appearances, but nothing came of his invitation.

Brahms agreed with Richarz that it was not necessary to provide Clara with a full account of his visit, but he felt that he must tell Joachim the truth. They would work together to help her through the next phase of the catastrophe.

Brahms told Joachim that he could not understand a single word that Schumann spoke. He kept muttering as if babbling, "bababa-dadada," apparently unaware that he was not making any sense. It was clear that his brain was affected. All the doctors could provide was nursing care. Brahms begged Joachim to be careful about what he told Clara.

In April 1856, Clara was still discussing with Brahms and Joachim the possibility of transferring Schumann to a different asylum. When it was clear that there was no possibility of doing so, Clara left for her long-planned concert tour to London. She wrote to Joachim on May 31: "I know very well that I must still work for my children, and for that reason continue to live, but my heart is broken. For him to be living still, but lost to us, the wonderful man—I do not know how I can bear it."

In spite of his decline, the patient continued to surprise the doctors. One day he wrote an entirely sensible letter to Peters, asking permission to play the piano and naming several compositions that he wished to play. He explained that he was writing because he knew that his speech was difficult to understand. Peters told him that he was welcome to play the piano at any time.

Later that week he burned letters from Clara. When questioned, he insisted that the scorched papers in the grate were official.

On one evening visit, Peters could not persuade the patient to eat anything; he said he was being given other people's *shite*. He could not be forced to eat; they would restrict his diet to jelly, broth, wine. The doctors agreed to keep their daily notes to a bare record of physical signs—pulse, temperature, bowels, pupil dilation, edema. They were now waiting for the end.

When Clara returned from England, she asked to meet Dr. Richarz in Bonn, where she planned to stay overnight with Johannes at the Deutsches Haus. She wished most earnestly to visit her husband. She knew he had very little time left. Richarz wrote that she must not expect him to live more than two or three months. He knew the end was more likely to be a matter of weeks. At their meeting in Bonn, Richarz told Clara that Schumann was unconscious and was having convulsions. She decided to return to Düsseldorf without seeing him. Richarz promised to cable if there was a sudden change.

On the 27th of July, Richarz cabled that Clara and Brahms must come at once if they wished to see Schumann alive. They arrived at Endenich in the early evening. Schumann had been unable to swallow and was in the final stages of pneumonia. He had been bedridden for four weeks and was severely emaciated and dehydrated.

When Clara entered his room, Schumann smiled weakly, and gestured as if to embrace her. This was according to Clara's account in her diary; Brahms told Joachim that Schumann was comatose. Clara stayed with her dying husband for an hour, lying at his feet, hardly daring to breathe. She was convinced that he knew her; she thought she could hear the word "my"—"my Clara," she thought he meant. She and Brahms spent the next day going in and out of his room, sometimes sitting with him, sometimes watching him through the open door. He seemed to be speaking with spirits. Clara fed him a few teaspoons of jellied consommé. She dipped her fingers in a glass of wine and he licked them. She was sure he knew that she was serving him.

Richarz told Brahms that he had increased the dose of morphine so that the patient would be free of pain. Clara and Brahms went into Bonn the next day to meet Joachim at the railway station. Schumann died while they were gone.

The funeral took place two days later. It was kept as simple as possible, according to Clara's wishes. Brahms, carrying a funeral wreath, led the way with Joachim and Albert Dietrich, the young men whose companionship had brightened Schumann's last months of normal life. Members of Bonn's Concordia Singverein carried the coffin, while a brass band played chorales. The pastor and the mayor of Bonn followed behind with Dr. Richarz, Dr. Hasenclever, Wasielewski, Christian Reimers, Ferdinand David, Ferdinand Hiller, and a few other close friends and colleagues. They walked along the Endenich Road to the lovely Old Cemetery on the outskirts of Bonn. Townspeople gathered as the funeral cortege passed, standing respectfully in silence, heads bared. Clara, who had waited at the chapel, wrote in her diary that the beautiful burial place had been planted with five plane trees. She stood at the back, "unnoticed," as the coffin was lowered into the grave and the mourners waited in turn to throw a handful of soil onto the coffin.

In August Clara took a month's holiday in Switzerland with her young sons Ludwig and Ferdinand and Brahms and his sister, Elise. They returned to Düsseldorf in mid-September, and soon afterwards Brahms returned home to his family in Hamburg. It seems clear that he had decided he must make his own way. It is also clear that Clara felt rejected. Perhaps she assumed that Brahms would remain nearby, at least as long as she needed him. On Brahms's part, the fact that she was an older woman—she was thirty-seven to Brahms's twenty-three years—with seven young children must have affected his decision. He needed to devote himself to his own career, composing, earning a living. He was happy to adore Clara, but a more intimate relationship would have meant marriage, which he was in no position to contemplate. Indeed, he was unable to commit himself to marriage in all of his later relationships with women. On Clara's part, her intensely physical relationship with Schumann, the frequency of pregnancy and childbirth, and a certain puritanical streak would all have argued against a sexual relationship with the young man who had been her unfailing support for two and a half harrowing years. The role of grieving widow was more natural for her, and she continued to wear widow's black for the rest of her life.

In a later letter to her children, since lost, she explained her relationship to Brahms, the friend she loved above all others. The children were to ignore those petty souls who were unable to understand such a loving friendship. Gossip there was, but it was baseless and ill natured. Still, Clara remained possessive of the young man who had so openly declared himself in love with her. She was jealous of Brahms's later relationships with women, and probably reinforced his reluctance to commit himself seriously to anyone else. They continued to be the closest of friends, visiting each other and spending summers in the same place, but they never lived together again.

Clara devoted much of her subsequent career to promoting Schumann's music in concerts and festivals across Europe. In 1873 she helped to organize a three-day music festival in Bonn, with an orchestra of one hundred players and a choir of close to four hundred singers. Joachim and his wife, Amalie; Brahms; Jenny Lind and her husband, Otto Goldschmidt; Ferdinand Hiller; Albert Dietrich; and many other musicians attended, along with the surviving Schumann children. On the first day, Schumann's D Minor Symphony and *Paradise and the Peri* were performed; on the second day, the Symphony in C, the Piano Concerto, played by Clara, the *Manfred* Overture, and the "Nachtlied" for choir and orchestra; and on the third day, the complete *Scenes from Goethe's "Faust."* A matinee of chamber music included the String Quartet in A Major, the Andante and Variations for two pianos, op. 46, and several of Schumann's most popular songs. These were the works Schumann himself would probably have chosen. The proceeds funded a grand marble monument that was erected on Schumann's grave in 1880. It featured a seated muse, her face meant to suggest Clara, holding a wreath in one hand and a scroll in the other, gazing at a winged Cupid playing a violin (signifying Schumann's instrumental music), on the opposite side a winged Psyche reading a book (signifying his vocal music), surmounted by a swan in flight (signifying his rich musical thoughts and songs). At the top, a bust of Schumann in profile, based on a double medallion by Ernst Rietschel, framed by a laurel wreath.

Clara died in 1896 of a series of strokes, aged seventy-six. Brahms outlived her by less than a year. For forty years he had consulted her about each of his compositions. They had had the closest of intimate friendships, marked by a few mutually distressing quarrels. Brahms's Four Serious Songs on biblical texts, including "O death, how bitter thou art," was composed shortly before the death of the woman he had revered above all others. He wrote to Joachim:

> I have often thought that Frau Schumann might survive all her children, and me—but I have never wished that she might do so. The thought of losing her cannot frighten us anymore, not even I who am so lonely and to whom so little is left in the world. And when she has left us, will not our faces light up with joy at the thought of the splendid woman whom it has been our privilege and delight to love and admire throughout her long life? Only thus let us grieve for her.

Of the seven surviving children, three daughters outlived Clara, remaining close to her during their long lives. Marie (1841–1899), who never married, served as her mother's chief assistant, her amanuensis, manager, and devoted companion. Elise (1843–1928) moved to Frankfurt as a young woman to work as a piano teacher. She married a businessman in 1877, lived for some time in America, and bore four children. Clara's youngest, Eugenie (1851–1938), never married; she worked for several years as a piano teacher in England and published two loving accounts of her parents and siblings. The beautiful Julie (1845–1872), whom Brahms thought seriously of courting, married an Italian count and died of tuberculosis at age twenty-seven, leaving two sons. Felix (1854–1879), the gifted youngest child, named after "the Unforgettable" Mendelssohn, also died of tuberculosis, aged twenty-four. Ferdinand (1849–1891) became addicted to the morphine that had been prescribed to him for rheumatism and died a broken man at forty-two, leaving a wife and six children. Ludwig (1848–1899), the "golden boy" whose slow development was of such concern to Schumann at Endenich, was incarcerated in the Colditz state asylum at the age of twenty-two, where Clara visited him only twice. He died there, blind, aged fifty.

In 1877 Clara signed a contract with Breitkopf & Härtel for an edition of Schumann's Collected Works, which appeared in thirty-one parts over the next several years as *Robert Schumanns Werke:* four volumes of piano works, two books of lieder, plus the four symphonies, the concertos for piano and for cello, and assorted chamber music. The full scores of *Genoveva, Manfred,* and *Scenes from Goethe's "Faust"* were reprinted, also the late fairy tales for chorus and orchestra, the Mass and the Requiem, and other works on religious themes. Clara worked in close consultation with Brahms, and her volumes have been reprinted many times. A new scholarly multi-volume Urtext edition of the collected works, collating all the early publications, Schumann's autograph scores, and manuscript drafts is close to completion.

The works contained in these volumes are Schumann's enduring gift to the world.

AFTERWORD

=====~◈◈◈~=====

Medical Diagnosis of Schumann's Illness

The medical diary Dr. Richarz maintained at Endenich suggests strongly that Schumann was suffering from tertiary syphilis (neurosyphilis) and its common manifestation, general paresis, or general paralysis of the insane (GPI). The syphilis microbe was not identified until 1905 and was not linked definitively to GPI until a few years later, though the connection was suspected long before. Physicians working with the insane during the nineteenth century were well aware of the relationship. The French physician Jean Alfred Fournier charted the typical course of syphilis by mid-century, and linked insanity to late-stage syphilis in a scientific paper in 1879. The British surgeon and pathologist Jonathan Hutchinson had earlier described syphilis as "the Great Imitator" because its symptoms during the period between the initial onset and the final stage mimicked so many other diseases, physical and mental. Of female inmates in the mental hospitals, the chief cause of dementia was postpartum psychosis. For male inmates, the chief cause was tertiary syphilis. The symptoms Richarz observed conform to the textbook definition of GPI: striking twenty to twenty-five years after the primary syphilitic infection, and often triggered by a violent fit of mania. Common symptoms include delusions, slurred speech, auditory problems, headache, dizziness, pupillary inequality (the *Anisokorie* noted several times in the medical diary), jerky movements of the limbs, tremors, spasms, and convulsions. Periods of remission are possible, but tertiary syphilis in Schumann's time was usually fatal within two to four years from its onset.

Why then, in the account he supplied to Wasielewski for his 1857 biography, did Richarz attribute Schumann's illness to "excessive mental exertion"? Perhaps he sincerely believed this to be a factor. He knew that Schumann had suffered a serious breakdown in 1844–1845, attributed to overwork, and he must have taken this into account. It is also likely that he wished to shield the family from scandal. Wasielewski's biography of Schumann was published a year after Schumann's death. Although he asked Clara for her help, she refused to share any letters or other material with him. At Wasielewski's request, Richarz supplied a brief medical report of the composer's illness and death, including postmortem findings of brain ossification and atrophy. He reports that Schumann suffered from organic disease taking root in early youth, but not manifesting itself as psychosis until many years later, when excessive mental exertion precipitated the final crisis. Unlike typical cases of this kind, Richarz reported, marked often by apathy or even gaiety, Schumann's unusual mental powers enabled him to preserve a characteristic melancholy and self-awareness until shortly before his death. The medical diary, as finally published in 2006, does not support this account.

Schumann's letters to Clara, Brahms, and Joachim suggest that in his first year at Endenich, up to March 1855, he was desperately trying to hold on to his sanity by recounting events of the past, still vividly present to him—his recent travels with Clara, the family and friends they had seen, his recent publications. He was also trying to maintain his most deeply established habits: keeping busy each day, reading, writing, playing dominoes, studying his friends' new compositions, improvising at the piano, taking long walks. He wrote to Joachim in March 1855, "I have been working a great deal, and it is not possible for me to remain inactive for a quarter of an hour." As his condition deteriorated, these efforts to hold on to his former life became sporadic, until they ceased entirely.

A number of misconceptions have been attached to Schumann's illness and death. Although biographers still disagree about how best to interpret the evidence of the medical diary, it seems virtually certain that the tragedy of Schumann's final years was caused by late-stage syphilis. While it is true that Schumann begged Clara and his doctors to be taken to an asylum, it is misleading to suggest that this was a rational decision. He was admitted to Endenich because there was no alternative; he was suicidal, experiencing an acute psychotic breakdown. It is often said that he died of self-starvation, as if he were deliberately repeating the suicide attempt begun with his leap into the Rhine. His emaciated state was caused by his inability to swallow, a result of progressive paralysis, which caused the doctors to restrict his diet to liquids and jellies. Clara failed to visit him at Endenich not because she was intent on pursuing her own career, but because she was told by the doctors that his only hope of recovery lay in avoiding agitation. She remained "faithful and true" to Schumann throughout his illness and after his death.

The promise of their early love was realized in music of surpassing beauty, reaffirmed passionately in the face of Schumann's recurrent illness, professional failure, and lack of public recognition. Clara Schumann was largely responsible for restoring her husband's music to its central place in the lives of music lovers today.

A NOTE ON PERFORMANCES AVAILABLE ON THE INTERNET

New interpretations of Schumann's music, live and on CD, are always being added to the Internet. In the following list, I recommend some great past performances, many dating back to the 1950s and 1960s. They provide fascinating evidence of Schumann's enduring magic.

Piano music

There are performances of virtually all Schumann's piano works by the great Russian pianist Sviatoslav Richter, sometimes recorded live. I also recommend performances of individual works by Claudio Arrau, Alfred Cortot, Annie Fischer (a live performance of the Piano Concerto), Walter Gieseking, Emil Gilels, Clara Haskil, Myra Hess, Vladimir Horowitz, Benno Moiseiwitsch, and Guiomar Novaes, who performed *Papillons* and *Carnaval* for Debussy as a thirteen-year-old—a link to an international tradition of Romantic piano music. There are magical performances by Clifford Curzon, Alicia de Larrocha, Arthur Rubinstein, and Solomon, each individual, poetic, and true to the composer.

Songs

The great song cycles of 1840—the Heine *Liederkreis,* op. 24, the Eichendorff, op. 39, and *Dichterliebe*—can be accessed in several performances by Dietrich Fischer-Dieskau, accompanied by Gerald Moore, including Fischer-Dieskau's debut recital in Salzburg in 1956. *Frauenliebe und Leben* has been sung by Kathleen Ferrier, Jessye Norman, Elly Ameling, and Lucia Popp, each interpretation superb in its own way; also by Lotte Lehmann with Bruno Walter and Elisabeth Schumann with Gerald Moore.

Chamber music

For the Piano Trios nos. 1 and 2, an early performance by Alexander Schneider, Fritz Busch, and Pablo Casals at the Prades Festival could hardly be bettered. The three String Quartets, op. 41, are beautifully performed by the Quartetto Italiano. For the popular Piano Quintet I recommend an early recording by Rudolf Serkin and the Busch Quartet. Equally fine is Clifford Curzon playing with the Budapest Quartet. Busch and Serkin also collaborate in the Violin Sonatas nos. 1 and 2. The Piano Quartet and the late fairy tales and romances for oboe, clarinet, viola, cello, or horn with piano can be found in excellent recent performances and recordings by leading contemporary artists.

The four symphonies present certain problems, including some reorchestration by Gustav Mahler and later conductors, which affects the pioneering version by George Szell and the Cleveland Orchestra. Leonard Bernstein conducting the New York Philharmonic is always exhilarating. Older versions by Toscanini, Furtwängler, Bruno Walter, Pierre Monteux, and Carlo Maria Giulini vary greatly in tempi and quality of sound, with outstanding performances by Rafael Kubelik and the Bavarian Radio Symphony. There are many fine performances of the Piano Concerto, including the 1948 and 1950 recordings by Dinu Lipatti. There is a superb live 1961 performance of the Cello Concerto by Mstislav Rostropovich with Benjamin Britten conducting; a later performance by Rostropovich's pupil Jacqueline du Pré is as heartbreaking as Schumann could have wished.

The major choral works, *Paradise and the Peri* and the *Scenes from Goethe's "Faust,"* are available in recent versions, reflecting a new appreciation of these long-neglected works. The Internet is a fine resource. But I hope the reader will be tempted to invest in the early remastered recordings of Schumann's works, along with new performances by a splendid range of artists who take his music to heart as if it were being heard for the first time.

ACKNOWLEDGMENTS

For new material about Schumann's early life and his circle, I am greatly indebted to Dr. Thomas Synofzik, director of Robert-Schumann-Haus, Zwickau. Dr. Synofzik read an early draft of my book and answered many questions, generously sending me unpublished archival material. The pianist Richard Goode, a superb artist as knowledgeable about literature as music, also read an early draft, and shared with me his profound understanding of Schumann's music.

Schumann has always evoked highly individual responses to the enigma at the heart of his music. Almost everyone who has written about him has contributed new insights, even when facts were few and speculation rampant—from early descriptions of the music as "neurotic" and "morbid" to theories that Schumann was "mother-fixated" or secretly homosexual. Among many attempts to explain the music and the life, I have learned most from the comprehensive account by John Daverio, *Robert Schumann: Herald of a "New Poetic Age"* (Oxford, 1997), with its illuminating analysis of key works. Misha Donat's program notes for a wide range of live concerts and recordings are always informative, as are Graham Johnson's notes to the Hyperion set of the *Complete Songs*. Jonathan Biss's online discussions of Schumann's works offer readings to a mass audience. The debate will continue as Schumann's music continues to be rediscovered and freshly interpreted.

My love of Schumann goes back to my childhood, when I found an old vinyl recording of the Piano Quintet in my parents' wind-up Victrola and played it to extinction. (The artists were Artur Schnabel and the Pro Arte Quartet.) My beloved aunt Ruth Lapidus, a Juilliard graduate, introduced me to Schubert's four-hand piano music, works which Schumann absorbed into his own early compositions. My French piano teacher, Madame Honoré, insisted that I struggle with *Papillons* and later with the Piano Concerto. With my first "best friend," Rita Loving, who became a superb singer and voice coach, I shared musical joys from our Brooklyn childhood to our professional lives in London and Munich.

I am fortunate in having many musicians as close friends. Tessa Uys and George Michell kindly played Schumann's four-hand music with me, including the delicious canons for pedal-piano set as piano duets by Bizet. The clarinettist Ian Herbert read through the late *Fantasiestücke* and *Märchenbilder* with me, works of great charm. Years before we became friends, I heard Caroline Palmer at a Guildhall master class playing Schumann's *Études symphoniques*—my first encounter with that extraordinary work. My dear friend Lani Chang cheerfully switched back and forth from violin to viola to read through Schumann's varied chamber works. The singer Stephanie Friedman introduced me to Schumann's songs—a revelation of their expressive beauty, confirmed again by Richard Stokes, who also directed me toward the late songs, often neglected. I've enjoyed conversation and correspondence with the pianist Imogen Cooper and the cellist Steven Isserlis, whose passion for Schumann's music, early and late, is a continual source of inspiration.

When I moved to London, I was introduced to the musicologist and Shakespeare scholar the late Eric Sams, who was as stimulating in conversation as in his publications; his interest in my work was formative. For several years I have been happily dissecting Schumann's music and his literary passions with John MacAuslan. The musicologist Eric Wen has been a welcome source of refined musical analysis.

My family have been hugely supportive. My sister Barbara Rosenstein and my brother Joel Sheffield both read and commented on chapters of my book. My son David and his wife Susan, accomplished professional musicians, played through much of the chamber music for me, and I gained immeasurably from David's special understanding of Schumann's unique poetry. My daughters Laura and Sara, both music lovers, and Sara's partner Peter Davies helped to sort out the workings of my ancient computer, including files for visual images, beautifully filmed by Sara. As always, I have relied on the unerring editorial judgment of my husband and life companion Warren Chernaik; he bore with me patiently as I worked my way at the piano and in recordings through Schumann's *Complete Works*.

As I came upon pieces new to me, I sometimes felt like the young Clara, terrified at the genius of the man to whom she had linked her life. It is, in truth, impossible to do justice to the music. I hope I have encouraged readers to deepen their own understanding of the works of one of our greatest tone poets.

My New York editor, Ann Close, has long been a source of encouragement, and in London, Belinda Matthews has been consistently helpful. I am grateful to Ann's multitalented assistant, Todd Portnowitz, and to my sympathetic literary agent David Godwin, who discovered Schumann's music on the Internet, just as I suggested. Antony Bye, editor of *The Musical Times*, kindly provided counsel for my published articles on Schumann, Chopin, and Mendelssohn. I must also thank my good neighbors, Franziska and Lars Gutsche, for advice on my translations of German sources.

It has been a privilege to consult the music collections of the British Library and Senate House Library (University of London). I must thank the distinguished publishers Bärenreiter, Breitkopf & Härtel, Dohr Verlag, and Schott for their permission to reprint material in copyright. Robert-Schumann-Haus, the Heinrich-Heine Institut, and the Beethoven House, Bonn, have kindly given permission to reprint images in their collections.

Above all, it is the musicians to whom I and others owe the greatest debt, for their passionate commitment to keeping the flame alive and glowing.

PRIMARY SOURCES

Schumann's musical works are available in reprints of the Collected Works edited by Clara Schumann, as well as more recent editions for use by students and teachers. For fully annotated texts and commentary, see the ongoing multi-volume publication: Robert Schumann, *Neue Ausgabe sämtliche Werke / New Edition of the Complete Works,* published by the Robert-Schumann-Gesellschaft Düsseldorf, edited by Akio Mayeda and Klaus Wolfgang Niemöller, in conjunction with the Robert-Schumann-Haus Zwickau. Mainz: Schott, 1991–. *Urtext* editions of single works have been published by Bärenreiter, C. F. Peters, Schott, and G. Henle Verlag.

The primary sources I have consulted include diaries, letters, and other writings by Robert Schumann; Clara Wieck Schumann; Friedrich Wieck; Felix Mendelssohn; Johannes Brahms; and Joseph Joachim. Translation from German into English is notoriously difficult. In presenting source material, I have tried to remain as faithful as possible to the writer's meaning. I take full responsibility for all errors.

SOURCES AND ABBREVIATIONS

Briefedition: Robert Schumann Briefedition, multiple volumes. Robert-Schumann-Haus, Zwickau. Cologne: Verlag Dohr, 2008–. Extracts from each volume of the *Briefedition* cited below have been trans-

lated and printed with kind permission of Verlag Dohr Köln, www
.schumann-briefedition.de.

*Briefedition I.2/I.3: Robert und Clara Schumann im Briefwechsel mit der Fami-
lie Wieck/Familie Bargiel,* ed. Eberhard Möller (2011).

Briefedition I.4–7: Braut-und Ehebriefwechsel Robert und Clara Schumann, ed.
Anja Mühlenweg and Thomas Synofzik (2012–2015).

*Briefedition II.1: Robert und Clara Schumann im Briefwechsel mit der Familie
Mendelssohn,* ed. Kristin Krahe, Katrin Reyersbach, and Thomas Synofzik (2009).

*Briefedition II.15: Briefwechsel Robert und Clara Schumanns mit den Familien
Voigt, Preusser, Herzogenberg und anderen Korrespondenten in Leipzig,* ed.
Annegret Rosenmüller and Ekaterina Smyka (2016).

Briefe NF: Jansen, F. Gustav, ed. *Robert Schumann: Briefe, Neue Folge,* 2nd
edition. Leipzig: Breitkopf & Härtel, 1904.

CS/JB Briefe: Litzmann, Berthold, ed. *Clara Schumann/Johannes Brahms:
Briefe,* 2 vols. Leipzig: Breitkopf und Härtel, 1927.

Endenich: Appel, Bernhard R., ed. *Robert Schumann in Endenich (1854–
1856): Krankenakten, Briefzeugnisse und zeitgenössische Berichte,*
Schumann Forschungen Band 11. Mainz: Schott, 2006.

FMB Briefe: Mendelssohn Bartholdy, Felix. *Sämtliche Briefe.* 12 vols. Kassel: Bärenreiter, 2008–2017.

GSK I, II: Kreisig, Martin, ed. *Robert Schumann: Gesammelte Schriften über
Musik und Musiker.* 5th edition. 2 vols. Leipzig: Breitkopf und Härtel,
1914.

JB/JJ: Moser, Andreas, ed. *Johannes Brahms im Briefwechsel mit Joseph
Joachim,* 2 vols. Berlin: Deutschen-Brahms-Gesellschaft, 1908.

Jugendbriefe: Schumann, Clara, ed. *Jugendbriefe von Robert Schumann.* 2nd
ed. Leipzig: Breitkopf & Härtel, 1886.

Lebenschronik: Burger, Ernst. *Robert Schumann: Eine Lebenschronik in Bil-
dern und Dokumenten.* Mainz: Schott, 1999.

Litzmann I, II, III: Litzmann, Berthold. *Clara Schumann: Ein Künstlerleben.*
3 vols. Leipzig: Breitkopf und Härtel, 1910.

NZfM: Neue Zeitschrift für Musik.

R-S-H: Robert-Schumann-Haus, Zwickau.

Tb I, II, III: Eismann, Georg, and Gerd Nauhaus, eds. *Robert Schumann:
Tagebücher,* 3 vols. Leipzig: VEB Deutscher Verlag für Musik, 1971–
1987.

Wasielewski: Wasielewski, Wilhelm Joseph von. *Robert Schumann: Eine
Biographie.* 3rd ed. Leipzig: Breitkopf & Härtel, 1906.

NOTES

Chapter One

3 There were three older brothers and a sister: Biographers have variously reported Emilie's year of birth as 1807 and 1796. According to the church register of Ronneburg, she was born on July 19, 1796 (early in the morning, four a.m.), in Ronneburg, where her parents lived before moving to Zwickau. R-S-H has a copy of the church register.

5 "Now, Robert dear": letter of 18 July 1824, *Lebenschronik*, 39.

5 "quiet madness": The death certificate attributes Emilie's death to "a nervous stroke."

5 "one who in a certain view": *Tb I*, 23 and editor's note.

7 "I was born in Zwickau": *Lebenschronik*, 32–33, first publication of the complete autograph and transcription; extracts reprinted in *Wasielewski*, 19, 22.

11 "I will go to bed": *Tb I*, 94.

12 "Be assured, honored teacher": *Jugendbriefe*, 78–85.

12 There is no further explanation: *Tb I*, 226ff.

12 Death to tyrants!: *Tb I*, 319, 323.

13 He was religious without religion: *Tb I*, 242–243.

13 He records "Attic nights": Peter Ostwald, *Schumann: Music and Madness* (London: Gollancz, 1985) suggests that "Attic nights" imply homosexual activities. It is more likely that Schumann was simply enjoying convivial late-night sessions of animated conversation with friends.

13 "How I am loved": *Tb I*, 223.

14 Technical skill was the foundation: *Lebenschronik*, 87, FW to RS's mother 9 August 1830.

14 "I confide entirely in you": *Wasielewski*, 62.

Chapter Two

16 Christel enters the romance: *Tb I*, 171ff.

17 Her name was Christiane Apitzsch: I am indebted to the superb scholarly research of Klaus Martin Kopitz for the identification of Christiane Apitzsch, i.e. "Christel," *Davidsbund* name "Charitas." See Klaus Martin Kopitz: "Christiane Apitzsch (1806–1838), Robert Schumann's *Geliebte 'Charitas': Eine Identifizierung*," in *Denkströme:* Journal der Sächsischen Akademie der Wissenschaften 13 (2014), 26–54.

17 "narcissus water": "Narcissus water" was an extract from the oil of the narcissus bulb, which like arsenic was a poison often used in traditional medicine. It is mentioned by Hippocrates and other classical authors as a topical treatment for cancerous ulcers.

17 "I sink, I sink": *Tb I*, 344.

19 They play charades and riddles: *Tb I*, 345–346.

20 Florestan and Eusebius: *Tb* I, 344.

20 "Tomorrow, at exactly eleven o'clock": *Jugendbriefe*, 62.

21 "my true 'I'": *Tb I*, 371.

21 "best friends": The last appearance of Florestan is as the author of a *NZfM* article in September 1843.

21 "Let Mozart and Bach": *Tb I*, 394–395.

21 "To Vienna!": *Tb I*, 399.

23 "Chopin is going well": *Tb I*, 344–346.

23 "The first variation expresses": *GSK I*, 5–7.

24 When Schumann sent: *Jugendbriefe*, 166–167.

25 He wrote to the critic Ludwig Rellstab: *Jugendbriefe*, 167–168. John Daverio, *Robert Schumann: Herald of a "New Poetic Age"* (New York: Oxford University Press, 1997), 493–501, provides a translation of the chapter from *Flegeljahre* with Schumann's markings and discusses its relevance: 79–90 and 493–501.

26 "An entire carnival": *GSK I*, 203.

27 A revised version: The symphony was rediscovered, published and performed in the twentieth century. See the sympathetic analysis in Daverio, op. cit., 103ff.

28 "He was a man through and through": *Tb I*, 389.

Chapter Three

29 "Why can I write nothing": *Tb I*, 417.

29 "The night of 17–18 October": *Tb I*, 419.

30 At his worst: *Jugendbriefe*, 227–228.

30 "the most significant of my life": *Tb I*, 419.

30 The masthead boasted a motto: *NZfM* I, 1. See Leon B. Plantinga, *Schumann as Critic* (New Haven and London: Yale University Press, 1967), 3–49, for a detailed account of the journal's founding and its aims.

31 "Our basic policy was clear": *GSK I*, 37–39.

31 To Franz Otto in Hamburg: *Jugendbriefe*, 222.

33 the astonishing genius of the young composer: See the full text of Schumann's review and two later reviews of Berlioz's works in Plantinga, *Schumann as Critic*, 235–250.

33 He introduced his essay: *GSK I*, 318–324.

37 "Belleville's playing": *GSK I*, 21.

38 Schumann had described Ernestine: *Jugendbriefe*, 70–71.

39 *Carnaval* captivated audiences: The ballet of *Carnaval* became world-famous after its 1910 production by Sergei Diaghilev's Ballets Russes, with sets and costumes by Léon Bakst, Lydia Lopokova as Columbine, and Vaslav Nijinsky as Harlequin. The ballet of *Papillons* was premiered in 1914.

39 His parting letter to her: *Jugendbriefe*, 71.

40 He wrote to Henriette Voigt: *Briefe NF,* 34.

42 "Summer of 1835": *Tb* I, 421.

Chapter Four

45 "I look up to him": *Jugendbriefe*, 76.

45 When Mendelssohn arrived in Leipzig: *Jugendbriefe*, 283.

45 "introverted, but a very good man": *FMB Briefe* VI, 462–463.

46 "I look forward greatly": The autograph of Chopin's note was published for the first time in *Lebenschronik*, 110–111.

47 "Dear and Honored Sir": *Selected Correspondence of Fryderyk Chopin*, tr. Arthur Hedley (London: Heinemann, 1962), 136–137.

47 "Just as I received your letter": *Wasielewski*, 345–346.

47 "I told her what an unforgettable sight": *GSK I*, 258.

48 "If the powerful autocratic Monarch": *GSK I*, 166.

49 He found Chopin's Sonata in B-flat: *GSK II*, 13.

49 "My earliest memory of you": *Litzmann I*, 207.

50 "How clearly I remember": *Briefedition I.5*, 207.

51 "Just as I was wending": *Litzmann I*, 87–88.

52 "engagement—happy hours": *Tb I*, 421.

52 "At the Zwickau post office": *Litzmann I*, 97–98, and *Briefedition I.4*, 50.

56 "In Easter 1821": *Litzmann I*, 2.

56 "Madam! I send you here": *Litzmann I*, 4.

57 "Never would I have believed": Georg Christian Tromlitz to Wieck, 22 March 1824, R-S-H 2466.a-A2, by permission of the director, R-S-H.

Chapter Five

60 "La Faneuse": *Tb II*, 28, 29, 34.

61 There seems little doubt: Kopitz, "Christiane Apitzsch," op. cit., speculates that the name David referred to Schumann's *Davidsbund*. The church register of the child's baptism describes Christiane as a *Dienst-mädchen* (servant girl), her occupation when Schumann first knew Christel in 1831.

61 "C. very sad and lovely": *Tb II*, 29, 30.

61 "C[lara] loves me as much as ever": *Wasielewski*, 348–349.

62 "Plans. Tears, dreams": *Tb II*, 30.

64 "Beethoven is not only the means": *Tb I*, 398.

65 "I know nothing whatever of harmony": *Briefe NF,* 6–7.

65 "I love it as I love you": *Litzmann I*, 186.

69 "the most passionate thing": *Litzmann I*, 224. See the comprehensive discussion in Nicholas Marston, *Schumann: Fantasie, Op. 17* (Cambridge: Cambridge University Press, 1992).

Chapter Six

75 She wrote to him later: *Litzmann I*, 117.

76 "13 August 37": *Litzmann I*, 118–119.

76 "All you need is a simple 'yes' "?: *Litzmann I*, 119–120.

76 "Today I am able": *Litzmann I*, 123–125.

77 "The meeting with your father": *Litzmann I*, 126–127, and *Briefedition I.4*, 106–107.

77 "Before I take farewell": *Litzmann I*, 129, and *Briefedition I.4*, 110.

78 Should he waver: *Litzmann I*, 129–130.

78 "Today I could think of nothing": *Briefedition I.4*, 120–121.

78 "If I improvise at the piano": *Litzmann I*, 133.

79 "the most blissful and purest days": *Tb II*, 32.

79 "In the afternoon, Mendelssohn": *Tb II*, 35, 36.

81 "When I am playing 'Night' ": *Briefe NF,* 120, and *Briefedition I.4*, 303.

81 Their specific literary meaning: See the intriguing links suggested by John MacAuslan, *Schumann's Music and E. T. A. Hoffmann's Fiction* (Cambridge: Cambridge University Press, 2016), passim.

82 "I meant, in the end": *Litzmann I*, 277.

86 "Who ordered you to love me": *Briefedition I.4*, 290–291.

Chapter Seven

88 First letter from Clara: *Litzmann I,* 140–141.

88 Schumann wrote back: *Litzmann I,* 141ff.

88 "In the midst of a thousand voices": *Litzmann I,* 163, and *Briefedition I.4,* 169.

89 "Come and sit beside me": *Litzmann I,* 83–85, and *Briefedition I.4,* 221–224.

90 "Everything that goes on": *Jugendbriefe,* 282.

91 "humorous things, Egmont stories": *Litzmann I,* 178.

91 To a fellow composer, Hermann Hirschbach: Hermann Erler, *Robert Schumann Leben, aus seinen Briefen geschildert* (Berlin: Ries and Erler, 1887), I, 206.

91 "Much of the battle": *Wasielewski,* 370.

93 The final piece ties the set together: See Alfred Brendel, "Testing the Grown-Up Player: Schumann's *Kinderszenen,*" *Alfred Brendel on Music: Collected Essays* (London: Robson Books. 2001), 218–228.

93 "There's a very wild love": *Litzmann I,* 206.

100 "First of all, congratulations": *Litzmann I,* 205, and *Briefedition I.4,* 280.

100 "One room dreamily dark": *Litzmann I,* 167.

102 "By good chance in the evening": *Tb II,* 56.

102 "I thought I saw you pass by": *Briefedition I.4,* 345.

102 "I am so desperate to see you": *Litzmann I,* 215.

103 "Be at our window": *Litzmann I,* 214–215.

103 "My twenty-eighth birthday": *Tb II,* 57.

103 "Imagine when I can walk": *Briefedition I.4,* 363.

104 "Can't we speak to each other": *Litzmann I,* 225, and *Briefedition I.4,* 420–421.

104 "About Friday night": *Jugendbriefe,* 291ff.

104 "I hardly know what to do": *Briefedition I.4,* 429.

104 "If only I could speak to you": *Briefedition I.4,* 429.

105 "I have to go away from here": *Litzmann I,* 238, and *Briefedition I.5,* 53.

Chapter Eight

107 "From everything I've experienced": *Jugendbriefe,* 291ff.

108 "The past two weeks": *Briefedition I.5,* 140, and *Litzmann I,* 254.

108 The verses continue: The verses were published in *Litzmann I,* 225–228; these are the verses Schumann asked Clara to send him when he was in Endenich asylum.

109 "This symphony reveals": *GSK I,* 459–464.

110 "All week I sat at the piano": *Litzmann I*, 297.

110 "not very merry": *Briefe NF*, 160.

115 "I want to tell you about last night": *Litzmann I*, 206.

116 "I dreamed I was lying": *Briefedition I.5*, 261.

Chapter Nine

117 "Honored Sir, Clara tells me": *Litzmann I*, 342.

118 "I have been so vividly reminded": *Litzmann I*, 359.

119 "At six she was there": *Tb II*, 93.

119 "I know no Fräulein Wieck": *Tb II*, 94, and *Litzmann I*, 373ff.

120 "They are love lilies": *Briefedition II.15*, 60. "Love lilies" (*Lilienliebe*),
in the new *Briefedition*, suggesting a bouquet held together by the
Schubert waltz, replaces the earlier *Linienliebe*, usually translated as
"love stories."

121 "Do not abandon me!": Wasielewski, 101.

121 "My dear friend—how I love": Wasielewski, 332.

121 "With trembling hand I write to you": *Briefedition II.15*, 71.

122 "Liebe . . . I think of you often": *Briefedition II.15*, 80.

122 "a change from then on": *Tb II*, 32–33.

122 "How much I have to tell you": *Briefedition II.15*, 84–85.

122 "Shall I then hear nothing more": *Briefedition II.15*, 85–86.

123 "I'd like to know what she thinks": *Briefedition II.15*, 78.

123 "Now I wish only": *Briefedition II.15*, 104.

124 "September 13th, 1836": *GSK I*, 446–452.

124 "If I didn't have you": *Briefedition I.6*, 517; *Litzmann I*, 386.

125 "You complement me": *Briefedition I.6*, 150–151.

125 "It will amuse you greatly": *Briefedition I.6*, 552.

125 "I thought for a long time": *Briefedition I.6*, 435.

125 "I am full of music": *Litzmann I*, 309.

134 "Without knowing each other": *Briefedition II.5*, 117.

135 In an earlier article: *GSK I*, 440.

Chapter Ten

142 Mendelssohn and his wife had kept: Mendelssohn's honeymoon diary
was published as *The Mendelssohns on Honeymoon: The 1837 Diary of
Felix and Cécile Mendelssohn Bartholdy*, ed. and trans. Peter Ward Jones
(Oxford: Clarendon Press, 1997). The diary includes Mendelssohn's
charming watercolor sketches.

142 The "true history": *Tb II*, 99–386. The marriage diary was published
in English as *The Marriage Diaries of Robert and Clara Schumann*, ed.
Gerd Nauhaus, trans. Peter Ostwald (London: Robson Books, 1994).

142 "I can truly say": *Tb II*, 102.

144 "since she must purchase my love": *Tb II*, 127.

144 In November Schumann noted: *Tb II*, 22.

144 "The whole town here is ringing": *FMB Briefe VII*, 340.

145 "Clara told me that I seemed to have changed": *Tb II*, 122–123.

146 "He played": *Tb II*, 132.

146 "Love and veneration": *Tb II*, 155.

146 "Hoorah! [*Juche!*] Symphony finished!": *Tb III*, 172, 173, 176; *Tb II*, 151.

146 Mendelssohn had described Schumann: *FMB Briefe VI*, 462–463.

148 "However old one is": *Tb II*, 139.

149 "Do not forget us": *FMB Briefe X*, 153.

150 "for your last loving lines": *Briefedition II.1*, 176.

150 "Laugh at this if you will": *FMB Briefe VIII*, 190.

150 "May you be happy": *FMB Briefe VIII*, 198.

153 "I totally reorchestrated the symphony": *Briefe NF,* 371–372.

153 Clara Schumann won that battle: Robert Schumann, Symphony no. 4, First Version, 1841, ed. Jon Finson (Leipzig: Breitkopf & Härtel, 2003).

Chapter Eleven

157 "It is absolutely necessary": *Tb II*, 206.

158 "It was really one of the most": *Tb II*, 206.

158 "the most terrible day": *Tb II*, 212.

162 The Finale, Allegro molto vivace: In Schumann's essay on "the character of keys," *GSK I*, 105–106, he cites a work by the poet Christian Schubart that assigns specific emotions to each key. Schumann argues that keys are evocative not because of intrinsic qualities but because of the well-known works with which they are associated: Beethoven's *Eroica* Symphony in E-flat, Mozart's Symphony no. 40 in G minor, Beethoven's Ninth in D minor. But he consistently associates certain keys with Clara, usually linked to the two "musical letters" in her name, C and A. Thus "Chiarina" in *Carnaval* is in C minor; the Fantasie in C portrays Clara in its radiant C major finale; and the concluding pieces of the two books of the *Davidsbündlertänze* are each in C. The single-movement Phantasie later expanded into the Piano Concerto is in A minor; Clara's F-minor theme in the Variations of the Sonata op. 14 is in the relative minor of A-flat. The three string quartets—in A minor, F major, and A major—all dance around these "Clara" keys and their close relatives.

164 Notable is the expressive power: For instance, in the opening bars, E-natural in the bass against D-flat in the middle voice; D against

E-flat in the piano middle voice, echoed as an accaciatura by the violin.

164 "They should remember": *GSK I,* 22.

167 "Dear Schumann": *Litzmann II,* 13. The original letter is reproduced in *Lebenschronik,* 218.

168 "Perhaps one could make": *Tb II,* 179.

169 "It is said . . . that you are engaged": Introduction to *The Corsair* in all editions of Byron's *Complete Poems.*

171 Moore writes in his notes: note 171 to *Lalla Rookh* in Thomas Moore's *Poetical Works.* My quotations are from Moore's original text; Schumann sets them in German translation.

175 "My husband speaks now": *Briefedition II.1,* 202.

175 Mendelssohn wrote to colleagues: *FMB Briefe X,* 52–53.

176 "No one could be more worthy": *FMB Briefe X,* 54–55.

176 "I have read and heard": *FMB Briefe* X, 54.

176 "its masterly musical perfection": *GSK I,* 322.

177 He set down in order the distances: *Tb II,* 304–305. Schumann lists German miles, which have been adapted to English/American convention.

180 "Now let heaven give me health": *Tb II,* 390.

181 "As soon as he concerned himself ": *Wasielewski,* 351–352.

Chapter Twelve

184 "I used to write most": *Tb II,* 402.

185 In April he began: A facsimile of Schumann's copy of the treatise, with occasional comments in his hand, has been published in the New Edition of the Complete Works.

190 "I am your tree, O gardener": See Thomas Synofzik, "Ein Rückert-Kanon als Keimzelle zu Schumanns Klavierkonzert Op. 54" (A Rückert Canon as Nucleus of Schumann's Piano Concerto, op. 54), in *Musikforschung* 58 (2005), 28–32. Synofzik has also published his own reconstruction of the duet in Robert Schumann, *Zwei Duette nach Friedrich Rückert (WoO)* (Cologne: Edition Dohr 17500, 2017). Schumann provided a new setting for the duet in 1849, in *Minnespiel aus Friedrich Rückerts "Liebesfrühling,"* op. 101.

191 "Dear Mendelssohn": *Briefe NF,* 247–249.

192 "It was a great joy for me": *FMB Briefe XI,* 41–42.

192 "Tendency to dizziness": *Tb II,* 393.

192 "My dear Robert": *Briefedition I.7,* 607–608.

193 "I cannot work": *Briefedition I.7,* 613–614.

195 "I sketched it out": *Wasielewski*, 206–207.

196 "Really, couldn't we": *Briefe NF,* 255–256.

196 "then perhaps in the afternoon": *FMB Briefe XI*, 71–72.

196 "If only I might stand": *Briefe NF,* 251–253.

197 "Thank you (and so heartily!)": *FMB Briefe XI*, 105.

198 "Her husband has behaved": *FMB Briefe XI*, 495.

204 Schumann consulted his diaries: Schumann's notes on Mendelssohn were transcribed and published with the manuscript as *Erinnerungen an Felix Mendelssohn Bartholdy,* ed. Dr. Georg Eismann (Zwickau: Predella, 1948).

Chapter Thirteen

207 "I have published": *Wasielewski*, 156–157.

207 His chief weakness: phrenological study by Noel, dated "June 1, 1846" in Maxen (just outside Dresden), *Tb III*, 403.

219 "Learn the fundamental laws of harmony": *GSK II*, 163ff. See *Robert Schumann's "Advice to Young Musicians," Revisited by Steven Isserlis* (London: Faber & Faber, 2016), a delightful tribute to Schumann's work by a fellow musician.

221 Schumann wrote to his publisher: *Briefe NF,* 491.

222 Recent studies suggest: Thomas Synofzik, *"Weltliche a capella-Chormusik"* in Ulrich Tadday, *Schumann Handbuch* (Stuttgart/Weimar: Metzler, 2006), 458–478, analyzes each choral song Schumann has written; English translations are published in CDs of the *Secular Choral Music I* (Carus Verlag 83.173) and *Complete Songs for Male Voices* (Musikproduktion Dabringhaus und Grimm 622 1316–2).

227 "There I found mentioned": *Briefe NF,* 323.

Chapter Fourteen

234 Schumann wrote to Horn: *Wasielewski*, 423.

235 "He wrote to Pohl": *Briefe NF,* 344.

236 "It is a kind of composition": *Wasielewski*, 433.

237 One way of looking: Dietrich Fischer-Dieskau, *Robert Schumann, Words and Music: The Vocal Compositions,* tr. Reinhard G. Pauly (Portland, OR: Amadeus Press, 1988); cf also Daverio, op. cit., 459–464.

238 The record in his household book: *Tb III.2*, 569, 571, 587.

239 "The ladies and gentlemen": *Litzmann II*, 240.

241 Schumann suffered another health crisis: *Tb III.2*, 592–601.

246 "It reminds me of the magician": *Briefe NF,* 374.

246 "Joachim astounds everyone": *Tb III*, 634.

248 seize the genuine: See Robert Schumann, *Klavierbüchlein für Marie,* ed. Bernhard R. Appel (Beethoven-Haus Bonn, 1998). Four pieces in the "*Klavierbüchlein*" were included in Robert Schumann, *Pezzi inediti dall'Album per la Gioventu'* Op. 68, ed. Jörg Demus (Milan: Ricordi, 1973). All these pieces and several others are published in the Urtext edition of *Album für die Jugend: 43 Klavierstücke,* ed. Holger M. Stüwe (Kassel: Bärenreiter, 2015).

Chapter Fifteen

250 "Toward the end of the year 1833": *GSK I,* 1–2.

253 "Yesterday for the first time": *Wasielewski,* 431–432.

255 The notorious essay: The essay was reprinted in Wagner's name as a pamphlet in 1869, and again in his *Collected Writings.*

255 "The article on 'Judentum in der Musik'": R-H-S 4601–A2, private communication from the director.

256 "Herr Brahms, from Hamburg": *Tb III,* 637.

257 "It is truly moving": *Litzmann II,* 281.

257 Brahms came from an extremely modest background: According to recent scholarship, Brahms's experience of low life, described by his first biographer, Max Kalbeck, has been exaggerated. He certainly played in respectable working-class restaurants or inns that provided musical entertainment. See Styra Avins, *Brahms: Life and Letters,* tr. Josef Eisinger and Styra Avins (New York: Oxford University Press, 1997), 3.

258 "The young eagle": 8 October 1853, *Briefe NF,* 380.

258 "What shall I write to you about": *JB/JJ I,* 8–9.

259 "Years have gone by": *GSK II,* 301.

261 "Shameless people": *Tb III,* 639, 641.

262 "They are musical pieces": *Endenich,* 51.

263 "We have been gone a whole week": *Briefe NF,* 391–392.

263 Schumann noted in his household book: *Tb III,* 648.

264 "Soon after we had gone to bed": *Litzmann II,* 207–209.

266 "Dear Clara": *Litzmann II,* 301.

Chapter Sixteen

269 In 1988 the documents: Extracts were first published in 1994 by the Academy of the Arts as *Robert Schumanns letzte Lebensjahre,* Archiv-Blätter 1 (Stiftung Archiv der Akademie der Künste, Berlin), tr. Judith Chernaik, "Guilt Alone Brings Forth Nemesis," *Times Literary Supplement,* August 31 2001.

269 The complete medical record: The records from RS's admission on 4 March to 6 April and from 28 April to 6 September were lost after the entry of Russian troops into Berlin in 1945. *Endenich*, 34.

269 The avenging Nemesis: See entry for 19 April 1854: "Restless at night, spoke loudly to himself until midnight of 'Veneris' [Venus, venereal], was unlucky, would go mad." *Endenich*, 95.

270 But he told Schumann's publisher: letter quoted in *Endenich*, 78.

274 "How happy I was": *Briefe NF,* 397–398; also in *Endenich*, 137–138.

276 "Dearest Clara, What joyful news": *Briefe NF,* 398–399.

277 "What joy, dearest Clara": *Briefe NF,* 399ff.

278 "Write to me even more": *Briefe NF,* 400f.

278 "Dear Klara and children": *Endenich*, 160f.

279 "Would to God it were permitted": *CS/JB Briefe*, 54–57.

279 "If only I could come to you": *Briefe NF,* 402 and *Endenich*, 176ff.

280 "It is indeed noteworthy": *Endenich*, 188.

280 "For the first five": [26] January 1855, *Endenich*, 205.

281 "I was with your beloved husband": *CS/JB Briefe*, 78–81.

282 "Doesn't Brahms let drums": *Briefe NF,* 389–390.

283 "He always speaks of the past": *Litzmann II*, 341.

283 "My own Clara, I feel": *Litzmann II*, 364, and *Endenich*, 203.

283 In March 1855, both doctors noted: *Endenich*, 222–248.

284 "To be away from here": *Briefe NF,* 406, and *Endenich*, 229.

286 "Why have I had no word": *Endenich*, 270–271.

286 "Dearest Clara, On the first of May": *Litzmann II*, 374, and *Endenich*, 270–271.

288 "To think of seeing him": *Litzmann II*, 387.

288 "In 1831 I was syphilitic": *Endenich*, 326 and fn. 1106, which summarizes the literature discussing Schumann's illness. In a diary entry of 1831 Schumann mentions being treated with "narcissus water" by his friend Glock. It is possible that he was also treated with arsenic, a common treatment for syphilis at the time.

292 "I know very well": *Endenich*, 377.

293 When Clara entered his room: *Litzmann II*, 414ff.

296 "I have often thought": *JB/JJ*, 285.

Afterword

300 "I have been working": *Endenich*, 226.

300 A number of misconceptions: The problem of diagnosing Schumann's illness was inevitably changed by the publication of the complete medical diary in 1999. Even after publication, however, two contrast-

ing diagnoses were offered by Franz Hermann Franken, arguing that the diary confirmed that Schumann was suffering from neurosyphilis, and by Uwe Henrik Peters, who argued that this diagnosis remained speculative. See *Endenich*, 442–480. John Worthen, *Robert Schumann* (New Haven: Yale University Press, 2007), 362–369, provides a full account of the history of this troubled question.

FURTHER READING

Abraham, Gerald, ed. *Schumann: A Symposium*. London: Oxford University Press, 1952.

Avins, Styra, ed. *Johannes Brahms: Life and Letters*, trans. Josef Eisinger and Styra Avins. New York: Oxford University Press, 1997.

Barthes, Roland. "Loving Schumann," in *The Responsibility of Forms: Critical Essays on Music, Art, and Representation*, trans. Richard Howard. Berkeley: University of California Press, 1985.

Brendel, Alfred. "Testing the Grown-Up Player: Schumann's *Kinderszenen*," in *Alfred Brendel on Music: Collected Essays*. London: Robson Books, 2001.

Byron, George Gordon, Lord. *The Complete Poetical Works*, ed. Jerome J. McGann. Oxford: Clarendon Press, 1986.

Chernaik, Judith. "Guilt Alone Brings Forth Nemesis." *Times Literary Supplement*, August 31, 2001.

———. "Schumann's Doppelgängers: Florestan and Eusebius Revisited." *Musical Times* 152.1917 (Winter 2011): 45–55.

———. "Schumann's *Papillons*, Op. 2: A Case Study." *Musical Times* 153.1920 (Winter 2012): 57–66.

———. "Schumann and Chopin: From *Carnaval* to *Kreisleriana*." *Musical Times* 157.1934 (Spring 2016): 67–78.

———. "Mendelssohn and Schumann: New Letters." *Musical Times* 156.1930 (Spring 2015): 89–100.

Daverio, John. *Robert Schumann: Herald of a "New Poetic Age."* New York: Oxford University Press, 1997.

Finson, Jon W., and R. Larry Todd, eds. *Mendelssohn and Schumann: Essays on Their Music and Its Context.* Durham, NC: Duke University Press, 1984.

Fischer-Dieskau, Dietrich. *Robert Schumann—Words and Music: The Vocal Compositions,* trans. Reinhard G. Pauly. Portland, OR: Amadeus Press, 1988.

Geck, Martin. *Robert Schumann: The Life and Work of a Romantic Composer,* trans. Stewart Spencer. Chicago: University of Chicago Press, 2013.

Goethe, Johann Wolfgang von. *Faust,* trans. Walter Arndt, ed. Cyrus Hamlin. Norton Critical Edition. New York: Norton, 1976.

Heine, Heinrich. *Buch der Lieder,* in *Sämtliche Schriften,* ed. Klaus Briegleb. Munich: Carl Hanser, 1968.

———. *Selected Verse,* ed. and trans. Peter Branscombe. London: Penguin Classics, 1986.

Hoffmann, E. T. A., *E. T. A. Hoffmann's Musical Writings: Kreisleriana, The Poet and the Composer, Music Criticism,* ed. David Charlton, trans. Martyn Clarke. Cambridge: Cambridge University Press, 1989.

Jensen, Eric Frederick. *Schumann.* Oxford: Oxford University Press, 2001.

MacAuslan, John. *Schumann's Music and E. T. A. Hoffmann's Fiction.* Cambridge: Cambridge University Press, 2016.

Marston, Nicholas. *Schumann: Fantasie Op. 17.* Cambridge: Cambridge University Press, 1992.

Mendelssohn, Felix. *Felix Mendelssohn: A Life in Letters,* ed. Rudolf Elvers, trans. Craig Tomlinson. London: Cassell, 1986.

Moore, Thomas. *Lalla Rookh: An Oriental Romance.* (1817) in *Poetical Works.* London: Longmans Green, 1841.

Musgrave, Michael. *The Life of Schumann.* Cambridge: Cambridge University Press, 2011.

Niecks, Frederick. *Robert Schumann,* ed. Christina Niecks. London: J. M. Dent & Sons, 1925.

Ostwald, Peter. *Robert Schumann: Music and Madness.* London: Gollancz, 1985.

Perry, Beate, ed. *The Cambridge Companion to Schumann.* Cambridge: Cambridge University Press, 2007.

Plantinga, Leon. *Schumann as Critic.* New Haven: Yale University Press, 1967.

Reich, Nancy B. *Clara Schumann: The Artist and the Woman,* revised ed. Ithaca: Cornell University Press, 2001.

Rosen, Charles. *The Classical Style: Haydn, Mozart, Beethoven.* London: Faber and Faber, 1972.

———. *The Romantic Generation.* Cambridge, MA: Harvard University Press, 1995.

Sams, Eric. *The Songs of Robert Schumann*. 3rd ed. Bloomington and Indianapolis: Indiana University Press, 1993.

Schauffler, Robert. *Florestan: The Life and Work of Robert Schumann*. New York: Dover, 1963; reprint of original edition (New York: Henry Holt, 1945).

Schumann, Clara and Robert. *The Complete Correspondence of Clara and Robert Schumann: Critical Edition*, ed. Eva Weissweiler, trans. H. Fritsch and R. Crawford. 3 vols. New York: Peter Lang, 1994, 1996, 2002.

Schumann, Robert. *Erinnerungen an Felix Mendelssohn Bartholdy*, ed. Dr. Georg Eismann. Zwickau: Förster & Borries, 1948.

———. *On Music and Musicians*, ed. Konrad Wolff, trans. Paul Rosenfeld. London: Dennis Dobson, 1947.

Storck, Karl, ed. *The Letters of Robert Schumann*, trans. Hannah Bryant. New York: Arno Press, 1907.

Taruskin, Richard. *Oxford History of Western Music: The Nineteenth Century*. Oxford: Oxford University Press, 2005.

Todd, R. Larry. *Mendelssohn: A Life in Music*. Oxford: Oxford University Press, 2003.

———, ed. *Schumann and His World*. Princeton: Princeton University Press, 1994.

Tovey, Donald Francis. *Essays in Musical Analysis*. 6 vols. London: Oxford University Press, 1935–1939.

Tunbridge, Laura. *Schumann's Late Style*. Cambridge: Cambridge University Press, 2007.

Walker, Alan, ed. *Robert Schumann: The Man and His Music*. London: Barrie & Jenkins, 1972.

Worthen, John. *Robert Schumann: Life and Death of a Musician*. New Haven and London: Oxford University Press, 2007.

INDEX OF SCHUMANN'S WORKS

KEYBOARD MUSIC

LIEDER

ORCHESTRAL WORKS
(including concertos)

GENERAL INDEX

ILLUSTRATION CREDITS

All illustrations are courtesy of Robert-Schumann-Haus, Zwickau, except where noted below. The following are organized by page for clarity; the insert does not include page numbers.

page 4: Caricature of Paganini's Vienna concert of 1828: Getty Images / ullstein bild Dtl.

page 6: Chopin, drawing by George Sand: Courtesy of the Library of the Fryderyk Chopin Institute / Object F. 2080 / Photograph by Franciszek Myszkowski. Mendelssohn, age twenty-one: Wikimedia Commons. Liszt, age twenty-five: Oil painting by Jean Gabriel Scheffer / Property of the Conservatoire de Musique de Genève.

page 7: Clara Wieck, age seventeen: Courtesy of the Stadtgeschichtliches Museum, Leipzig / Inventory number L 27. Pauline Viardot Garcia drawing of Friedrich and Clara Wieck, with Clara's friends: Sächsische Landesbibliothek—Staats und Universitätsbibliothek (SLUB) Dresden / Mus.Schu.309cc.

page 10: Manuscript draft of "Ich bin dein Baum": Courtesy of Heinrich-Heine-Institut, Düsseldorf.

page 12: Watercolor of Clara, age thirty-four: Carpentras, Bibliothèque-musée Inguimbertine, Jean-Joseph-Bonaventure Laurens, Clara Schumann, DES 35 (crédit photo Chaline).

page 13: Silver pencil drawing of Brahms, age twenty-one: Copyright Stadtarchiv Bonn / Copyright Photo, StadtMuseum, Bonn.

page 14: Düsseldorf Piano Trio: Künstlerverein Malkasten (Archiv), Düsseldorf. Joseph-Bonaventure Laurens drawing of Schumann, age forty-four: Carpentras, Bibliothèque-musée Inguimbertine, Jean-Joseph-Bonaventure Laurens, Robert Schumann, DES 36 (crédit photo Chaline).

page 15: Manuscript of a theme supposedly dictated by angels: Beethoven-Haus, Bonn.

page 16: Schumann's final letter to Clara: Beethoven-Haus, Bonn.

A NOTE ABOUT THE AUTHOR

Judith Chernaik was born and grew up in New York City. She graduated from Cornell University and received a PhD from Yale University. She has taught at Columbia, Tufts, and after moving to London with her husband and children, at Queen Mary College, University of London. In 1986 she founded London's popular Poems on the Underground, imitated in cities around the world. Her books include *The Lyrics of Shelley* and four novels. Most recently she has published essays on Schumann, Mendelssohn, and Chopin in the English journal *Musical Times*. She lives in London with her husband, Warren Chernaik, Emeritus Professor at the University of London.

A NOTE ON THE TYPE

This book is set in Schneidler, a typeface originally designed for the Bauer Foundry in 1936 by F. H. Ernst Schneidler. Born in 1882 in Berlin, Schneidler is regarded as the founder of the Stuttgart School and recognized as one of Germany's most important twentieth-century typographers and calligraphers. This sturdy and highly readable Venetian-style font is distinguished by even, classical proportions and cupped serifs.

Composed by North Market Street Graphics,
Lancaster, Pennsylvania

Printed and bound by Berryville Graphics,
Berryville, Virginia

Designed by Betty Lew